THE CHRISTIAN LIFE

THE CHRISTIAN LIFE

Baptism and Life Passages

Using *Evangelical Lutheran Worship*
Volume Two

Dennis L. Bushkofsky
Craig A. Satterlee

Augsburg Fortress

Using *Evangelical Lutheran Worship*
  Volume 1, *The Sunday Assembly*
  Volume 2, *The Christian Life: Baptism and Life Passages*
  Volume 3, *Keeping Time: The Church's Years*

Other *Evangelical Lutheran Worship* Leader Guides
  Indexes to Evangelical Lutheran Worship
  Musicians Guide to Evangelical Lutheran Worship
  Hymnal Companion to Evangelical Lutheran Worship

The Christian Life: Baptism and Life Passages
Using *Evangelical Lutheran Worship,* Volume Two
Copyright © 2008 Augsburg Fortress. All rights reserved.

Cover art: Nicholas T. Markell, Markell Studios, Inc. Copyright © 2006 Augsburg
Fortress.

Manufactured in the U.S.A.

ISBN 978–1–5064–2511–5 (paperback edition)
ISBN 978–0–8066–7014–0 (hardcover edition)

CONTENTS

Preface to the *Evangelical Lutheran Worship* Leader Guides

Evangelical *Lutheran Worship* includes a number of related print editions and other resources developed to support the worship life of the Evangelical Lutheran Church in America and the Evangelical Lutheran Church in Canada. The core print editions of *Evangelical Lutheran Worship*, released in 2006, include the following:

Pew (Assembly) Edition

Leaders Edition and Leaders Desk Edition

Accompaniment Edition: Liturgies

Accompaniment Edition: Service Music and Hymns

An encounter with these core editions and their introductions is important to an understanding of the goals and principles embodied in *Evangelical Lutheran Worship*.

In addition to the core materials, *Evangelical Lutheran Worship* includes other published resources that are prepared to extend the usefulness of the core editions and to respond to the developing needs of the church in mission. The Evangelical Lutheran Worship leader guides, which include the present volume, supplement the core editions in a variety of ways.

These resources are intended to provide worship leaders and planners with support for *Evangelical Lutheran Worship* in ways that would not be possible within the core editions themselves. Although the assembly edition includes more interpretive material than its predecessors, such as the annotated patterns for worship that complement the notes within the services, it provides only minimal guidance for leading worship in a variety of settings. Although the leaders edition includes a more extensive section titled Notes on the Services, it is not designed to accommodate deeper historical context, theological reflection, or extensive practical counsel for those who want to lead worship with understanding and confidence.

The leader guides include a set of three volumes, Using *Evangelical Lutheran Worship*. This set addresses as its primary audience pastors, seminarians, and church musicians—people who together take the lead in preparing the assembly's worship week by week. In a time when many congregations have implemented a broader sharing in worship leadership and planning, however, the contents of these three volumes will be valuable also for assisting ministers with various roles, altar guilds and sacristans, worship committees, and worshipers who are seeking deeper understanding.

The Sunday Assembly, the first book in the set of three volumes, includes a general introduction to worship that is evangelical, Lutheran, and ecumenical. That is followed by in-depth historical, theological, and practical reflections on the service of Holy Communion and the Service of the Word. This book, *The Christian Life: Baptism and Life Passages,* is the second volume in the set and takes up the service of Holy Baptism and related services such as Affirmation of Baptism, together with the services of Healing, Funeral, and Marriage. *Keeping Time: The Church's Years,* the third volume in the set, addresses the church's calendar of Sundays, festivals, and seasons; the place of the lectionary and other propers; and the cycle of daily prayer.

The leader guides also include two volumes focused on assembly song. *Musicians Guide to Evangelical Lutheran Worship* presents essays on the musical leadership of assembly song in a variety of styles and genres and offers music performance helps for each piece of liturgical music and every hymn in *Evangelical Lutheran Worship*. The *Hymnal Companion to Evangelical Lutheran Worship* includes detailed background on the words and music of the hymns, together with an overview of the role of hymnody in the church's worship. Both of these volumes, while having particular appeal to church musicians, will be useful also to pastors, seminarians, worship committees, choir members, and other worshipers.

Other reference and interpretive resources will be included among the leader guides as needed. *Indexes for Worship Planning* is one such volume, with an extensive list of suggested hymns for the church year and an expanded set of other indexes.

Many of the church's gifted teachers have contributed to the writing and assembling of the leader guides. They have sought to discern and give additional focus to the vision for worship among Lutherans that emerged from the five-year Renewing Worship process (2001–2005), which engaged thousands of people across the Evangelical Lutheran Church in America and the Evangelical Lutheran Church in Canada in encountering provisional materials, sharing creative gifts, and evaluating various stages of the proposal. To be sure, this vision is one marked by a great diversity of thought and practice, a diversity the contributors seek to reflect in these volumes. Yet these gifted teachers also bring to this work their own distinctive points of view, shaped by their own experiences and by their encounters with other teachers, rostered leaders, and worshiping communities around the world.

The *Evangelical Lutheran Worship* leader guides thus do not intend to provide definitive answers or official positions in matters related to worship among Lutherans. In these volumes, however, we are invited to engage in conversation with teachers of the church, to consider how their insights and guidance may best inform and inspire the many different contexts in which local leaders guide the worship life of their communities. In so doing, these leader guides in their own ways seek to do what also the core editions set out to do: "to make more transparent the principle of fostering unity without imposing uniformity" so that ultimately all these resources might "be servants through which the Holy Spirit will call out the church, gather us around Jesus Christ in word and sacrament, and send us, enlivened, to share the good news of life in God" (*Evangelical Lutheran Worship,* Introduction, p. 8).

1

Holy Baptism
and Related Rites

CHAPTER ONE

Baptism: Wellspring of the Christian Life

O ne of the most noticeable outcomes of the renewal of worship taking place in many parts of the church is a renewed awareness of the centrality of baptism. Congregations that are building or renovating worship spaces are considering how to reflect this centrality in the size and placement of the font. Newer worship resources in many denominations have given greater accent to baptism and related rites, and baptism more frequently has a central place in primary worship services. Educational materials and preaching helps give greater attention to baptism. Individuals and families are encouraged to remember and give thanks for their baptism and its significance for their whole lives.

Evangelical Lutheran Worship continues and extends this movement toward a renewed emphasis on baptism, especially in the context of worship. Lutherans and many other Christians regard holy baptism as a sacrament equal in importance to holy communion, even as it has a different function in the Christian life. Thus, the first volume in this series, *The Sunday Assembly,* focuses primarily on the church's primary weekly gathering around the word of God and the sacrament of holy communion. And this volume focuses primarily on the church's gathering in worship around the sacrament of holy baptism—in services where the sacrament itself is offered and in other settings where the connection of baptism to the Christian life is lifted up.

What is so important about baptism? And what has led to a renewed appreciation of its centrality? In this chapter, we will examine some of what lends baptism its weight within the Christian life, aided by a number of significant resources and documents: *Evangelical Lutheran Worship* itself, both the assembly/pew edition (AE) and the leaders edition (LE); one of its primary foundations, a statement called *The Use of the Means of Grace* (UMG), adopted for guidance and practice by the Evangelical Lutheran Church in America in 1997 and included as an appendix to *The Sunday Assembly* in this leader guide series; the writings of Martin Luther and other reformers as translated in *Luther's Works*

(LW) and in the *Book of Concord* (BC); and an influential ecumenical study called *Baptism, Eucharist, and Ministry* (BEM), which originated in the Faith and Order Commission of the World Council of Churches in 1982.

Other chapters will address how baptism intersects with the church's worship (chapter 2), look in detail at the service of Holy Baptism in *Evangelical Lutheran Worship* (chapter 3), and proceed on to the other services closely related to baptism (Welcome to Baptism, chapter 4; Affirmation of Baptism, chapter 5; and Individual and Corporate Confession and Forgiveness, chapter 6). This book will conclude with considerations of three further expressions of the baptismally founded Christian life, jointly referred to as Life Passages: Healing (chapter 7), Funeral (chapter 8), and Marriage (chapter 9). The scope of the material covered in chapters 4 through 9—the wide range of ways in which holy baptism flows through the Christian life—is evidence that the chords struck by this sacrament reverberate widely in the church.

Among Martin Luther's greatest contributions is lifting up what *Evangelical Lutheran Worship* calls "the baptismal life"—a baptismal spirituality, or even a baptismal way of living. From a Lutheran perspective, this washing with water in the name of the triune God among the gathered Christian assembly is at the center of one's whole life as a Christian. We might describe baptism as the wellspring from which the entire Christian life flows. Jesus' words to the woman at the well in John 4:14, promising "a spring of water gushing up to eternal life," are often applied to baptism. This spring gushes up from the font, where, as Romans 6 assures us, we are liberated from sin and death by being joined to Jesus' death and resurrection. From the font, God's spring of living water flows freely and powerfully throughout the gathered assembly, its ripples extending into every day of the Christian's life. The streams of the baptismal spring include nurture, formation, initiation, return, affirmation, vocation, remembrance, and, ultimately, the completion of God's promise in the life to come, when the wellspring of baptism overflows in new life.

Between the moment of our baptism and the moment of our death, we continually do that which baptism attests. "By God's gift and call, all of us who have been baptized into Christ Jesus are daily put to death so that we might be raised daily to newness of life" (UMG 17).

Evangelical Lutheran Worship helps us by making connections between baptism and various aspects of our lives as Christians. Our dying to sin and rising to new life is most vividly expressed in the various forms of confession and forgiveness. Yet returning to and living out of the promise of our baptism is equally important when significant transitions occur in Christians' lives. At these times the service of Affirmation of Baptism helps the church express the ongoing significance of baptism in the lives of Christians. While this order is most often associated with confirmation and when receiving or restoring people into congregational membership, it is an especially meaningful way of marking other important moments in life. In addition, three particular times in Christians' lives—need for healing, the time of death, and (for some) the entry into marriage—are considered so important that the church through the ages has developed baptismally centered rites for these times.

The baptismal life in all its expressions reflects several emphases. First, baptism gives physical expression to our Lutheran understanding of salvation as justification by grace through faith. Second, this promise is as important to the life of the church as it is to the life of the individual Christian. In addition to being the source of the Christian life, baptism is also the wellspring from which congregations are gathered and in which Christian denominations find their shared life in Christ. Third, our baptismal unity accommodates a diversity of practice, so that celebrations of the baptismal life may reflect a particular community, context, and culture. Fourth, God's gift in baptism is so great that a wealth of scriptural images and metaphors are needed to deepen and enliven our understanding of the baptismal life. In this chapter, we explore these four emphases related to holy baptism: we consider baptism as a consistent Lutheran theme, a point of ecumenical convergence, a complex of rites that reflect culture and context, and a reality best appropriated through rich images for God's many gifts.

A Consistent Lutheran Theme

Luther's entire life was a celebration of baptism because he found in baptism both lifelong assurance that God has forgiven our sin and daily motivation to live as those who belong to Christ. For Luther, baptism is a sign, promise, and participation in what God does for humanity and all creation in the life, death, and resurrection of Jesus Christ. Though we may wander away from the baptismal life for a time, God's promise remains. For this reason, Luther argued that God's promise in baptism "should swallow up your whole life, body and soul, and give it forth again at the last day, clad in the robe of glory and immortality" (LW 36:69).

Luther was genuinely overwhelmed by God's grace in baptism. In a sermon on baptism, he declared, "there is no greater comfort on earth than baptism." Baptism is "so great, gracious, and full of comfort, we should diligently see to it that we ceaselessly, joyfully, and from the heart thank, praise, and honor God for it" (LW 35:34, 42). Luther is said to have made the sign of the cross over himself daily while reminding himself that he was baptized. By remembering that he was baptized and trusting the promise God made to him through water and the word, Luther found the courage to face each day. He encouraged Christians to "regard baptism and put it to use in such a way that we may draw strength and comfort from it when our sins or conscience oppress us, and say: 'But I am baptized! And if I have been baptized, I have the promise that I shall be saved and have eternal life, both in soul and body'" (BC 462). The goal of Luther's entire ministry was that all Christians might live each day trusting in the assurance that they are baptized.

Baptism is foundational to a Lutheran understanding of the Christian life because it is nothing less than the promise that we share in Christ's death and resurrection and, therefore, are justified by grace through faith. In his monumental treatise on the sacraments, *The Babylonian Captivity of the Church*, Luther wrote, "Baptism, then, signifies two things—death and resurrection, that is, full and complete justification" (LW 36:67). In a sermon on baptism, he taught that in baptism the Christian dies to sin and rises in the grace of God. The old Adam, conceived and born in sin, is drowned, and a new Christian, born in grace, comes forth and rises. Through this spiritual birth the Christian is a child of grace and a justified person. Sins are drowned in baptism, and in place of sin, righteousness comes forth (LW 35:30). Through baptism, God establishes a new relationship with the Christian. In Luther's words, "We must humbly admit, 'I know full well that I cannot do a single thing that is pure. But I am baptized, and through my baptism God, who cannot lie, has bound himself in a covenant with me. He will not count my sin against me, but will slay it and blot it out'" (LW 35:36).

That salvation is God's gracious act toward humanity is made plain when infants and young children are baptized. Luther initially defended infant baptism as the traditional practice of the church, on the grounds that infants are aided by the faith of those who bring them for baptism, and because Christ received children and blessed them. However, in the Large Catechism Luther subsequently taught that "we pray God to grant [the child] faith. But we do not baptize on this basis, but solely on the command of God" (BC 464). The baptism of infants and young children makes it clear that salvation in Christ is first and foremost God's gracious act of justifying the sinner. Through water and God's word, those baptized are declared righteous before God on the basis of the life, death, and resurrection of Christ, and nothing else.

Faith, then, is not intellectual assent to doctrine or right living but trust in God. Faith simply means trusting that God will do what God promises to do in baptism, namely granting forgiveness of sins, deliverance from death and the devil, and eternal salvation. Even this trust is God's gift. Our faith results from the work of the Holy Spirit in the proclamation of the gospel and the administration of the sacraments in the church. Luther states this eloquently in his explanation of the third article of the Apostles' Creed in the Small Catechism (AE p. 1162). In a similar vein, the Augsburg Confession declares:

> To obtain such faith God instituted the office of preaching, giving the gospel and the sacraments. Through these, as through means, he [God] gives the Holy Spirit, who produces faith, where and when he [the Holy Spirit] wills, in those who hear the gospel. It teaches that we have a gracious God, not through our merit but through Christ's merit, when we so believe. [BC 40]

The infants we bring to the font can claim no faith or personal decisions of their own. They are completely dependent and completely trusting. In this regard they powerfully witness that salvation is entirely God's act, that we in no way cooperate with God in baptism, and that faith and repentance are lifelong consequences of and not preconditions for baptism.

In addition to providing assurance, baptism initiates a way of life motivated and directed by God's promise that our sins are forgiven, that we belong to Christ, and that God's action in baptizing us is effective for the rest of our lives. "Baptism conforms us to the death and resurrection of Christ precisely so that we repent and receive forgiveness, love our neighbors, suffer for the sake of the Gospel, and witness to Christ" (UMG 14A). The Christian life is lived in the aftermath of being conformed to Christ in baptism and is a continual remembrance of this promise made to us in baptism. All Christians need to remember this promise, since we "are at the same time sinners and justified. We experience bondage to sin from which we cannot free ourselves and, at the same time, 'rebirth and renewal by the Holy Spirit'" (UMG 17A). The Christian life is one long returning to and then living out our baptism. It is daily dying to sin and being raised to live before God. In the community of faith, we die to sin and are raised to new life when we seek the consolation of our brothers and sisters in Christ, confess our sins and receive forgiveness, hear the word and receive Christ's supper, proclaim the gospel in word and deed, and strive for justice and peace in all the world. To help worshipers remember their baptism, Lutherans typically place their baptismal fonts either in the front of the church, often near the place of the word and the table of the meal, or at the entrance to the worship space. In our individual Christian lives, we remember and return to baptism—among other ways—by reading scripture, praying, professing the creed, making the sign of the cross, and encountering the catechism. As we remember that we are baptized, God's promise in baptism becomes a wellspring of confidence and renewal every day of the baptismal life.

From the time of Luther through the dawn of the eighteenth century, the so-called period of Lutheran orthodoxy, Lutheran Christians maintained Luther's baptismal emphasis. Lutheran church architecture emphasized the entire assembly seeing and hearing everything that happens at altar, pulpit, and font. Those three came to be the central foci of Lutheran church buildings; they were placed close together in front of the assembly. The period of the Enlightenment (roughly 1700–1800) tended to suppress spirituality based on the sacraments. Sacraments were understood as biblical commands and therefore obligatory, but they were celebrated infrequently and with minimal ritual and no sense of festivity. A stated goal of *Lutheran Book of Worship* was "to restore to Holy Baptism the liturgical rank and dignity implied by Lutheran theology" (Introduction, p. 8), an emphasis grounded in Luther's own baptismal spirituality. *Evangelical Lutheran Worship* reinforces and builds upon this return to Luther's emphasis on baptism. "Baptism is set within the principal gathering for worship, and its themes are reflected in other services. Materials are newly included to help congregations welcome adults and children to formation in faith, to baptism, and to the baptismal life" (AE p. 7).

Ecumenical Convergence

The second half of the twentieth century witnessed an extraordinary ecumenical convergence as several of the world's Christian churches moved toward a greater consensus on both baptismal practice and interpretation, like springs of baptismal water flowing into a common stream. Lutherans around the globe joined with others, including member churches of the worldwide Anglican communion, Presbyterians, Methodists, and Roman Catholics, in conversation about baptism and its place in the life of the church. Rites were developed and shared; the churches borrowed from and informed one another as they sought to reflect this conversation and growing consensus in their worship life. A significant catalyst for this ecumenical endeavor was the Constitution on the Sacred Liturgy of the Roman Catholic Church's Second Vatican Council (1963–1965), which resulted in the creation of renewed rites for the baptism of children, confirmation, and the Christian initiation of adults.

In keeping with another stated goal of *Lutheran Book of Worship*, "to continue to move into the larger ecumenical heritage of liturgy while, at the same time, enhancing Lutheran convictions about the Gospel" (Introduction, p. 8), the major North American Lutheran church bodies produced new services of Baptism and Affirmation of Baptism for that worship book. These services drew deeply upon the ecumenical conversation and convergence of the time, yet the extensive pan-Lutheran dialogue and review of provisional materials ensured that "Lutheran convictions about the Gospel" were well represented in the final versions. The baptismal services in *Lutheran Book of Worship* subsequently became the standard of practice in the vast majority of congregations of the Evangelical Lutheran Church in America and the Evangelical Lutheran Church in Canada.

Beyond these services, an order titled Enrollment of Candidates for Baptism was included in *Occasional Services* (1982). In following years, various North American church bodies, including Lutherans,

Episcopalians, and Methodists, continued work on principles and resources related to the formation of youth and adults leading to baptism, in conversation with Roman Catholics who were implementing their Rite of Christian Initiation of Adults. The work of the ELCIC and the ELCA in this arena is ongoing; it is notably visible in *Evangelical Lutheran Worship* through the inclusion of the order for Welcome to Baptism.

The theologies of baptism and baptismally-related worship resources in several Christian churches had so much in common that in 1982, in a significant document entitled *Baptism, Eucharist, and Ministry*, the Faith and Order Commission of the World Council of Churches provided an overview of the widespread denominational consensus on both baptismal theology and the shape of baptismal rites. According to this document, baptism is the one sacrament for which no church questions the validity of the practices of other Christians. The churches agree that baptism is rooted in the ministry, life, death, and resurrection of Christ. They affirm that baptism is God's gift of incorporation into Christ and entry into the new covenant. Yet the statement agrees with Luther that the life of baptism also encompasses human response: that baptism is a lifelong process of growth into Christ and that the Christian life involves both struggle and continuing in the experience of God's grace. The commission lifts up and attempts to bring together the various scriptural emphases on the meaning of baptism (see Images of Baptism, p. 16), without favoring one over the others.

Turning to practice, *Baptism, Eucharist, and Ministry* specifically addresses the differences between believers' baptism—baptism only of those able and willing to confess their Christian faith—and the baptism of infants. Rather than attempting to resolve these differences, the statement affirms that both are rooted in the faithfulness of Christ and within the faith and life of the believing community. The statement lifts up the merits of a variety of practices. It advises churches, both those that practice believers' baptism and those that practice infant baptism, to reconsider certain aspects of their practices. Churches that practice believers' baptism may seek to express more visibly the fact that children are placed under the protection of God's grace. Those that practice infant baptism must guard themselves against the practice of apparently indiscriminate baptism and take more seriously their responsibility for nurturing baptized children so that they grow to mature faith in and commitment to Christ.

Finally, *Baptism, Eucharist, and Ministry* spells out six implications of this ecumenical consensus for baptismal practice. They include the following:

(1) identifying the essential parts of services of baptism,
(2) encouraging the generous use of water in baptism,
(3) administration in the name of the triune God as essential to the sacrament,
(4) endorsing the use of additional symbols and actions to help communicate the meanings of baptism,
(5) highlighting baptism as a communal act, and
(6) connecting baptism and the festivals of the church.

These implications are affirmed in *The Use of the Means of Grace* and are reflected in *Evangelical Lutheran Worship*.

First, *Evangelical Lutheran Worship* incorporates the elements identified as essential in an order of baptism. As *Baptism, Eucharist, and Ministry* notes,

> Within any comprehensive order of baptism at least the following elements should find a place: the proclamation of scriptures referring to baptism; an invocation of the Holy Spirit; a renunciation of evil; a proclamation of faith in Christ and the Holy Trinity; the use of water; a declaration that the persons baptized have acquired a new identity as sons and daughters of God, and as members of the Church, called to be witnesses of the Gospel. Some churches consider that Christian initiation is not complete without the sealing of the baptized with the Holy Spirit and participation in holy communion. [BEM 6]

How do we see these essential elements in *Evangelical Lutheran Worship*'s baptismal service? Biblical images abound in the thanksgiving at the font. The Holy Spirit is invoked twice, in the thanksgiving—"Pour out your Holy Spirit, the power of your living Word"—and again in the prayer accompanying the laying on of hands. By God's grace we "profess [our] faith in Christ Jesus, reject sin, and confess the faith of the church" through the renunciations and the creedal affirmations that follow. A generous use of water is encouraged. Each of the newly baptized is named "child of God" and is welcomed by the assembly into the mission of the whole church. The baptismal rite in *Evangelical*

Lutheran Worship also includes the declaration that the newly baptized are sealed by the Holy Spirit, an action that may be accompanied by anointing with oil. *The Use of the Means of Grace* (37D) provides for the possibility that the newly baptized, including infants, receive holy communion in the service at which they are baptized.

Second, *Evangelical Lutheran Worship* encourages generous use of water at baptism: "Water is used generously" (Notes on the Services, LE 28). This recommendation flows from an awareness that the symbol of water speaks most eloquently when it is plentiful and visible rather than minimal. Toward this end, pouring and immersion are especially valuable ways of administering baptism. Each mode accents a particular image of what God is doing in baptism: pouring suggests cleansing from sin, immersion communicates dying and rising with Christ. *The Use of the Means of Grace* asserts that water, as a sign of cleansing, dying, and new birth, "is used generously in Holy Baptism to symbolize God's power over sin and death" (26). This statement goes on to affirm that God's word, not the amount of water, is the power at work in baptism, and that God can use any amount of water we may have. However, citing Luther, the statement emphasizes that "we wish to make full use of water, when it is possible" (26A).

Third, *Evangelical Lutheran Worship* reflects the ecumenical consensus that baptism is administered in the name of the Holy Trinity and that reference to Matthew 28:19 is integral to the baptismal order. *The Use of the Means of Grace* states that "Holy Baptism is administered with water in the name of the triune God, Father, Son, and Holy Spirit" (24), and *Evangelical Lutheran Worship* uses these words at the baptism. *The Use of the Means of Grace* goes on to state, however, that baptism into the triune God involves confessing and teaching the meaning of the Trinity. Teaching that meaning occurs within the community of faith. The goal of this instruction is to help the baptized understand the name not merely as a formula but as "the power and presence of the triune God and of that teaching which must accompany every Baptism" (24B) This teaching ought to help the baptized distinguish between what the doctrine of the Trinity does and does not convey, including continually reexamining what *Father* and *Son* mean in biblical and creedal perspective. In this way, the church will "maintain trinitarian orthodoxy while speaking in appropriate modern language and contexts" (24A).

Fourth, *Evangelical Lutheran Worship,* continuing what was included in *Lutheran Book of Worship,* affirms the early church's practice of using additional gestures and symbols to signify the gift of the Holy Spirit in baptism. Such actions engage the various human senses and serve as vivid expressions of what God is doing in baptism. *The Use of the Means of Grace* agrees that interpretative signs—including the laying on of hands, prayer for the Holy Spirit, signing with the cross, and anointing with oil—proclaim the breadth of the meaning of baptism and the gifts that God's promise gives. Scripture provides the key for interpreting these signs. The baptismal service in *Evangelical Lutheran Worship* includes these symbols and gestures, as well as the possibility of clothing the newly baptized in baptismal garments and presenting each with a lighted candle.

Fifth, *Evangelical Lutheran Worship* highlights the communal nature of baptism. Baptism is intimately connected with the corporate life of the church, in and through a congregation. This relationship with a particular congregation leads to baptism best, and normally, being administered during public worship. The wisdom of this accepted practice is twofold. First, celebrating baptism within worship helps the members of the congregation recognize the centrality of baptism, remember their own baptism, and live the baptismal life. Second, the members of the congregation can support the newly baptized, their sponsors, and families, and can express their commitment to nurture those being baptized and welcome them into community. The connection to the church further implies that, under normal circumstances, baptism is administered by an ordained minister.

Sixth, *Evangelical Lutheran Worship* carries forward the ecumenical encouragement to link baptism and the church's major festivals. This is a continuation of the counsel of *Lutheran Book of Worship:* "It is appropriate to designate such occasions as the Vigil of Easter, The Day of Pentecost, All Saints' Day, and The Baptism of Our Lord for the celebration of Holy Baptism. Baptismal celebrations on these occasions keep Baptism integrated into the unfolding of the story of salvation provided by the church year" (Ministers Edition 30). *Baptism, Eucharist, and Ministry* says that baptism "is appropriate to great festival occasions such as Easter, Pentecost, and Epiphany, as was the practice in the early Church" (23). *The Use of the Means of Grace* includes All Saints Day and the Baptism of Our Lord as worthy of consideration and identifies the Vigil of Easter as an especially appropriate time to celebrate baptism, because it emphasizes that the source of all baptisms is the death and resurrection of Christ. The notes on Holy Baptism in *Evangelical Lutheran Worship* (LE 27) rightly observe that designating festivals as baptismal celebrations will amplify baptism's imagery and significance. This approach to scheduling baptism also links the story of Christ's life and our salvation.

We might think of these six characteristics of baptismal celebration as manifestations of the ecumenical convergence around the theology and practice of baptism, which have been making their way into the church's life since the middle of the twentieth century. This ecumenical consensus is both a gift of the Holy Spirit and a powerful Christian witness. It was influential in the development of *The Use of the Means of Grace* and both *Lutheran Book of Worship* and *Evangelical Lutheran Worship*. These considerations guide this volume and can helpfully inform pastoral practice.

Baptism in Culture and Context

Christian worship occurs within a given community, context, and culture. Preaching, baptism, and communion cannot exist without a gathered assembly of Christians. "The congregation assembles in God's presence, hears the word of life, baptizes and remembers Baptism, and celebrates the Holy Supper" (UMG 6A). What assemblies do when they gather to worship is, for the most part, shared across time, space, history, and culture; however, the ways congregations worship also take seriously the local context, and thus they can foster the expression of local Christian unity.

The Worship and Culture Study undertaken from 1993 to 1998 by the Lutheran World Federation (LWF) provided biblical and historical foundations for celebrating Christian worship, particularly baptism and eucharist, in culture and context. It also outlined contemporary issues facing Lutheran churches. The Study's "Nairobi Statement on Worship and Culture: Contemporary Challenges and Opportunities" (Appendix A), published with supporting essays in *Christian Worship: Unity in Cultural Diversity,* outlined a fourfold dynamic of Christian worship and culture. Christian worship is and should be *transcultural*, the same substance everywhere, transcending culture. It is *contextual* in the ways the substance of Christian worship is expressed locally, adapted from the cultural and natural contexts. At the same time, Christian worship is *countercultural* as it challenges and transforms cultural patterns that are inconsistent with the gospel. Finally, Christian worship is *cross-cultural* as it seeks to share among and between local cultures.

The LWF Study's fourth international consultation, related to baptism and other rites of life passages, developed the "Chicago Statement on Worship and Culture: Baptism and Rites of Passage" (Appendix B). This statement summarizes the consultation's principles and conclusions and was published with the papers presented in *Baptism, Rites of Passage, and Culture* (1999). The Chicago Statement examines baptism and three rites of passage (healing, marriage, and funeral) in cultural context.

The Chicago Statement begins by defining the relationship between baptism and rites of passage or rites related to the life cycle. It calls baptism the "foundational event in the life of any community" and summarizes the many meanings of baptism, which are discussed in the next section. Of particular note, baptism introduces the newly baptized into life both in a local community of Christians and in communion with all the churches of God. Baptism also gives Christians the lifelong dignity and responsibility of their vocation in Christ. The statement then relates other life passages to baptism by asserting, "All other changes and transitions in the life of the Christian must be seen as to reflect this basic transition and this basic dignity: 'Once you were not a people, but now you are God's people' (1 Peter 2:10). Baptism thus informs and shapes rites related to the life-cycle" (1.1).

Rites of passage are communal and symbolic processes and acts that are connected with important or critical transitions in the lives of individuals and communities. The statement observes that in almost all cultures, giving birth, coming to adulthood, marrying, reconciling, leave-taking, passing into and sometimes through sickness, and dying and grieving are among those life transitions. Cultures observe these transitions with diverse communal rites, which express the transitional process of separation or ending, *liminality* or the in-between stage, and incorporation or new beginning. As in virtually all communities, the Christian community celebrates rites of passage, chiefly those associated with sickness, funerals, and marriage, as a way of invoking God's care and blessing and accompanying people in these significant life transitions. The Chicago Statement observes that Christians understand these rites of passage as extending, renewing, or concluding their original and essential rite of passage through the waters of baptism. The statement then endorses remembering and affirming baptism in diverse rites associated with the life cycle and celebrating these rites within the community of the baptized.

Next, the statement suggests two approaches that the churches may use when considering how baptism and other rites of passage may be celebrated in ways that are attentive to a given community, culture, and context. One approach involves the reexpression of components of Christian worship with elements from a local culture that have an equal meaning, value, and function *(dynamic equivalence)*. A second approach involves the addition of elements from the local culture to the pattern of the rite, which enrich its original core *(creative assimilation)*. The statement astutely advises that the design of the worship space, the selection of music, and all other dimensions of rites should be considered as important ways of communicating and celebrating the gospel. These elements should not be dismissed out of indifference or decided solely by personal taste. Rather, all elements should be in accordance with the gospel, making clear the baptismal value and connection of the rites.

The statement continues with sections devoted to baptism, healing rites, funeral rites, and marriage rites. Each section elucidates the transcultural, contextual, countercultural, and cross-cultural dimensions of the rites. These insights are included in the discussion of the rites in this volume. In the statement's final section, "Call to the Churches," the study team exhorts member churches of the LWF to embrace the challenge of developing and using forms of worship that are both authentic to the gospel and relevant to local cultural contexts. The team calls the churches to undertake intentional study related to the fourfold dynamic of worship and culture, while recovering the centrality of baptism for their life and worship and as the foundation of rites of passage.

Images of Baptism

What is baptism? In the Small Catechism, Luther answers: "Baptism is not simply plain water. Instead, it is water used according to God's command and connected with God's word" (AE p. 1164). This classic definition, which concisely and accurately summarizes baptism, has served Lutheran Christians well for generations. Yet, as we continue to grow in our understanding of baptism toward celebrating the entire Christian life as a return to and living out of the promise of our baptism, images and metaphors—especially those from scripture—add rich dimensions of meaning to a simple definition.

The New Testament scriptures and the liturgy of the church unfold the meaning of baptism in multiple images that express the riches of Christ and the gifts of salvation. Sometimes these images are linked with the symbolic uses of water in the Old Testament. Scripture teaches that in baptism we share in Christ's death and resurrection (Rom. 6:3-5; Col. 2:12); we are washed clean from sin (1 Cor. 6:11), born anew (John 3:5), enlightened by Christ (Eph. 5:14), clothed with Christ (Gal. 3:27), and renewed by the Spirit (Titus 3:5). Scripture compares baptism to salvation from the flood (1 Pet. 3:20-21), exodus from bondage (1 Cor. 10:1-2), and unity that transcends barriers of division (1 Cor. 12:13; Gal. 3:27-28).

Echoing these scriptural references, *The Use of the Means of Grace* describes baptism as deliverance, death, birth, adoption, and membership. "In Holy Baptism, the Triune God delivers us from the forces of evil, puts our sinful self to death, gives us new birth, adopts us as children, and makes us members of the body of Christ, the Church" (14). *The Use of the Means of Grace* also describes God's action in baptism as liberating, joining, sealing, marking, inaugurating, and conforming.

These descriptions help us take seriously that, more than anything else, the sacrament of baptism is a mystery. We can never fully grasp, completely define, or thoroughly exhaust all that God does by water and the Word. At most, we point to, hint at, and glimpse the depth of God's love for us in baptism. Images for baptism help us to expand our understanding and appreciation of all that baptism is, so that we do not reduce baptism by confining it to either an essential definition or just one of its many interpretations.

For the purpose of this discussion, we can identify six chief ways in which scripture speaks of baptism:

(1) participation in Christ's death and resurrection,

(2) new birth,

(3) forgiveness of sins,

(4) reception of the Holy Spirit,

(5) membership in the church, and

(6) entrance into the reign of God.

This list is not intended to be exhaustive. Others might construct it differently. Yet, rather than considering every image of baptism, our aim is to stimulate evocative thinking that will expand and enliven baptismal practice and living.

Participation in Christ's Death and Resurrection

Through baptism we participate in the life, death, and resurrection of Jesus Christ. In the Small Catechism, Luther quotes Romans 6:3-5 about being buried with and rising with Christ. By baptism the old person in all of us is drowned, the power of sin is broken, and we are raised now, confident that we will share in Christ's resurrection. Elsewhere Luther says that this death and resurrection are "not [to] be understood only allegorically as the death of sin and the life of grace, as many understand it, but as actual death and resurrection. For baptism is not a false sign" (LW 36:68). Luther said, "the life of a Christian, from baptism to the grave, is nothing else than the beginning of a blessed death. For at the Last Day God will make [the Christian] altogether new" (LW 35:31).

For this reason, as we have seen, Luther preferred baptism by immersion. Immersion has a strong reference to death, to drowning and burial. It is not surprising that early baptisteries often imitated the form of a mausoleum and that baptismal fonts are often stone and tomblike. As going into the water and being submerged signifies drowning and death, so emerging from the water and coming out of the baptismal pool signifies life. In the early church, the connection of baptism with Christ's death and resurrection was reinforced by the timing of baptism. By the fourth century, most baptisms occurred at Easter, when the image of the candidates' dying and rising with Christ was most vivid. By the Middle Ages, the connection of baptism and Christ's death and resurrection at Easter was mostly lost, due in part to the emergence of a piety that emphasized baptizing infants as soon after birth as possible, out of fear that they might be lost to God if they died before baptism. The gradual erosion of the practice of baptism by immersion further weakened the image of the sacrament as death and resurrection. But today this image of baptism is experiencing a widespread revival in popularity, in part because of the renewed understanding that all Christian worship celebrates Christ's death and resurrection. The gradual recovery of the Vigil of Easter in some parts of the church is also contributing to a renewed emphasis on this fundamental New Testament image.

In addition to dying to sin and rising to new life, participating in Christ's death and resurrection also means that we share in Christ's work. We are united to Christ's priestly ministry. The Christ to whom we are united in baptism is our high priest (Heb. 9:11) and, as a result, we become a priestly people (1 Pet. 2:9)—that is, we are people who carry out Christ's ministry in the way Christ did, by offering ourselves for the life of the world.

Luther wrote, "For whoever comes out of the water of baptism can boast that he [or she] is already a consecrated priest, bishop, and pope. . . . We are all priests of equal standing" (LW 44:129). Luther proclaims a radical equality on the basis of baptism. There are not multiple categories of Christians; there is not a hierarchy of spiritual standings before God; rather, in baptism we are all members of one body, serving one another and the world through our respective and differing vocations. Baptism inaugurates the Christian community's ministry to the individual Christian. It inaugurates the individual Christian's ministry to the Christian community. In baptism, God calls all Christians to minister to one another and to the world in whatever station they find themselves.

Such baptismal equality provides an important foundation for a Lutheran understanding of worship. Worship is the work of God, who gathers people by the Holy Spirit, speaks to them through the living word, feeds them with the bread and cup of heaven, and sends them forth to continue God's mission. Yet God's work in worship is not mediated to the masses, as though they were passive recipients, by a limited group of spiritual experts. God's work in worship is carried out through the whole people of God. Through their respective and differing roles, each of the baptized contributes for the benefit of all. Luther determined that, for the people of God to be a priestly people who share in the work of worship, worship must be accessible to them. The vernacular allowed the assembly to pray together so that all could hear and speak as one body. Music, particularly the singing of hymns, permitted all Christians to join their voices in adoring God and witnessing to one another. Worship also requires many different people. Some serve as readers of scripture, cantors, musicians, and leaders of prayer. Some serve as ushers and greeters; others prepare and serve at the altar. Many serve as the common voice of the assembly, proclaiming the word through hymns, liturgy, and creed, and enacting the word by offering, praying, greeting one another with the peace of Christ, and receiving that same Christ in the holy supper. Finally, someone serves the whole body by preaching and administering the sacraments. By calling forth the gifts of each and requiring the participation of all, Christian worship both celebrates the radical equality of baptism and forms the people of God to carry out Christ's radical priesthood, offering their lives to the world as those who are joined to his death and resurrection.

Assembly song in *Evangelical Lutheran Worship* frequently reflects this image of being joined to Christ's death and resurrection. We sing, "Buried with Christ in death, you are raised with him to life" ("Springs of water, bless the Lord," #214). "We are baptized in Christ Jesus, we are baptized in his death, that as Christ is raised victorious, we might live a brand new life" (#451). "Awake, O sleeper, rise from death, and Christ shall give you light" (#452). "We share by water in his saving death. Reborn, we share with him an Easter life" ("We know that Christ is raised," #449). "We were baptized in Jesus, into his death and grave, to resurrection's promise: praise and eternal life" ("Seed that in earth is dying," #330). These are among the newer songs that are helping assemblies not only to recover an awareness of this image but also to restore a baptismal dimension to the seasons of Lent and Easter, when these hymns are often suitable for use.

New Birth

In John's gospel, Jesus says to Nicodemus, "No one can enter the kingdom of God without being born of water and the Spirit" (3:5). The baptismal image of new birth, of being born anew, born again, or born from above, has a rich history in the church. For example, Cyril of Jerusalem said of baptism, "In one and the same action you died and were born; the water of salvation became both tomb and mother for you." Theodore of Mopsuestia calls the water of baptism the awesome womb of the second birth; all who go down into the water are formed again by the grace of the Holy Spirit and are born again in another, higher nature. In both the Large Catechism and the Small Catechism Luther refers to baptism as birth. In both places he quotes Titus 3:5 to describe baptism: God "saved us . . . through the water of rebirth and renewal by the Holy Spirit."

Today, new birth as an image for baptism is subject to a variety of interpretations. Although some Christians consider new birth to be an apt description for the unilateral gift of God in baptism, others think of being born again or born from above as a moment or process of conversion in which the one being born actively participates—and which may have little to do with the sacrament of baptism. The image of baptism as new birth has nonetheless grown in popularity in recent years, in part because it is the most explicitly feminine metaphor the church has. Calling baptism a new birth brings to mind aspects of God's nature and our experience of grace that correspond to women's role as bearers of children. This scriptural image provides needed balance to an abundance of masculine metaphors and invites the church to reclaim an image of baptism that enables the church to celebrate it in new and powerful ways. For example, the baptismal font once again may be regarded not only as a tomb of death from which we rise with Christ but also as a womb through whose waters God bears us forth into new life.

Several newer hymns explore this image of baptism as new birth. "Mothering God, you gave me birth" (#735) can be understood to refer not only to creation but also to the new creation in baptism. "O living Breath of God, bearing us to life through baptismal waters" (#407), we sing, recalling the work of the Holy Spirit in baptism and the fact that in Hebrew the word for breath or spirit is a feminine noun. But the image is also present in the venerable German chorale "Dearest Jesus, we are here": "You must all be born again, heart and life renewing truly, born of water and the Spirit, and my kingdom thus inherit" (#443).

Forgiveness of Sins

Baptism is the "washing of water by the word" (Eph. 5:26) by which we are forgiven, cleansed, and made holy in Christ. From a Lutheran perspective, forgiveness of sins is perhaps the predominant way of describing the gift of baptism. The Small Catechism names it first among the "gifts or benefits" of baptism: "It brings about forgiveness of sins, redeems from death and the devil, and gives eternal salvation to all who believe it, as the words and promises of God declare" (AE p. 1165). For the central theological statement of his baptismal rite of 1523, Luther assembled his famous flood prayer, a version of which is included in the *Evangelical Lutheran Worship* baptismal rite (AE p. 230). This prayer relates God's use of water in cleansing the world through Noah and the ark, the deliverance of God's people from bondage through the Red Sea, and the baptism of Jesus in the Jordan. Here, water serves as "a rich and full washing away of sins" (LW 53:97). The metaphors of cleansing and washing for the forgiveness of sin make it clear that God acts in baptism. God enters into a covenant relationship with humanity and forgives us. Through baptism God creates and effects this new relationship. For Luther, baptism was such a powerful expression of the gospel that he produced the "Order of Baptism" in the German language three years before publishing the German Mass.

Understanding baptism as the forgiveness of sins also has a strong missional emphasis. As the gathering of people forgiven by Christ, baptism identifies the Christian community with Jesus, who identified himself with those considered outcasts and sinners and gave his life for the needs of the world. The church is called to proclaim the forgiveness we receive in baptism to the whole world (see Luke 24:47).

Baptism as the forgiveness of sins has a long history in both scripture and the church's tradition. Forgiveness of sins was already present in the baptism of John: "John the baptizer appeared in the wilderness, proclaiming a baptism of repentance for the forgiveness of sins" (Mark 1:4; see Luke 3:3). The apostle Peter preaches, "Repent, and be baptized every one of you in the name of Jesus Christ so that your sins may be forgiven" (Acts 2:38; see Acts 22:16, 1 Cor. 6:11). Both 1 Peter 3:21 and Hebrews 10:22 compare baptism with an outward washing and an inward cleansing to create "a good conscience" (1 Peter) or "hearts sprinkled clean" (Hebrews). Baptism as the forgiveness of sins became church doctrine in the Nicene Creed: "We acknowledge one baptism for the forgiveness of sins." After the fourth century, this understanding of baptism was reinforced by the concept that children bore the guilt of original sin, transmitted to all humanity from Adam. Baptism canceled the guilt of original sin, though not the human tendency to sin. Baptism also removed the guilt of the actual sin that anyone of accountable age had committed. By the late Middle Ages the forgiveness of sins was the dominant way of understanding baptism. The medieval church determined that all infants should be baptized no later than the eighth day after birth, for fear that salvation was impossible without baptism. John 3:5 was interpreted to mean that the kingdom was unattainable without baptism, and this threat was applied to people of all ages. Language and imagery about the forgiveness of sins remains a central theme in baptismal orders now in use. However, the theological history associated with this theme, as alluded to above, suggests the importance of holding other images alongside this dominant understanding.

Assembly song that connects baptism with the forgiveness of sins is plentiful, including newer hymn texts such as "Wash, O God, our sons and daughters, where your cleansing waters flow" (#445); "Baptized in water . . . freed and forgiven . . . God's praise we sing" (#456); and "The cleansing was for certain, with water and the Word" ("Waterlife," #457).

The Gift of the Holy Spirit

God pours out the Holy Spirit on those being baptized. Jesus' own baptism includes the descending of the Holy Spirit, visible as a dove (Matt. 3:16). Acts 2:38 says, "be baptized . . . and you will receive the gift of the Holy Spirit." Baptism includes God's promise that the same Spirit who revealed Jesus as the Son and empowered the disciples at Pentecost is at work in the lives of Christians. The Spirit draws the baptized into communion with the triune God and with one another. This communion creates the church, as well as providing and empowering Christians for their participation in Christ's ministry. Other New Testament passages describe the Holy Spirit's activity in baptism as illumination, enlightenment, and sanctification (Heb. 6:4; 1 Cor. 6:11). Yet the relationship of baptism and the gift of the Spirit is complicated by passages in Acts, where the Holy Spirit arrives both before baptism and afterward with the laying on of hands (10:47; 19:6). The point is not that God *only* gives the Holy Spirit through baptism, but that God *does* give the Holy Spirit in baptism.

Both in words and actions, the early church celebrated baptism as the gift of the Holy Spirit. Symbolic gestures, including the laying on of hands, anointing with oil, and the presentation of a lighted candle underscored the connection of the outpouring of the Holy Spirit with baptism. In his treatise *On Baptism* (c. 200), Tertullian tells us that the baptized were anointed and received the laying on of hands, "inviting and welcoming the Holy Spirit." In the fourth century, Theodore of Mopsuestia relates the signing of cross on the foreheads of the newly baptized to the presence of the Holy Spirit at Jesus' baptism and Jesus' claim of being anointed by the Spirit (Luke 4:18). By the fifth century in the West, although a priest could baptize, the signing with the cross after baptism was restricted to the bishop and, consequently, removed from baptism. By the sixteenth century, the gift of the Holy Spirit evolved into a separate rite, known as confirmation, and was administered after children attained the age of reason, which was defined as twelve years of age. Luther, though, explicitly maintained that confirmation is not a sacrament since it contains no divine promise. The work of the Holy Spirit is not prominent in Luther's baptismal piety. In fact, in Luther's baptismal orders, the unclean spirit being exorcized is emphasized almost as much as the Holy Spirit. Contemporary baptismal orders seek to restore a clear articulation that the Holy Spirit is given in baptism. These rites furthermore understand confirmation as a renewal or reaffirmation of what God has done for us in baptism, in which we ask God to stir up rather than pour out the Holy Spirit.

The activity of the Holy Spirit in baptism is expressed in hymns such as "This is the Spirit's entry now: the water and the word" ("Remember and rejoice," #448). We are "forever traced by water sign, and sealed by Spirit flame" (#454). We pray, "Baptize with joy and power, give, O Dove descending, life never ending" ("Praise and thanksgiving be to God," #458).

Incorporation into the Body of Christ

Closely related to the images of participation in Christ's death and resurrection and the giving of the Holy Spirit is the image of incorporation into Christ's body. Baptism makes Christians members of the church, the community joined to Christ in and through which the Spirit is active. The classic text for this image of baptism is Paul's statement that "We were all baptized into one body" (1 Cor. 12:13). This theme is also found in several other passages, where Paul states that for those "baptized into Christ . . . there is no longer Jew or Greek, there is no longer slave or free, there is no longer male and female; for all of you are one in Christ Jesus" (Gal. 3:27-28).

As early as the New Testament, baptism was seen as the means of becoming a part of the church. By the fourth century, this transition was made explicit. The newly baptized, who had never before witnessed the holy supper, went immediately from the font to the altar. There the assembly greeted them with the sign of peace, and they received communion for the first time. When church and society were synonymous, as in Europe during the late Middle Ages, baptism lost much of its sense of being an entrance rite into the Christian community. For this reason, Luther, who has so much to say about the personal dimension of baptism, downplays the communal aspect. For example, in a long exposition of the meaning of baptism in the Large Catechism, he sums up the communal dimension of baptism as "the sacrament by which we are first received into the Christian community" (BC 464).

In recent decades, as Christians have become increasingly aware that the church is a distinct community, baptism as incorporation into the church has received renewed attention. In some quarters, the church is coming to understand baptism as initiating a distinct way of life that invites people to undergo radical and lasting transformation. As we have seen, baptism also has become an ecumenical rallying point because most Christian traditions accept the validity of other communions' baptisms. Our common baptism is a basic bond of unity, a sign and seal of our common discipleship, and a clear call to end divisions. Our baptismal unity in Christ also provides the theological basis for seeking justice for all members of the body of Christ. To highlight baptism as entrance into the church, fonts are sometimes placed near the doors of churches.

One of the baptismal acclamations in *Evangelical Lutheran Worship,* suitable for singing immediately after baptism, proclaims this understanding: "You belong to Christ, in whom you have been baptized" (#212, #213). The image of incorporation is married with other scriptural images in the hymn "O blessed spring, where word and sign embrace us into Christ the Vine," which concludes, " . . . word and water thus revive and join us to your Tree of Life" (#447). And in the ancient "breastplate" attributed to St. Patrick, this binding to Christ and his community is manifold: "Christ be with me, Christ within me, Christ behind me, Christ before me, Christ beside me . . . Christ in hearts of all that love me, Christ in mouth of friend and stranger" ("I bind unto myself today," #450).

Entrance into the Reign of God

Baptism initiates the reality of a new life in the reign or kingdom of God, given amid the reality of the present world. God's reign is a new order of creation, which embraces the whole of life, extends to every people and nation, and anticipates fulfillment in the life of the world to come, where Christ "fills all in all" (Eph. 1:23). Jesus proclaimed, "Repent, for the kingdom of heaven has come near," and commissioned the disciples to proclaim this good news as well (Matt. 4:17; 10:7). In baptism the kingdom of God comes near to us. Baptism functions as the transition from the old order to the new; in baptism we move into a new age in which we are already part of the reign of God that is breaking into our world. Baptism makes us citizens of the coming kingdom of God on earth.

In baptismal orders, this transition is expressed most clearly in the strong statements of renunciation of evil. These renunciations are intended to stress the nature of sin as social and systemic and not merely as personal action and private temptation. By renouncing evil, the baptized reject everything in the world that is contrary to the gospel.

In the early centuries of the church's life, renouncing evil and entering God's coming reign meant rejecting the dominant culture. This rejection was enhanced as candidates for baptism faced west, the direction of the setting sun, to renounce the devil, and then turned east, toward the new day, to profess faith in Christ. Baptism as entrance into God's reign also meant becoming a member of a tightly disciplined, countercultural community, the church, which understood itself as a colony on earth in which the first fruits of God's reign are found. By the Middle Ages, when church and society were synonymous, baptism lost its significance as entrance into God's reign through rejecting the forces at work in the world and becoming part of a distinct community. Baptism became a sacrament of individual salvation, and the reign of God was defined strictly as heaven.

In our time, where in many places church and society do not walk so closely hand in hand, baptism is increasingly regarded as entering a communal way of life that sometimes stands in contrast to the surrounding society. "Christians profess baptismal faith as they engage in discipleship in the world. God calls Christians to use their various vocations and ministries to witness to the Gospel of Christ wherever they serve or work" (UMG 52). Home and school, community and nation, daily work and leisure, citizenship and friendship, all belong to God and are places where God calls Christians to serve. The connection of baptism and social justice is an essential aspect of Christian service.

Baptism engenders a profound sense of responsibility for other members of the household of faith, for all people, and for all creation. In baptism we undertake a serious responsibility not only for people's spiritual welfare but also for their material welfare. The fact that people, many of whom are baptized into the same body with us, lack the essentials for life is a contradiction of our baptism. The deprivation of our neighbor and exploitation of creation are indications of our failure to take our baptism seriously. On the other hand, deeds of love and charity are a form of living out our baptism as citizens of God's reign.

The expansion of baptismal hymnody in *Evangelical Lutheran Worship* allows for additional emphasis on this theme of baptism as entrance into the reign of God. "We pledge ourselves anew . . . to cling to Christ's community, in justice, peace to dwell" ("Remember and rejoice," #454). "Let water be the sacred sign that we must die each day to rise again . . . as followers of [Christ's] way" ("This is the Spirit's entry now," #448).

In the Large Catechism, Luther says that in baptism, every Christian has enough to study and practice all his or her life. For the blessings of baptism are so boundless that we might doubt whether they could all be true (BC 461). So that we might not doubt but live every day trusting in the promise of our baptism, we have a deep well of images, in scripture and in the church's liturgy and song, from which we may draw strength and fresh understanding. Immersed in these rich images for what God is doing in this sacrament, the church gives the baptismal life central place in all of its worship.

CHAPTER TWO

The Place of Baptism in the Church's Worship

Not so long ago, baptism might have been observed quietly, especially in denominations that have had a tradition of baptizing infants. Within the living memory of many Lutherans today, baptism might frequently have occurred apart from their congregation's usual worship space and not at a primary worship service.[1] Baptism was scheduled primarily for the convenience of a given family, often within a few days following the birth of an infant, and sometimes took place at home rather than in a space associated with public worship.

The occasion for baptism, in a society where it was presumed that nearly everyone was Christian, was the birth of a child. In such a situation one became a Christian by being *born* into the church, in nearly the same way that a person becomes a citizen of a country. For centuries—at least from Augustine's time in the fifth century throughout most of the twentieth century—with the doctrine of original sin paramount in church leaders' and parents' minds, people were particularly afraid of what might happen if an unbaptized child were to die. So began the custom of *quamprimum* baptism—as soon as possible after birth. Baptism often followed birth by no more than a week. Children were baptized so quickly following birth that sometimes the mother was not present because she had not recovered from the delivery.[2]

With the significant decrease of infant mortality in the past century or so, the fear of death—and the subsequent fear about what might happen to a child's eternal soul if it has not been baptized—is less often the great motivation for seeking a prompt baptism. Infant baptism is increasingly experienced as a gift and a celebration rather than an obligation to be performed out of fear. These days even active members of churches may not feel pressured to schedule a baptism within a few days or even weeks following a child's birth. Parents are often able to adjust to a variety of aspects of a child's presence in their lives prior to bringing a child to the church for baptism, and the day is often planned for some time in advance so that it might be marked with much celebration among family and friends.

At the dawn of the twenty-first century, a majority of Lutheran congregations in North America generally observe baptism within the context of a congregation's primary worship space and during the time of a regular Sunday service. This fundamental sacrament of Christian identity has grown more visible in recent decades, even apart from its celebration during primary worship services. A number of pastors regularly preach about what baptism means for all of life. Contemporary baptismal fonts are often larger than their predecessors of previous generations, and they may be located in places that are more prominent and accessible to people as they enter and leave the worship space.

Liturgical language, even apart from baptismal services, seems to refer to baptism more frequently than just a few decades ago. A greater quantity and variety of baptismal hymns are in *Evangelical Lutheran Worship* than in previous hymn collections: *Evangelical Lutheran Worship* (2006) has a baptismal section of eighteen hymns; *Lutheran Book of Worship* (1978) had nine baptismal hymns; while *Service Book and Hymnal* (1958) had only four hymns in the section on baptism. Simply stated, baptism has been growing in prominence within church life in recent years, as well it should! Something that is so fundamental to Christian identity and growth in that identity deserves to have great attention paid to it.

The remainder of this chapter will explore a number of specific ways in which baptism is an integral part of worship—not only during the baptismal liturgy itself but also in many moments of the church's life.

Holy Baptism and Holy Communion

Holy baptism and holy communion are linked together as the church's two sacraments. Both sacraments are means by which God confers grace, and they are practices of the church that are carried out in response to Christ's command. The two sacraments differ chiefly in that baptism is performed once in the lifetime of a Christian—though believers may remember it daily—while communion is repeated regularly. Baptism initiates reception into the body of Christ, and members of the body of Christ regularly celebrate that reality through communion. In an explanation of communion, Augustine preached that when Christians receive the body of Christ and say "Amen," they affirm what they already are, together: the Body of Christ.

Confession and Forgiveness

For the baptized, confession and forgiveness may be understood as a return to baptism. Though baptism is once for all time in the life of every Christian, there are a number of ways for people to continue to be aware of God's baptismal grace. A brief order of confession and forgiveness in the Sunday assembly is but one way in which the baptized return to baptism. Additional possibilities are described in the sections that follow.

It must be said that although an order for confession and forgiveness may be related to baptism, it also invites the participation of all present, whether or not they are baptized or perceive a connection to baptism. An awareness of brokenness in one's own life and of disorder in the world may lead people who have not been baptized deeply into this act of confession. And the word of forgiveness is God's gift to all.

Preparation for holy communion

Brief congregational forms of confession and forgiveness have been used at the outset of services of holy communion in several generations of Lutheran worship books. While it is true that Martin Luther taught that simply believing in the words "given for you" and "shed for you for the forgiveness of sin" make a person worthily prepared for communion (see AE p. 1166), an order of confession and forgiveness is often pastorally appropriate at the communion service.

Several forms for confession and forgiveness as a part of the assembly's gathering for holy communion are included in *Evangelical Lutheran Worship.* The order includes this introductory note: "All may make the sign of the cross, the sign that is marked at baptism, as the presiding minister begins" (AE p. 94). With the use of this tactile symbol connecting the two sacraments, holy communion may be experienced as the repeatable act of grace that holy baptism first inaugurates in a believer's life.

Evangelical Lutheran Worship also provides a thanksgiving for baptism (AE p. 97) as an alternative way to begin the service. This form includes the same note about making the sign of the cross. The thanksgiving for baptism is a more overt reminder of the baptismal liturgy itself, with a prayer of thanksgiving that is very similar to one used in Holy

Baptism (AE p. 230). Yet it also sounds the note of forgiveness: the opening address reminds us that "we are clothed with God's mercy and forgiveness," and we ask God in the prayer that follows to "renew our lives with your forgiveness, grace, and love."

Although either the confession or the thanksgiving may be led from the baptismal font, the sprinkling of water that may occur following the prayer of thanksgiving is a strong physical reminder of baptism. These portions from the Gathering section of the service of Holy Communion are described more thoroughly in *The Sunday Assembly,* the first volume of Using *Evangelical Lutheran Worship.*

Other ways in which the Holy Communion service may relate to baptism include these:

- scripture readings where water is a central theme provide opportunities to make a baptismal connection;
- preachers weaving frequently into their proclamation references to God's grace in baptism and to baptismal living in vocation and service;
- the Nicene or Apostles' creeds, when used, are declarations of the trinitarian faith received at baptism;
- the sign of the cross, when used by the presiding minister in blessing the assembly during the Sending, or when used by members of the assembly themselves, is a reminder of the cross of Christ traced on the forehead of the newly baptized (AE p. 231).

Other experiences of confession and forgiveness

The primary experience of confession and forgiveness for most worshipers will likely be during a congregational service of holy communion, yet confession and forgiveness may be experienced in a number of other ways.

The Apology of the Augsburg Confession enumerated confession and forgiveness as a third sacrament, since along with baptism and the Lord's supper it has "the command of God and the promise of grace" (BC 219). For this reason, as well as for pastoral reasons, confession and forgiveness ought to have a prominent use within the worship life of a congregation. In some seasons of the church year, weekly services of holy communion might begin regularly with a brief confessional liturgy (AE pp. 94–96). Even when the service does not include a specific form of confession and forgiveness, the cleansing power of baptism can be experienced in other ways. The presence of a baptismal font filled with water is a strong nonverbal sign. The prayers of intercession might include specific prayers of confession or ask for God's restorative gifts. Chapter 6 of this book will demonstrate how corporate confession and forgiveness, as well as individual confession and forgiveness, might be used in some situations to give voice to the confession of certain sins and to experience the proclamation of God's forgiveness in a specific way. Each of these liturgies is rooted in the grace bestowed in baptism.

Seasonal use of confession and forgiveness

Some seasons of the year invite a specific use of an order for confession and forgiveness, even if this is not routinely part of the worshiping assembly's pattern of gathering. The Ash Wednesday liturgy provides an extended litany of confession (AE pp. 252–253) that names several sins, many of which are corporate misdeeds or systemic forms of injustice. The imposition of ashes that may follow highlights the reality of human brokenness even further with its proclamation "Remember that you are dust, and to dust you shall return." The assurance of forgiveness announced on Ash Wednesday is stated in the form of a fervent invocation of God's action in our lives: "Almighty God have mercy on us, forgive us all our sins through our Lord Jesus Christ, strengthen us in all goodness, and by the power of the Holy Spirit keep us in eternal life."

In many ways the Maundy Thursday liturgy reflects what happened on Ash Wednesday and provides a strong announcement of the forgiveness that was invoked in the earlier liturgy. Either form of the forgiveness that is used (AE p. 259) announces a clear forgiveness of sins now: "I therefore declare to you the entire forgiveness of all your sins . . ." or "In the name of Jesus Christ, your sins are forgiven." The opportunity to come forward for the laying on of hands is a tangible sign of that gift of forgiveness.

Worship gatherings between Ash Wednesday and Maundy Thursday might regularly include a confession and forgiveness liturgy, even if this is not always the standard practice throughout the year. The season of Lent provides ways for the entire assembly to accompany those who are preparing for baptism, and in so doing everyone is invited to remember the journey to baptism: "Returning to God's mercy and grace, marked with the cross of Christ, we make our way through Lent, longing for the baptismal waters of Easter, our spiritual rebirth" (AE p. 248).

If the entirety of the season of Lent—from Ash Wednesday through Maundy Thursday—provides a prolonged experience of confession and forgiveness, as well as a time of baptismal renewal, the Three Days provides this in microcosm. Particularly if the solemn reproaches are used on Good Friday (LE 639–641), worshipers will be mindful of the myriad ways in which Christians have failed to live up to the teachings and the love of Christ. Perhaps the only fitting response to these reminders of our inadequacies is: "Holy God, holy and mighty, holy and immortal, have mercy on us." After this rehearsal of the many ways in which we "have prepared a cross for [our] Savior," the Good Friday liturgy ends with a simple but profound statement: "We adore you, O Christ, and we bless you. By your holy cross you have redeemed the world" (AE p. 265).

The Vigil of Easter provides a grand announcement of forgiveness in the Easter proclamation: "The holiness of this night puts to flight the deeds of wickedness; washes away sin; restores innocence to the fallen, and joy to those who mourn; casts out hate; brings peace; and humbles earthly pride" (LE 647). How is wickedness put to flight? Where is sin washed away? Here in the waters of baptism: "At this font, holy God, we pray: Praise to you for the water of baptism and for your Word that saves us in this water. Breathe your Spirit into all who are gathered here and into all creation. Illumine our days. Enliven our bones. Dry our tears. Wash away the sin within us, and drown the evil around us" (LE 589).

Because of its place in the church's year, the Vigil of Easter announces the saving death and resurrection of Christ in a most particular way. For this reason the Vigil of Easter is an especially suitable day to celebrate baptism, for on this day the joining of new Christians to Christ's death and resurrection is dramatically reinforced through the whole liturgy. If there are no candidates for baptism, at least the assembly might join in the order for Affirmation of Baptism (AE p. 234, using the conclusion on p. 237).

Seasonal use of thanksgiving for baptism

If the forty days of Lent are a season that calls to mind human frailties and weakness, the fifty days of Easter are a time to announce God's power to make new and to restore life. Taken together, an entire quarter of the year celebrates the paschal mystery—the passage with Christ through death into life—in a focused way. The forgiveness of sins is among the ways that Christ's death and resurrection is experienced in the lives of the faithful: "Shower us with your Spirit, and renew our lives with your forgiveness, grace, and love" (AE p. 97). Throughout the season of Easter, and particularly on the Sundays of Easter, the service might fittingly begin with a thanksgiving for baptism. Thanksgiving for baptism might be used at other times as well, though it does have a particular resonance throughout the season of Easter or on those festivals that have often been associated with baptism, particularly the Day of Pentecost, The Holy Trinity, All Saints Day, and the Baptism of Our Lord.

Omitting confession and forgiveness or thanksgiving for baptism

Confession and forgiveness, or thanksgiving for baptism, are supportive rather than central elements of the service, and may be omitted. For example, when baptism is celebrated—and even more so if baptism takes place at the Gathering—confession and forgiveness may be omitted. Under most circumstances, it seems redundant and potentially confusing for a separate thanksgiving for baptism to be scheduled at the same service in which baptism itself will be celebrated.

Baptismal Echoes in Other Services

Most liturgical orders have one or more connections with baptism: words that recall God's promises for the baptized, greetings and blessings that recall God's trinitarian name given in baptism, or the use of water as a specific baptismal sign. While some connections to baptism may be more obvious than others, baptism has echoes through the lives of Christians, and this is especially obvious in the forms used for corporate worship.

Affirmation of Baptism

Affirmation of Baptism bears an obvious connection to baptism. While its primary use in many congregations may be to celebrate adolescent confirmation, this worship form may actually be used in a number of occasions in people's lives, as well as with the congregation as a whole. When youth have undergone a period of study and faith formation, their experience may culminate with affirmation of baptism as a way of recognizing the previous and more fundamental event in their lives but also as a way of committing themselves to a life of devotion to God, of communion with the church, and of service to others.

Other moments may also be appropriate times for making an affirmation of baptism: entering into and identifying with a particular faith community and its mission, following a time of significant renewal in faith, returning to the church, or at the time of a significant life passage. Affirmation of baptism by the assembly might occur on traditional baptismal festivals (Vigil of Easter, Day of Pentecost, All Saints Day, and the Baptism of Our Lord) when there are no candidates for baptism.

Affirmation of Christian Vocation

The call to serve God comes to all Christians fundamentally through baptism. This call to serve God may be exercised in part through a variety of occupations, voluntary responsibilities in the church and the community, and in settings within the home and family. The brief order for Affirmation of Christian Vocation (AE p. 84) provides one way to build on the concept of baptismal vocation for all people while at the same time identifying specific forms of service that people exercise in their daily lives. This rite may be used as part of the Sending in the service of Holy Communion. It could recognize a particular individual or groups of individuals (such as those preparing to leave on a mission trip or people who have similar occupations or ways of exercising their baptismal vocation).

This concise order may also be used on the festival of the Baptism of Our Lord as a way to affirm the ministries of the baptized in the new year. It might also find a use on a Sunday near a day on the secular calendar that recognizes and honors people's daily engagement in work and other vocations that benefit society.

Healing

Resources for healing prayer are included in *Evangelical Lutheran Worship* (AE p. 276, LE 660) as well as in related pastoral-care resources. The prayers of intercession include the petition "Renew in us the grace of baptism, by which we share in Christ's death and resurrection" (LE 661). The signs that may accompany the prayers for healing—laying on of hands, the sign of the cross, anointing with oil—are strong echoes of the use of these same actions in the baptismal service.

Funeral

Nowhere else is the promise of baptism clearer than in the funeral liturgy. The thanksgiving for baptism that may be used at a funeral makes it abundantly clear that baptism is a participation in the eternal life of Jesus Christ (AE p. 280). All who are baptized have already been united to Christ's death and resurrection. While death is a reality that every person faces, the promise of Christ's resurrection is certain for all believers as well.

The use of a funeral pall is itself an allusion to the clothing that is often literally, but at least figuratively, received by all of the baptized. The funeral pall not only proclaims that this child of God is clothed with Christ in life and in death, but it anticipates the final clothing in glory that God's children will one day receive. If the lighted paschal (Easter) candle is carried in procession during the service, or if it is simply placed near a coffin or urn holding the remains of the deceased, it also is a reminder of baptism, since the paschal candle is normally used whenever a baptism occurs. Furthermore, if the congregation's worship space makes it possible to hold the thanksgiving for baptism next to the baptismal font, the font may also serve as a concrete reminder of the eternal life that begins at baptism.

Prayers of intercession at the funeral liturgy may also incorporate petitions that offer a thanksgiving or a remembrance of baptism. The first petition in the model prayers of intercession at the funeral liturgy (LE 670) recalls that in baptism God has knit the communion of saints into the body of Christ. The second petition asks "that all who have been baptized into Christ's death and resurrection may die to sin and rise to share the new life in Christ."

In the committal section of the funeral liturgy, the gift of baptism is implied in the prayer that recalls how Jesus destroyed the power of death through his death and burial. The words spoken while the coffin is lowered or set into place ("In sure and certain hope of the resurrection to eternal life . . .") end with a blessing and with the presiding minister making the sign of the cross (AE p. 284–285). Here the sign of the cross echoes the cross that may have been signed upon the person in baptism (or in welcome to baptism).

Marriage

Though the service of Marriage may be the least likely of the life passage rites to contain a connection to baptism, some of the texts provided in the leaders edition do acknowledge this relationship, though their use requires pastoral sensitivity to the context. The third option for the declaration of intention that is spoken by the presiding minister and addressed to each individual to be married acknowledges the primacy of baptism in this way: "_Name_, living in the promise of God, [joined to Christ in baptism,] will you give yourself to _name_ in love and faithfulness?" (LE 677). The first form of the prayers of intercession also contains a petition that prays "for the life and ministry of the baptized" (LE 681). Though the linkage between marriage and baptism is a subtle one, the text of the marriage service makes clear that even the exclusive relationship that is established in marriage is nevertheless connected to Christ and to the entire community of Christian believers.

Daily Prayer

In the Small Catechism, Martin Luther encouraged people to remind themselves about baptism at the beginning and at the end of each day when he provided the instruction to make the sign of the cross and say "God the Father, Son, and Holy Spirit watch over me. Amen" (AE pp. 1166–1167). Many Christians will recognize the sign of the cross and the invocation of the triune name as echoes of significant elements from the baptismal liturgy.

In the service of Morning Prayer, either form of the opening provides a trinitarian doxology (AE pp. 298–299). In keeping with Luther's encouragement in the catechism, either order for the opening might be accompanied with worshipers making the sign of the cross upon themselves.

Following scripture reading and reflection at Morning Prayer, one of the dialogue options has a baptismal focus: "You have been born anew through the living and abiding word of God" (AE p. 302).

A thanksgiving for baptism may also conclude Morning Prayer. The prayer provided in the first form of thanksgiving is rich in baptismal imagery. Meanwhile, the optional provision to have a sprinkling with water is a tangible reminder of the gift of baptism. A baptismal hymn and the blessing that concludes the thanksgiving for baptism at Morning Prayer provide further ways to give thanks for God's sacramental grace.

Though the connections with baptism at the service of Evening Prayer may not be as obvious as they are at Morning Prayer, the simple theme of light guiding the world amid the darkness is a reminder of the light of Christ that often accompanies baptism. The thanksgiving for light that may be a part of evening prayer echoes the Easter proclamation that is a part of the Vigil of Easter, a day in the year that is a prime occasion for baptisms.

Following scripture reading and reflection at Evening Prayer, one of the dialogue options uses a text similar to the one that may be used in giving a lighted candle to the newly baptized at the baptismal service: "Jesus said, I am the light of the world. Whoever follows me will never walk in darkness" (AE p. 314; see p. 231).

The service of Night Prayer, too, abounds in subtle references to the parent-child relationship we have with God through our baptism. It also includes confession and forgiveness, which as we have seen is often helpfully understood as grounded in baptism.

Worship in the home

Worship in the home, or in other settings apart from a primary gathering of the Christian assembly, may echo baptism in a number of ways. Occasions for prayer in the home may be as simple as Luther's provision in the Small Catechism for morning and evening blessings (see the previous section above) or they may use various liturgical forms or adaptations of daily prayer.

One way to encourage individuals to remember their own baptismal anniversaries is to include names of people observing baptismal anniversaries that week in the Sunday prayers of intercession. A card (or email message) with a scripture verse, a prayer, and a brief handwritten note could be sent to all members of the congregation on their baptismal anniversaries as a reminder of the occasion and with an encouragement to remember their baptismal anniversaries and reflect on their various opportunities for ministry in daily life.

At home, whether one lives alone or with others, a baptismal anniversary may be remembered during daily devotions by lighting the candle often given to the newly baptized. The thanksgiving for baptism from the communion service or the morning prayer service might be used to acknowledge a baptismal anniversary. An order for marking a baptismal anniversary is also included among the pastoral care resources accompanying *Evangelical Lutheran Worship*.

In addition to lighting the baptismal candle (if a person does not have a candle given at baptism, a new one may be designated as a baptismal candle), a bowl of water may be placed on a table nearby, and each person may dip a hand into the bowl and make the sign of the cross upon herself or himself as a tangible connection with baptism. Parents may help younger members of the family in remembering their baptism by tracing the cross upon their foreheads for them.

Architectural Spaces for Baptism

The physical space used for baptism may stand as a regular testimony to the gift of baptism, even when baptism itself is not celebrated. Many Christian worship spaces in use today are evidence of the evolution in liturgical thought and practice in recent decades. Some of the changes have been prompted by a renewed appreciation for descriptions of baptism in the New Testament, as well as within certain periods of the church's history. Many contemporary congregations have also realized the importance of sacramental signs that are larger and more accessible to people as they gather for worship.

Historical considerations regarding the place of baptism

When a place for baptism is specified in the New Testament, it is invariably a natural body of water. John baptized at the river Jordan, and it was that body of water into which Jesus entered for his own baptism. The book of Acts does not record specifically where—or how!—3,000 people were baptized on the day of Pentecost (Acts 2), but it must have been an amazing sight. Presumably the baptism of the Ethiopian eunuch (Acts 8) was in a natural body of water, though not much is mentioned about it other than that "they came to some water" (8:36) along the road from Jerusalem to Gaza. No mention is made in the New Testament of a pool or other human-made container being used specifically for baptism.

Evidence from churches in the first three centuries of the Christian era demonstrates that early in the church's life baptism did occur in buildings containing fonts or pools large enough to accommodate adult baptism. The baptistery at Dura-Europos in modern-day Syria (search the Internet for an image of it) was shaped like a tomb and was likely constructed in the early part of the third century.

Some fonts in early church history were shaped in the form of a cross, undoubtedly conveying the message that the Christian is buried with Christ in his death and joined to him in his resurrection. Steps leading down into cruciform fonts gave allusion to being buried with Christ, while steps leading out on the other side indicated the resurrection. The artwork that introduces the Holy Baptism section in *Evangelical Lutheran Worship* is a contemporary interpretation of this design (AE p. 223). Fonts have also been given hexagonal or octagonal shapes, respectively symbolizing the sixth day (Good Friday) or the eighth day (Easter).

Images of the baptism of Clovis depict the first French king being baptized around the year 500 in Reims. The monarch is depicted (in various versions available on the Internet) kneeling in a font that is on a pedestal, perhaps in water that would have been waist high. Though the baptism of an adult may be accommodated in such fonts, the trend toward the development of smaller containers of water for baptism is already visible at this time.

By the late Middle Ages, baptismal fonts were constructed almost exclusively for use with infants, though many were substantial enough that they could have accommodated the immersion of an infant. Even in Martin Luther's day it would have been common for infants to have been immersed three times in the font.[3] Fonts constructed since the Middle Ages through much of the twentieth century (at least for traditions where infant baptism has been common) have typically only been intended for pouring water over the head of a baptismal candidate.

Contemporary baptismal spaces

In recent decades, with the recovery of a fuller use of sacramental signs, fonts have grown larger in size among many denominations. While large immersion fonts have been primarily associated with traditions that practice only the baptism of adults or of young people who are at least able to give a testimony to the faith on their own, even fonts used by churches that generally practice infant baptism have grown larger in size, and their location may be more prominent within the congregation's worship space.

Baptism by immersion offers a powerful experience of the old self (the "old Adam") being drowned, as Martin Luther referred to in his Large Catechism (BC 465). Baptism by immersion is a vivid symbol of being joined to Christ's death and resurrection in this sacrament, calling to mind a central teaching of baptism by the apostle Paul in his Letter to the Romans: "Therefore we have been buried with him by baptism into death, so that, just as Christ was raised from the dead by the glory of the Father, so we too might walk in newness of life" (Rom. 6:4).

Congregations that are building new worship spaces or making major renovations to old ones should consider how a large enough space can be provided to accommodate the immersion of both infants and adults. Providing enough open space around a font so that several candidates, sponsors, parents, and worship leaders may gather there is also an important consideration. Having enough space so that a significant number of people from the assembly may gather near the font would also be helpful, especially for baptismal festivals when a significant portion of the liturgy may be focused on the font.

Temporary fonts

Although a font large enough for baptism by immersion will ordinarily be a permanent installation in a congregation's worship facilities, congregations that have not been able to renovate their space or that are in the process of acquiring their own worship space may wish to consider how an adequate baptismal space can be improvised.

Some congregations have provided temporary baptismal spaces either to accommodate the baptism of adults upon occasion or to celebrate major baptismal festivals throughout the year, particularly at the Vigil of Easter. On those occasions when the assembly may experience a stational liturgy (such as the Vigil of Easter, when the assembly may be moving from a place outdoors for the lighting of the new fire to other spaces inside the church building for the service of readings, baptism, and the celebration of the meal), it is not even necessary that a baptismal space be within the room in which the assembly normally worships.

A fellowship hall or gathering space may provide a suitable location for a temporary font. Set a portable wading pool (as plain as possible), a large galvanized tub, or a sturdy water tank on the floor, with plenty of space for an assembled congregation to gather around. Through the container may not be able to accommodate the full immersion of an adult, it may be possible for baptismal candidates to kneel in the water while the presiding minister pours water from a pitcher or a baptismal ewer over their heads. Candidates for baptism may be dressed in swimwear for the baptism itself and may also have a bathrobe that they use prior to and immediately following the baptism (allow them time to change from and into an alb or street attire for other portions of the service).

Make the space surrounding a temporary font visually appealing. Gather large green plants (but not much taller than whatever is used to hold the water) around the temporary font, while still making it easy for candidates and ministers to approach the font. Ideally the water in the font would be slightly warmer than room temperature. Partially fill the container with water hours (or even a day) in advance of when it is to be used. Then add warmer water to the font within an hour ahead of time so that it is up to 95°F/35°C (a gauge designed for testing the temperature of a baby's bath water could help).

Any size font and any amount of water may technically do the job for the celebration of baptism. However, the fullest use of water that is possible will convey an image of God's abundant grace in this sacrament in an expansive and vivid way, exemplifying the words and actions of the baptismal service.

CHAPTER THREE

The Shape and Practice of Holy Baptism

The pattern for worship for Holy Baptism in *Evangelical Lutheran Worship* (AE pp. 225–226; LE 581–582) consists of seven parts: Presentation, Profession of Faith, Thanksgiving at the Font, Baptism, Prayer for the Holy Spirit, Sign of the Cross, and Welcome. This pattern provides the reference points for our discussion of the order of Holy Baptism in *Evangelical Lutheran Worship* (AE pp. 227–231; LE 583–591). The pattern for worship clearly reveals that Holy Baptism in *Evangelical Lutheran Worship* carries forward the essential aspects of the rite in *Lutheran Book of Worship*. As we have seen, the rite also incorporates the gifts of other Christian traditions as the whole church works toward a common understanding and expression of its unity. The service underscores the unitary character of baptism of people of all ages and expands the profession of faith. The optional prayers for the thanksgiving at the font strengthen the connection between the celebration of baptism and the story of salvation that is told by the church year. The welcome highlights the relationship of baptism to the sending of the Christian community to share in Christ's mission. The order of baptism provides freedom, flexibility, and possibility, which invite congregations to reflect carefully on their baptismal practice.

In thanksgiving for God's immeasurable gift, congregations are encouraged to "celebrate Baptism in such a way that the celebration is a true and complete sign of the things which Baptism signifies" (UMG 25, paraphrasing Martin Luther, LW 35:29). The church has long understood that the manner in which baptism is administered is the most powerful teacher of what the church believes and how the church values this sacrament. A Lutheran understanding of baptism as God's gift and promise of salvation, and as the wellspring of Christian faith, community, and life, demands a strong and intentional baptismal practice. "Those who plan baptisms attend to the use of faithful words and gracious actions, to including the event within the Sunday service, to the architectural or natural setting, to the regular preparation of

Baptism

God brings those who are baptized out of death and into life.

Presentation

The Holy Spirit calls and invites us to receive God's grace. Sponsors present those to be baptized, and we promise our support.

Profession of Faith

Only by God's grace can we renounce the forces of evil and the power of sin. With the whole church, we confess our faith in the triune God.

Thanksgiving at the Font
Baptism

With thanksgiving, God's saving deeds are remembered. Dying with Christ in baptism, the child of God is raised to new life through water and the Word.

Prayer for the Holy Spirit
Sign of the Cross

Additional signs proclaim the meaning of baptism. We pray that the gift of the Holy Spirit sustain the baptized. The baptized are marked with the cross of Christ forever.

Welcome

The baptized are called to follow Jesus, the light of the world. We welcome new companions in the mission of God.

candidates, sponsors, parents, and congregation for Baptism, to post-baptismal teaching that strengthens us for mission, and to the possibility of great festivals as times for Baptism" (UMG 25A). To facilitate this attention on the part of all who plan baptism, the Notes on the Services for Holy Baptism (LE 27–29) place the order in the contexts of the Christian assembly, baptismal preparation, the congregation's worship, and the church year. The notes make clear that this rite is to be used with candidates of all ages. Lastly, the notes provide helpful guidance on preparing for and leading the service, which is included in the discussion of the individual parts of the service in this chapter.

A Communal Act

God is the actor in holy baptism. In every baptism God joins a life to Christ's dying and rising, gives birth to a new creation, and breathes the holy and life-giving Spirit. Every baptism proclaims Christ's active faithfulness and love for us and for all creation. Yet scripture teaches that God rarely acts alone. Most often God acts in partnership through and with human beings. God worked with Noah and his family to save the world from the flood, and with Moses and Miriam to bring Israel through the sea. God entrusted the infant Jesus to a human family and Jesus shared his ministry with disciples and others. The risen Christ gave the church authority, entrusted the church with the gospel, and commanded it to make disciples and baptize. In every baptism, the risen Christ makes disciples in partnership with the community of believers. Jesus acts in and through the gathered Christian community. Though God is the actor, and God's saving word is the sole source of the salvation offered through this sacrament, baptism is a corporate or communal act.

The order of Holy Baptism reflects this communal sense. Candidates for holy baptism, sponsors, and an ordained minister called by the church gather around the font with the assembly to administer the sacrament within the corporate worship of the church (UMG 21). All participants play an essential role. Sponsors accompany and guide the candidates and, as appropriate, their families in preparation for baptism. As they stand at the font, sponsors give tangible expression to the congregation's commitment to support the baptized in their life of faith, to welcome them into the life of the community of believers, and to include them in the congregation's work of proclaiming the gospel for the sake of the world. The pastor acts as baptizer in the midst of the assembly but makes it clear that she or he baptizes on behalf of the church and not out of any sense of individual authority. The entire assembly prays for and assists those preparing for baptism and their sponsors, reaffirms its faith in God, welcomes the newly baptized into the congregation and into Christ's mission, and pledges itself to provide an environment of witness and service. Together the entire assembly participates in and witnesses to God's faithfulness and love.

In the way it celebrates baptism, the congregation also embodies or incarnates God's love and faithfulness. A communal celebration vividly expresses God present in the midst of God's people, bringing life and salvation in and through this gathering of believers. Every Christian assembly incarnates baptism in a unique way. Every congregation has its own way of teaching and passing on the faith to baptismal candidates and their families. Every congregation has its own baptismal space, way of administering the sacrament, and way of involving the entire assembly in that celebration. In addition to deciding the manner of baptismal washing, each congregation determines how best to use symbols that express the gift of the Spirit, the claim of Christ upon each child of God, the dignity and vocation of the baptized, and the sense of belonging to the church and sharing in its mission. Although God's action in baptism is not effected by the manner of administration, every congregation distinctively communicates something (whether positive or negative) about God's love and faithfulness in the way it celebrates baptism. As congregations consider their baptismal practice, they might ask how their celebration of the sacrament embodies and proclaims the gospel.

Sometimes, in extraordinary circumstances such as an emergency or the prospect of imminent death, baptism outside the assembly is requested; in such cases, any Christian may administer baptism. Yet so-called private baptism is not the church's normal way of administering the sacrament. During the Middle Ages, the practice of baptizing infants outside of the assembly became more prevalent when the church began to emphasize baptism of an infant before it might die. The teaching (reflected later in the Augsburg Confession, Article IX) that baptism is necessary for salvation was often interpreted so narrowly as to foster an atmosphere of fear and urgency. The church required that baptism occur within eight days of birth, making the administration of baptism within the Sunday assembly more infrequent, so that the sacrament was unintentionally transformed into what was often a private, family ceremony.

Thankfully, the church by and large has come to understand that baptism is an expression of God's unconditional love in Jesus Christ, not a precondition for receiving that love. Jesus does not abandon or reject those who are not baptized. Even when sudden death prevents baptism, we commend the person to God with prayer, trusting in God's grace and mercy (UMG 23). In cases other than emergencies, baptism apart from the Christian community may reinforce the unfortunate impression that we are acting out of fear and haste to appease an angry God. It suggests that the Christian stands before God alone, rather than being welcomed, embraced, and surrounded by God in and through a community of believers. Private baptism may even reinforce values contrary to the gospel, including privatized faith, individualism, consumerism, and convenience. For all these reasons, the notes for Holy Baptism observe: "Ordinarily, baptism is celebrated within the primary service of the congregation" (LE 27).

The community is so important in a Lutheran understanding of baptism that, when pastoral considerations require that baptism take place outside of corporate worship, representatives of the congregation are present if at all possible, and a public announcement is made in worship the following Sunday. The notes in *Evangelical Lutheran Worship* are even more specific. They call for both a public announcement and prayer at the Sunday service should baptism occur at another time. Furthermore, when a person is baptized in extraordinary circumstances, such as when death appears to be imminent, the *Evangelical Lutheran Worship* pastoral care resources provide an order for Public Recognition of a Baptism, to be used in the assembly should the person survive.

Locating Baptism in the Pattern for Worship

As an expression of its central place in the life of the Christian community, baptism has a natural home within the pattern of the assembly's worship. Because we understand baptism as the wellspring of Christian living, we can see significant parallels between the celebration of baptism and the pattern for Christian worship. At the Gathering, worship may begin with actions that echo the service of baptism. Confessing sin, we again renounce the power of evil and the ways of sin that draw us away from God; or, giving thanks for baptism, we ask God again to shower us with the Holy Spirit. At the liturgy of the word, then, the good news Christians hear in scripture and sermon is none other than the promise made at baptism. Turning to the Meal and Sending sections of the pattern of worship, baptism raises Christians to sit at the Lord's table and commissions them to serve as Christ's body in the world.

Baptism may take place at one of several points in the worship service. "Within the service of Holy Communion, this order normally follows the hymn of the day. Or, it may replace the thanksgiving for baptism in the gathering rite" (AE p. 226). Within the foundational pattern of gathering, word, meal, and sending, baptism after the proclamation of God's word emphasizes baptism's connection to faith in the promise of the gospel and leads the baptized to the eucharistic table. When infants are baptized in a service where adults are not, the baptism may be part of the Gathering rite. This placement of baptism in the pattern of worship signifies the nature of baptism as entrance into the community where instruction, formation, and nurture will follow. At the Vigil of Easter, an alternative placement for baptism is between the vigil readings and the New Testament reading and gospel.

Congregations are invited to consider whether to locate baptism regularly in its primary placement following the hymn of the day or whether to vary its location depending on the circumstances. The age of candidates for baptism is an important factor when considering where to place baptism in the service. When adults are among the candidates, baptism follows the hymn of the day, since adults and older children come to the font in response to God's word. The season of the church year in which baptism is celebrated is another helpful consideration. For example, when infants are baptized on Pentecost, locating baptism in the gathering rite might reinforce that all Christians receive the Holy Spirit and are incorporated into the church by water and God's word. Wherever the sacrament is located in the pattern for worship, people in the assembly give thanks for the gift of baptism in their own lives even as they welcome new sisters and brothers into the household of God through the waters of baptism.

The Importance of Baptismal Preparation

Whether the candidates are infants or adults, the order for baptism normally concludes a period of baptismal preparation. In the baptismal liturgy, the question asked by the presiding minister when candidates are presented for baptism assumes that baptismal preparation has occurred. For infants and young children, baptismal preparation involves prayer and explanation. The pastor, sponsors, and congregation pray for and with parents prior to birth or adoption. They continue to offer prayers anticipating baptism after the child is born or adopted. These prayers are a natural part of pastoral visitation and the congregation's prayer ministry and are included in the prayers of intercession during the Sunday assembly. Preparation also includes sessions with the parents and sponsors prior to baptism, at which the pastor or a representative of the congregation explains the significance of baptism, the Christian responsibilities of parents and sponsors, and the liturgy of baptism itself. In fact, using the liturgy of baptism—particularly the questions addressed to parents and sponsors, as well as the images and actions contained in the service, may be the best way of explaining the significance of baptism and the responsibilities of parents and sponsors. When children are baptized, the readiness of parents and sponsors to answer the questions addressed to them with confidence and their sense of comfort about participating in the service are perhaps the best indication that they grasp the significance of baptism. For older children and adults, baptismal preparation ordinarily includes a period of faith formation and instruction, guided by catechists, sponsors, pastors, and other leaders in the congregation. Chapter 4 discusses a rich and transforming approach to preparing adults and older children for baptism.

For recent generations of Christians, the church frequently minimized and even overlooked opportunities for careful baptismal preparation, in part because congregations and pastors assumed that the vast majority of the persons to whom they ministered grew up in the church and understood the meaning and significance of baptism. "In many large European and North American majority churches infant baptism is practiced in an apparently indiscriminate way."[1] As a result, baptism has sometimes been commonly understood as something parents *do* when a child is born, comparable to getting a baby vaccinated, rather than as participation in the death and resurrection of Christ, incorporation into the church, and initiation into a distinctive way of life. In some instances, the indiscriminate practice of baptism could even be seen as harmful, as when baptismal practice required adopting a Christian name not rooted in one's culture and setting aside the name given at birth.

Increasingly, congregations minister to adults who have not been evangelized or baptized and to parents with serious questions about the meaning of baptism for their children. Administering baptism indiscriminately can be perceived as discounting their experience and questions, as well as disrespecting the religious pluralism that characterizes contemporary culture. *The Use of the Means of Grace* observes, "Our times require great seriousness about evangelization and readiness to welcome unbaptized adults to the reception of faith and to Baptism into Christ. Our children also need this sign and means of grace and its continued power in their lives." (18A)

One Rite for All Ages

Following the practice established in *Lutheran Book of Worship*, the order for Holy Baptism emphasizes an understanding of baptism as God's gift, which makes all Christians equal, by providing a single rite designed to be used with candidates of all ages. At several points in the service, options are provided, depending on whether the candidates can answer for themselves. The most obvious alternative is found in the presentation. The presiding minister directly questions candidates who can answer for themselves; the presiding minister questions the parents or others who bring infants, young children, or other candidates who are unable to answer for themselves. Two different questions are provided in the rite.

In other places in the service, options do not reflect variations based on the age of the one being baptized but offer alternatives as to how the rite is administered. For example, in the welcome, when the candidate is an infant, a representative of the congregation presents a lighted candle to a sponsor. The unitary character of the rite demonstrates that, since baptism is God's overwhelming gift of grace, "we baptize infants as if they were adults, addressing them with questions, words, and promises that their parents, sponsors, and congregation are to help them know and believe as they grow in years. We baptize adults as if they were infants, washing them and clothing them with God's love in Christ" (UMG 18A).

Baptism and the Church Year

The notes suggest designating certain festival days in the church year as baptismal celebrations. The Vigil of Easter and Day of Pentecost are the ancient days for celebrating baptism in the Western church; baptism is celebrated on Epiphany in the East. *Evangelical Lutheran Worship* (LE 27) lists the Vigil of Easter, the Day of Pentecost, All Saints Day, and the Baptism of Our Lord as appropriate occasions for celebrating baptism. Some congregations find that when the Easter Vigil is not celebrated, including baptism in the service on Easter Day is a powerful experience of resurrection for the entire assembly. Other congregations designate the Second or Third Sunday in Advent (depending on the lectionary year), with gospel readings that emphasize the preaching and baptizing ministry of John the Baptist, as a baptismal celebration. In most congregations, designating five days as baptismal festivals, distributed throughout the year and well publicized long in advance, is sufficient to accommodate most if not all baptisms.

Celebrating baptism on festivals of the church year connects the order of baptism to the aspect of the story of salvation that the church remembers on those occasions. The readings, hymns, sermon, and prayers all amplify the imagery and significance of the sacrament, even as the order for baptism reinforces the festival. For example, in addition to the general prayer of thanksgiving at the font included in the rite, the four alternative prayers (AE pp. 70–71; LE 587–589) emphasize the images and themes of different seasons and festival days. The connection of baptism and the occasion on which it is celebrated can be enhanced by the manner in which it is celebrated, specifically the choices made among the alternatives provided in the service. In addition to strengthening the relationship of baptism and the church year, designating baptismal festivals also emphasizes other important aspects of baptism. The communal nature of baptism is reinforced when several candidates are baptized on the same day. The equality Christians share in Christ is evidenced when adults and infants are baptized in the same service.

Congregations that move toward baptismal festivals may experience some confusion and resistance from members, especially if the change is not adequately prepared for. Both responses are understandable and to be expected. Scheduling baptism on specified occasions, which in some instances may be months after a child is born or adopted, may conflict with a "popular" theology of baptism and produce anxiety in parents. Some parents seek baptism soon after a child is born or adopted as a way of securing God's love and protection for their child and guaranteeing the child's salvation. Delaying baptism might cause parents to wonder whether their child is somehow in jeopardy. Parents' eagerness for baptism for their children is not to be discounted. It will be important to explain (and to demonstrate in the services) that the change is more than simply a congregation's or its leaders' preference for a certain festival. Rather, thoughtful baptismal instruction, such as that described above, enhances the parents' experience of God's love and the congregation's concern for their child. Additional time can be interpreted positively in the way it allows for greater preparation, in which parents and other family members are reassured that baptism is a genuine welcome into a supportive Christian community, and not insurance against being condemned by God. Then, if the whole congregation together with the families of those to be baptized is indeed prepared for the baptismal festival, and it is designed as a joyful, faith-affirming event, it will have a positive impact on the understanding and lives of all involved.

Scheduling the occasions on which the congregation celebrates baptism is also a countercultural act. In our mobile society, many people want baptism to be scheduled at times when it is convenient for family members, particularly grandparents and godparents, to gather. This expectation may be a vestige of the earlier practice of baptism as primarily a family celebration. It may reflect not so much a fear of postponing baptism as a desire to bring a geographically scattered family together for a milestone event. Or, it may be that families feel that having their child share a baptismal celebration with other children somehow makes it less personal and special.

Scheduled baptismal festivals suggest that the rhythm of the church's life and worship take precedence over individual and family preferences. In our highly individualized society, many look upon baptism as *their* day. Baptizing several candidates on the same occasion suggests that God's action in water and word is bigger than any individual and that what for many is a family celebration is, in fact, a celebration of God's entire family. Scheduling baptism in a way that encourages proper preparation and mutual commitment challenges the consumerism that encourages people to get what they want when they want it. In subtle ways baptismal festivals reflect the baptismal renunciation of "the powers of this world that rebel against God" and the distinctive nature of baptismal living.

People may be helpfully encouraged to consider a family celebration of the baptism at another time if they are not able to gather on the scheduled baptismal festival, perhaps using elements from an order for the anniversary of a baptism.

Singing around the Font

As an important relational aspect of Lutheran worship, music—and congregational song in particular—can greatly contribute to the joy and meaning of the celebration of holy baptism in at least four ways.

First, singing reinforces the communal nature of the sacrament by uniting the members of the congregation and the whole church. The assembly, though made up of many individual voices, sings in one voice, and its song is added to the song of the church throughout the world and throughout the ages.

Second, congregational singing teaches and nurtures faith. Singing teaches Christians the story of salvation and provides language for expressing faith. Singing has the additional power of repetition when hymns and songs are sung over the course of weeks, seasons, years, and lifetimes. Songs that employ different images for baptism help the congregation appreciate the boundless nature of God's gift.

Third, congregational singing helps to connect baptism and daily life by forming communal memory. Songs sung in worship are among the most powerful ways that faith remains with people throughout their baptismal lives; songs return us to our baptism in ways other expressions of faith cannot, give life meaning, and are a source of comfort in death.

Fourth, music and singing are especially powerful ways of calling upon the Holy Spirit, and these elements frequently open doors for people to experience the Spirit's presence in the community in profound ways.

The order for Holy Baptism includes several opportunities for including congregational hymns, songs, and acclamations, depending on where baptism is placed within Holy Communion. When baptism is placed within the liturgy of the word, the hymn of the day might be chosen in the awareness that it is to help the assembly respond to the gospel by participating in the celebration of baptism. When baptism is part of the Gathering, the assembly in its song may ask the Holy Spirit to be present and surround the candidates, their families, and sponsors with prayer, love, and support. Within the baptismal service, provision is made for the assembly to respond to each baptism with a sung alleluia or another acclamation, and a sung acclamation, hymn, or psalm may conclude the rite as part of the welcome.

Evangelical Lutheran Worship includes sung acclamations (#209–213) that are particularly suited to baptism. The words are easy to remember, and the melodies are easy to sing. Congregations might select a baptismal acclamation and use it consistently over time so that the assembly learns to sing it without needing to look at the worship book (and away from the baptism). In this way, sung acclamations become a way the congregation actively assents and responds in the service and celebrates baptism as a communal act.

New songs and an established core of music connect the celebration of baptism to the whole church and daily life in different ways. Songs that have a history of being part of the congregation's celebration of baptism (perhaps #444, "Cradling children in his arm," or #781, "Children of the heavenly Father") stimulate awareness that the Christian community is part of the gathering of God's people of *every* time, including all of the saints who ever have gathered around the font in this or that particular congregation. These songs also strengthen the connection of baptism and daily life by evoking memories of times when they were sung at other significant moments and transitions in the lives of both individual Christians and the congregation. Newer songs, particularly those that come from beyond the congregation's culture and from other places, strengthen the congregation's connection to the church throughout the world. See, for example, "Gracious Spirit, heed our pleading" (#401), a hymn from Africa that may precede baptism, perhaps using the refrain alone. Such songs also highlight the relationship of baptism and justice: singing the songs of other members of Christ's body may help to deepen concern for their lives. By balancing songs with a rich history in the congregation and songs that the congregation may experience as new, the inclusion of congregational song in Holy Baptism can broaden the congregation's awareness of baptism as a celebration of the whole church and deepen its appreciation of the connection of baptism and daily life.

Finally, assembly song within the baptismal order can support a spirit of joy and festivity in the celebration. The enthusiastic participation of the entire people of God is, for many, a sign of the Spirit's presence and an assurance of Christ's embrace through the community that is his body. Selecting assembly song that a given assembly can sing and teaching them to sing with confidence is an important part of preparing the congregation to participate actively in the sacrament of baptism.

Preparation

Congregations are increasingly discovering that, where it is possible, there is logic and value in giving the place of baptism space comparable to that provided for word and meal. *Evangelical Lutheran Worship* notes that "keeping the font open and filled with water at worship services, whether or not baptism is to be celebrated, is a strong symbol of the importance of this sacrament" (LE 27). When the font is located near the entrance of the worship space, worshipers may be encouraged, both in words and by the example of worship leaders, to remember their baptism by dipping their fingers into the baptismal water and making the sign of the cross on their foreheads as they enter or exit the worship space. At services when baptism is to be celebrated, if the font is not regularly kept filled with water it may be filled either before the service begins or as part of the thanksgiving at the font. If the font is to be filled during the thanksgiving, a pitcher (ewer), often made of metal or glass, is filled with a sufficient amount of water to fill the font and placed nearby. Experienced altar guild members recommend that the water be warm, even hot when baptism is to be celebrated after the hymn of the day, since it will cool during the service.

Placing the paschal candle, which represents the risen Christ, near the font during most of the year reinforces the scriptural image of baptism as participation in Christ's death and resurrection. Lighting the paschal candle when baptism is part of the service provides a visible reminder of the church's celebration of Christ's death and resurrection at Easter. Some congregations add to the baptismal environment in other ways— such as adorning the space with plants or flowers, or incorporating a baptismal banner—to signal the festive character of the service and to highlight various images for baptism.

Other items necessary for baptism are also placed near the font. These include towels or napkins for drying those who are baptized, and a baptismal shell or basin for pouring, if one is to be used. Depending on which, if any, additional symbols are to be used, oil for anointing, baptismal garments, and candles are all put in their proper places or given to appropriate leaders. If certificates for the newly baptized and sponsors are to be presented during the service, they are prepared and put in place as well.

As part of baptismal preparation, it is helpful for candidates, sponsors, family members, the pastor(s), and representatives of the congregation who will participate in the baptism to gather in the baptismal space and walk through the service together. Participants can also determine how and when they will gather at the font, and plan the movements in the service so that where they stand and how they move maximizes the congregation's participation by permitting as many people as possible to see and hear what is happening. This kind of rehearsal also lessens participants' anxiety so that they worry less about what they are supposed to do and can concentrate more on what God is doing in baptism. When those around the font are comfortable and confident, the assembly participates in the service more fully and easily.

Presentation

As the assembly sings the hymn of the day (or a gathering song), candidates for baptism and sponsors, together with parents of young children and perhaps other family members, gather around the font with the presiding and assisting ministers who will participate in the baptism. This movement may be informal or a procession led by the cross and, optionally, torches. Such a procession is especially appropriate when the baptismal space is a focal point of the room equal to and at a distance from the places of the word and of the meal. Even when the baptismal font is close to these other centers, some congregations find it helpful to bring the processional cross to the font to visually signal that the movement of the service is now to baptism and that the assembly is to face the font. Those participating in the baptism arrange themselves so that the assembly sees and hears as much of the service as possible. It is helpful if an assisting minister holds the book from which the order of Holy Baptism will be led.

Where space permits, the assembly, and especially children, may gather around the font as well. Many congregations find it helpful when young children are accompanied by a parent or someone is designated to attend to them at the font. In many spaces, having the assembly remain in place affords the best visibility and acoustics and, therefore, the best congregational participation. If the font is located so that it is not visible to the assembly, the presentation and profession of faith could take place in the chancel, and the baptismal party would move to the font for the thanksgiving. If the assembly remains in place as the order begins, they may be seated at the conclusion of the hymn.

The presiding minister may address the assembly using what is essentially an explanation of the meaning of baptism as found in scripture. Two alternatives are provided. Both include the metaphors for baptism discussed in Chapter 1 and point to the lifelong nature of the sacrament. The first option emphasizes new birth and God's actions—giving us new birth, delivering us from death and raising us to new life in Christ, and anointing us with the Holy Spirit. It also refers to anointing with the Holy Spirit and being joined to Christ's mission. These emphases may suggest that this is a fitting choice for baptism at Epiphany and Pentecost. The second option emphasizes participation in Christ's death and resurrection, humanity's fallen nature, freedom from sin and death, and membership in the church. These emphases may commend this option as appropriate for baptism at Easter. Alternatively, the presiding minister might use other words that explain baptism from scripture in a similar fashion. Under certain circumstances, as when more than one minister participates in baptism, this address may be said by someone other than the presiding minister.

Fig. 3.1. Gathering around the font. *Those participating in the baptism arrange themselves in a way that maximizes the assembly's ability to see and hear. Where there is sufficient space, children and others in the assembly may also gather around the font.*

The appropriate sponsors, in turn, present each candidate to the assembly, using the words provided. In the case of candidates unable to answer for themselves, parents may join the sponsors in speaking the words of presentation. The full name of each candidate may be used in the presentation. At other points in the service, including baptizing, praying for the Holy Spirit, and signing with the cross, only the given name (the Christian name) is typically used, as a reminder that we are baptized into the one family of God. Because the sentence in which the sponsors present the candidates comes directly after a page turn in the assembly edition, it is wise to alert the sponsors, who may be reticent anyway, so that they will be prepared to speak out the declaration. In some situations the presiding minister may find it necessary to frame the presentation as a question—"Who presents this candidate / _name_ for holy baptism?"—and to prompt the response, "We/I do."

The Use of the Means of Grace (20A) encourages congregations to select at least one baptismal sponsor for each candidate from among the members of the congregation. By selecting a baptismal sponsor for each candidate, the congregation exercises and expresses its lifelong commitment to those baptized by providing a companion, guide, and mentor in faith formation, baptismal living, and participation in the congregation's life and mission. Additional sponsors may be selected by parents of candidates. Baptismal sponsors are baptized Christians who participate in the life of the Christian community, understand the responsibilities they undertake as sponsors, and commit themselves to the joys and duties of sponsorship.

The presiding minister continues with questions addressed to the candidates, sponsors, and assembly. Beginning with these questions, plural forms are used throughout the order and are indicated with italics within the text. If only one candidate is presented, these words are modified appropriately. The first question is addressed to the candidates or, in the case of candidates unable to answer for themselves, their parents or guardians. The form of these questions is essentially the same. The presiding minister addresses candidates individually using the given name; parents are questioned as a group. The phrase, "called by the Holy Spirit, trusting in the grace and love of God," which begins the presiding minister's question, makes clear that the desire for baptism is a response to God, who calls through the gospel, and does not result from personal understanding or strength. Thus, the commentary in the pattern for baptism observes that "the Holy Spirit calls and invites us to receive God's grace."

The order indicates that the presiding minister then addresses the parents and others who bring for baptism children who are not able to answer for themselves. In some instances, such as when younger candidates can answer for themselves and express their desire to be baptized but still need their parents' help to grow in Christian faith and life, it may be pastorally sensitive to include this address after the first form of the question asked after candidates are presented, which asks candidates directly if they desire to be baptized. Speaking on behalf of Christ and the church, the presiding minister entrusts parents (or guardians) with responsibilities related to helping their children grow in the communal, lifelong, and missional dimensions of the baptismal life. Regardless of the age of the candidates, the presiding minister then asks sponsors and the assembly to pledge to pray for and support the candidates in their baptismal covenant and new life in Christ. The distinct questions for parents, sponsors, and the assembly increase participation in the rite and symbolically strengthen the assembly's commitment to those baptized. After responding, "We do," the assembly stands for the profession of faith.

Profession of Faith

The presiding minister asks the candidates, sponsors, and parents of younger children to profess faith in Christ, reject sin, and confess the faith of the church. The assembly joins the whole church in confessing faith in the triune God, using the words of the Apostles' Creed, and may also join in renouncing sin. When baptism is celebrated at the Easter Vigil, it is fitting for everyone to reject sin and profess faith, as a way of recalling that they have died and been raised with Christ. It is also appropriate for the assembly to reject sin when only infants are baptized, as an expression of the whole church speaking on their behalf. The presiding minister should indicate to the assembly if they are to participate in the renunciation, perhaps by using words such as, "I ask you, *together with all the people of God here assembled*, to profess your faith. . . ."

The pattern for baptism (AE p. 226) affirms that "only by God's grace can we renounce the forces of evil and the power of sin." The leaders edition provides two options for the renunciation (LE 585). In both options, the presiding minister asks questions and the baptismal party (and assembly) responds, "I renounce them." Both options are identical in content and communicate an understanding of sin and evil that is larger than individuals' thoughts, words, and deeds. Christians renounce the devil—the archetype of evil—and forces that defy God; powers that rebel against God; as well as sinful ways that draw us away from God. Sin and evil are corporate, societal, and systemic, as well as individual, personal, and incidental. Baptism initiates a life that makes no distinction between a commitment to social justice and personal faithfulness. The first option for the renunciation, which is included in the assembly edition, consists of three questions that correspond to the three professions of faith in the three articles of the creed. This form demonstrates that, as the gospels suggest, rejecting evil and embracing God are two sides of a single action. (See Matt. 12:43-45; Luke 11:24-26.) The second option (in the leaders edition only) is simpler in that the three renunciations are combined in a single question with one response. The first option produces a symmetric effect and increases participation, particularly when the assembly joins in the response. The second option gives greater weight to faith than to sin, particularly when this option is compared to the profession of faith using the creed. Though the longer question in the second option may be easier to see on the page, the three shorter questions are easier for the baptismal party to hear and comprehend without the aid of the book. Regardless of which form is used, the renunciation of evil, together with the profession of faith that follows, is a public declaration; therefore, the candidates and their sponsors respond boldly.

The presiding minister then addresses the candidates and the assembly in the profession of faith. In three questions, the presiding minister asks if the candidates, sponsors, and the assembly believe in God the Father, Jesus Christ the Son of God, and God the Holy Spirit. The assembly responds to each question using the words of the appropriate article of the Apostles' Creed. This ancient baptismal creed unites those to be baptized and the assembly gathered around them with the church of all times and places. The use of the creed enacts the baptismal metaphor of incorporation into Christ's body.

Thanksgiving at the Font

The presiding minister then leads the assembly in the prayer of thanksgiving at the font. From a Lutheran perspective, this prayer said at the baptismal font is best understood as the church recalling and giving thanks that God's word here is connected to the water of baptism. In the Small Catechism, Luther says that baptism "is not simply plain water. Instead, it is water used according to God's command and connected with God's word" (AE p. 1164). Luther further points to God's command and promise recorded in scripture, noting that Jesus commands, "Go therefore and make disciples of all nations, baptizing them in the name of the Father and of the Son and of the Holy Spirit," and promises, "The one who believes and is baptized will be saved" (Matt. 28:19; Mark 16:16). In the Large Catechism, Luther explains what it means when God's word is added to the water: "[Baptism] is not simply a natural water, but a divine, heavenly, holy, and blessed water—praise it in any other terms you can—all by virtue of the Word, which is a heavenly, holy Word that no one can sufficiently extol, for it contains and conveys all that is God's" (BC 458). For when the word of God, by which God created heaven and earth and all things, is present, God's name is in it, and where God's name is, life and salvation are present. For Luther, God's word is nothing other than the active, life-giving power of God, which in other contexts we call the Holy Spirit.

According to Luther, adding God's word is not something *the church* does by blessing baptismal water. Rather, God's word was added when *Christ,* God's incarnate Word, sanctified all water by being baptized for all in the Jordan. Luther makes this theology explicit in the "flood prayer," which replaced the blessing of the font in Luther's 1526 baptismal rite. In this prayer, Luther says that God, "through the baptism of thy dear Child, our Lord Jesus Christ, hast consecrated and set apart the Jordan and all water as a salutary flood and a rich and full washing away of sins" (LW 53:107). At the font, the church recalls and gives thanks for God's saving action in water and, trusting in God's promise, asks God to do with *this* water all that God has promised to do in baptism. Through praise, remembrance, and petition, the thanksgiving prayer celebrates baptism at the font as part of God's saving work, which includes deliverance from the waters of the flood, safe passage through the sea on the way to the promised land, as well as the baptism of Jesus' death and resurrection.

Five forms for the thanksgiving at the font are provided in *Evangelical Lutheran Worship.* In the assembly edition, the first is part of the order for Holy Baptism; the other four are included in Prayers for Worship (pp. 70–71). Prayer IV includes responses by the assembly. These prayers use the same themes found in Luther's flood prayer and in many ancient writers on baptism. They are rooted in Jewish prayers of thanksgiving, which regularly recall before God all that God has done out of grace and mercy. The abbreviated preface dialogue and the structure of these prayers, as well as the way they combine thanksgiving and proclamation, parallel thanksgivings at the table. Like the prayers said at the communion table, these prayers begin with praise to God for creation and mighty acts recorded in the Hebrew scriptures. They continue by proclaiming the saving work of Christ and inviting the Spirit's presence. They conclude in praise for the triune God. These parallels to the great thanksgiving indicate the importance the church places on baptism.

The five prayers differ in their images, which may suggest varying possible uses. For example, in Prayer II, the references to God leading Israel through the sea to the promised land and Christ bringing us through the waters of baptism to the land of promise may suggest its use at Easter. Similarly, Prayer III, which seems particularly appropriate for Pentecost, includes *spirit*, *breath*, and *adoption*, and recalls Jesus' promise to send the Spirit to us. By examining these prayers for images found in the readings for the day, those who plan baptism can strengthen the relationship of baptism and the church year.

Whichever of the five prayers is selected, it will be important that presiding ministers are familiar enough with it that the thanksgiving is an authentic prayer and proclamation rather than the mere reading of a text. Presiding ministers also determine in advance what, if any, liturgical gestures they will use to embody the thanksgiving. Historically, the gestures used for the thanksgiving at the font are similar to those used for the thanksgiving at the table. Thus, at the beginning of the thanksgiving at the font, the presiding minister could use a gesture of greeting as may be used with the parallel words in the Meal section (Fig. 3.2). During the prayer itself, a prayer posture with uplifted hands (the ancient *orans* posture, Fig. 3.3) would be appropriate. Such decisions, of course, are not essential to the rite.

If water is to be poured into the font, either immediately before or as part of the thanksgiving, the assisting minister who will pour the water gets the ewer from its place. (A second assisting minister or acolyte may be assigned this task, since the principal assisting minister will

Fig. 3.2. Gesture at the thanksgiving at the font. *The presiding minister may extend open hands toward the assembly when announcing the opening words of the dialogue: "The Lord be with you."*

likely be needed to hold the book for the presiding minister.) When the font is filled (fully or in part) at this time, it is best done in such a way that the sight and sound of the water as it is poured is a strong sensory reminder of the significance of baptism. And it is best if it is the sound of pouring, not dribbling—if the pouring accompanies the prayer, it need not continue through the whole thanksgiving.

If the font is already filled with water, as in the case of a font with a circulating system or an immersion pool, the pouring of water in connection with the prayer of thanksgiving is not needed. In any case, this action may be omitted, and the font may be filled with water before the service or during the hymn preceding the baptism.

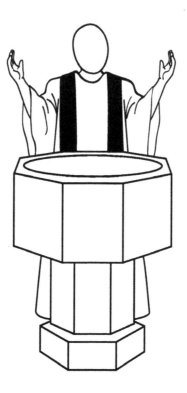

Fig. 3.3. Posture during prayer at the font. *In the prayer of thanksgiving at the font it would be appropriate, although not essential, for the presiding minister to pray with uplifted hands (the ancient* orans *posture).*

As in the great thanksgiving, the presiding minister begins the thanksgiving at the font with the preface dialogue. Looking at the assembly with her or his hands extended in a gesture of greeting, the presiding minister says, "The Lord be with you." At the congregation's response, the presiding minister may join his or her hands. (Ancient practice limits the line "Lift up your hearts" and the assembly's response, "We lift them to the Lord," to the thanksgiving at the table, which was considered the most joyful act of praise.) When the presiding minister says, "Let us give thanks . . . ," the hands may be extended as at the first exchange or they may remain joined.

After the interaction of the preface dialogue, the presiding minister looks at the font or at the book, which may be held by an assisting minister, as a way of calling the assembly to common prayer. The prayer of thanksgiving is a single unit, and this unity is maintained when the presiding minister keeps gestures simple and avoids change in voice during the prayer. In praying the prayer, the presiding minister endeavors to interpret God's work of creation, redemption, and sanctification in ways that are meaningful to the assembly.

The presiding minister may begin the prayer of thanksgiving by lifting the hands in a posture of prayer (Fig. 3.2). Except where specific gestures are desired, the presiding minister may maintain this posture throughout the prayer. Using broad gestures that are visible to the assembly is an important way the presiding minister can pray with the body as well as the voice.

As the presiding minister recounts creation and God's saving acts in and through water, an assisting minister might pour water from the ewer into the font. In Prayers II and IV, at the phrase, "baptizing . . . in the name of the Father, and of the Son, and of the Holy Spirit," the presiding minister may trace a cross in the water with the hand or dip a hand in the water and let it flow back into the font. Such gestures are ways of symbolizing physical contact with God's saving work with water, as it is recalled and proclaimed in the prayer.

The presiding minister may resume a posture of prayer with hands uplifted for the remainder of the thanksgiving. Some presiding ministers extend their hands over the water at the invitation to the Holy Spirit, which is expressed in the *Evangelical Lutheran Worship* prayers with the words "Pour out your Holy Spirit" or "Breathe your Spirit." Such a gesture of invocation is an ancient expression of the certainty of the presence of the Holy Spirit. However, if a similar gesture is not customarily used when praying for the Spirit in the thanksgiving at the table, it may not be wise to include it in the thanksgiving at the font; it is not necessary in either case. The presiding minister may instead continue the prayer to its conclusion with hands uplifted, joining them again for the assembly's Amen.

The Baptism

Each candidate is then baptized. The presiding minister (or an assisting minister) may invite the assembly to be seated when there are several candidates or when sitting facilitates the assembly's participation by making it easier to see and hear. Where circumstances allow, standing for baptism is another alternative. Standing may be understood as an expression of respect and an act of participation, and it may suggest the assembly's solidarity with those who are baptized and being raised to new life with Christ.

For practical reasons, especially when there are several candidates being baptized, the presiding minister may choose to ask the name of each candidate immediately before she or he is baptized, so that no mistake is made at this important moment in the baptismal liturgy and the Christian life. Such a question may be asked quietly of the candidate, sponsor, or parent; a second formal presentation is not needed. As part of the preparation for the baptismal service, the presiding minister may wish to alert those in the baptismal party that such a question may be asked, so that they are prepared to prompt the presiding minister as needed. It is customary that only the given (Christian) names are used in the administration of baptism: "Pedro Carlos Guillermo, I baptize you . . ."—rather than "Pedro Carlos Guillermo Rodriguez de Sanchez, I baptize you . . ." The name given in baptism is a new name, a sign of the new life in Christ and of being incorporated into a new family, for all the baptized belong to God's one family.

Two variations of the words for baptism are provided. The Western form (_Name_, I baptize you . . .), grammatically active, acknowledges the role of the baptizing minister. The Eastern form (_Name_ is baptized . . .), grammatically passive, lifts up God's action. The second form is provided in a footnote in the assembly edition, in recognition of the common usage of the first form among Lutherans. It is best if the same form is used at every baptism in the same service, since changing forms raises questions and undermines the equality of baptism. In the course of the church year, congregations can choose to use both forms as a way of expanding their understanding of baptism by recognizing both God's action and the role of the assembly through its pastor(s). The availability of two forms also indicates that precise words do not themselves make baptism. Rather, baptism is the word and Spirit of God, signified in the use of the triune name of God, connected with the water. Thus, "Holy Baptism is administered with water in the name of the triune God, Father, Son, and Holy Spirit" (UMG 24). Although the use of other names for God is encouraged in preaching and other parts of the service, such as the prayers of intercession, no adaptation to or alternative for this name of the triune God is recommended for use in connection with the administration of the water of baptism.

Water is used three times for each candidate, once for each person of the triune God. Both the Notes on the Services and *The Use of the Means of Grace* recommend that water be used generously, to symbolize God's power over sin and death and God's actions of washing, drowning, saving, and birthing. The Notes on the Services state, "The action of baptism may be immersion of the candidate in one of its several forms or the pouring of water on the candidate's head." Though the manner in which baptism is administered has no bearing on God's action in the sacrament, Luther advised that "we should . . . do justice to its meaning and make baptism a true and complete sign of the thing it signifies" (LW 35:29). Since Luther thought of baptism largely in terms of forgiveness of sin, he wanted to highlight the element of cleansing and washing. This is more obvious with an abundant rather than a minimal use of water.

Immersion helps to communicate dying and rising with Christ, the drowning of the old person, and new birth. In the ancient church, candidates for baptism of all ages and both genders were naked when they were immersed. Today, modest swimsuits are appropriate for those older than infancy. Infants may be immersed by being dipped into the baptismal water up to their chins.

Three forms of immersion are variously used with older children and adults. First, the candidate might stand or kneel in water of moderate depth with the head inclined forward. The baptizing minister, standing alongside the pool or beside the candidate in the water, pours water over the candidate's head so that the excess falls back into the baptismal pool. A second form provides for the candidate to kneel in the water. With one hand, the baptizing minister raises the person's clasped hands to protect the nose and mouth. With the other hand, the baptizing minister helps the candidate incline the head and shoulders into the water and out again. In the third form, both the candidate and the baptizing minister stand in the water. The minister stands a little behind the candidate. Again, the baptizing minister uses one hand to raise the person's clasped hands to protect the nose and mouth. The minister then places the forearm across the candidate's upper back, lowers the candidate into the water backward, and then raises the candidate up again. When baptism is administered by immersion, provision is made for candidates to change into dry clothing. This might be a time for the assembly to sing a hymn or approach the baptismal pool, dip a hand into the water and sign themselves with the cross in remembrance of their own baptism.

Administering baptism by pouring suggests cleansing from sin. This image is reinforced when the action is visible and audible to the assembly, so that all may see and hear what is being done. A dignified and substantial pouring of water helps symbolize the "water of rebirth and renewal by the Holy Spirit" (Titus 3:5). To insure a generous quantity of water, the presiding minister might consider baptizing with two cupped hands. The presiding minister may instead pour water from the a ewer or an ample baptismal shell, filled from the font. Don't worry too much about messes. Water spilled on the floor of the baptismal space can be seen as a reflection of the abundance of God's grace ("my cup is running over"), the uncontrollable nature of the Holy Spirit, and even the messiness of the Christian life. A towel—preferably one larger and more absorbent than the napkins sometimes used—is provided for each person who is baptized, and other towels may be needed to dry the floor. Towels used at baptism have a strictly utilitarian function and no ritual significance. Attaching visual symbols to them or giving them as gifts may distract from other, more central symbols of baptism.

For older candidates, enough water is poured so that it runs over their heads and even onto their clothing. An infant's head is held so that water can be poured over the child's head and fall back into the font. As part of baptismal preparation, parents should be advised that their children—and the clothes their children are wearing—and possibly the parents themselves—will get wet.

When baptism is administered by pouring, it is not necessary for the presiding minister to hold infants while baptizing them, and it is often impractical to carry out a hand-off at this juncture in the service. A more communal way of administering baptism may be demonstrated by having a parent or sponsor hold the child, leaving the presiding minister's hands free for pouring the water and for the actions that will follow.

Congregations might choose to vary the mode of administering baptism depending on context and circumstances. For example, when adults or older children are baptized at the Easter Vigil, congregations might construct a temporary baptismal space that permits a form of immersion as a way of enacting baptism's dying and rising with Christ. Or on All Saints Day water might be poured over the heads of infants at the congregation's baptismal font, symbolically connecting these new saints with all the saints of the congregation baptized in this font.

As indicated in the order, the assembly responds to each baptism with a spoken amen. Additionally, the assembly may respond after each baptism with one of two acclamations provided in the service, "Blessed be God, the source of all life" (#209–210) or "You belong to Christ" (#212–213); an alleluia, perhaps repeating the one sung as part of the day's gospel acclamation, or using one of the service music settings #168–175 without a proper verse; or another appropriate acclamation. As described earlier in this chapter, these and other sung acclamations, hymns, and songs provide a meaningful way for the assembly to assent to and share in the baptism of each candidate.

During or after the acclamation, a representative of the congregation may give each of the newly baptized a baptismal garment and say, "All who are clothed in Christ have put on Christ" or similar words. Alternatively, the common voice of the assembly might sing "You have put on Christ" (#211) as a representative of the congregation presents the baptismal garment to each of the newly baptized.

The baptismal garment may be a simple oval or rectangular piece of fabric with an opening in the center for the head (see fig. 3.4). The opening should be large enough to fit easily over the head. The garment itself is the symbol; incorporating additional words or symbols into the design of the garment is not necessary.

Traditionally, baptismal garments have been white, recalling the biblical image of being clothed with the righteousness of Christ and acknowledging that those who are baptized have joined the host of those who have "washed their robes and made them white in the blood of the Lamb" (Rev. 7:14). Alternatively, the baptismal garment might be an alb—especially for youth and adults—that the newly baptized wear for the remainder of the service. While this option may not convey the sense of a gift, it adds to the symbolic meaning of participation in the congregation's mission. The pall placed over the coffin or urn in the Funeral service is an echo of the baptismal garment and another reminder that in life and in death we are clothed with Christ.

Some households have found that the gift of a baptismal garment may play a meaningful part in celebrating an anniversary of baptism with children, especially if the garment is large enough so that a child may put it on well into the childhood years.

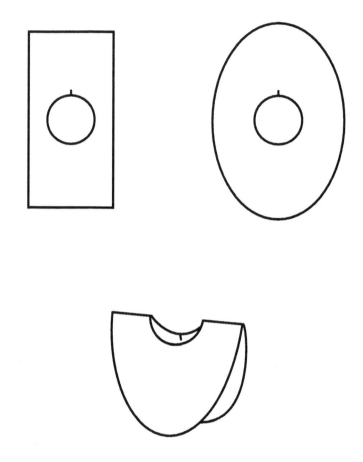

Fig. 3.4. The baptismal garment. *The congregation may give each of the newly baptized a baptismal garment, an oval or rectangular piece of fabric with a hole in the center for the head.*

In some cultures, dressing infants, either after the baptism or throughout the service, in a baptismal gown, perhaps handmade or handed down, is another adaptation of the tradition of the baptismal garment. If such a gown is worn throughout the service, a simple baptismal garment as described above may still be given and placed over the gown.

If the place of baptism is removed from the view of the assembly, the baptismal party may move in front of the table or to another place in view of the assembly for the remainder of the baptismal liturgy. The assembly may mark this transition by singing a hymn or psalm, or continue to sing the acclamation, particularly if the font and the table are at a distance from each other. Hymns inviting the Holy Spirit are particularly appropriate at this point in the service.

If, however, the place of baptism is accessible and visible to the assembly, such movement is not necessary and may in fact suggest a greater separation of the various elements in the baptismal service than is helpful. The place of baptism is a liturgical center equal in importance to the place of the meal; conducting part of the baptismal service near the table may suggest a hierarchy of the sacraments that does not exist.

Prayer for the Holy Spirit

After the baptismal party is reassembled, especially when time has been needed for the clothing of candidates after the baptism, the order continues with a prayer for the Holy Spirit. This prayer asks that the Holy Spirit, given through baptism in water with God's word, will sustain the baptized in the gift of baptism that has just been received. "Sustain *name* with the gift of your Holy Spirit. . . ." Praying for the Holy Spirit is neither a distinct nor an additional part of baptism. Instead, this prayer, accompanied by the laying on of hands and followed by signing with the cross and the presentation of a lighted candle, is part of what might be called the symbolic overflow of baptism.[2] "These interpretive signs proclaim the gifts that are given by the promise of God in Baptism itself" (UMG 28A). God's gifts in baptism are so overwhelming that, as the church reflected on baptism over time, certain of God's gifts came to be acknowledged and expressed with additional words and actions. Since humans grasp a number of concepts more easily when they are presented in sequence rather than simultaneously, associating different dimensions of baptism with distinct symbolic acts helps the assembly appreciate the many gifts of grace that God bestows in baptism. In this case, prayer with the laying on of hands helps the newly baptized and the assembly acknowledge the outpouring of the Holy Spirit and the Spirit's sevenfold gifts.

As recommended for the thanksgiving at the font and baptism, an assisting minister may hold the book so that both of the presiding minister's hands are free. After the invitation to prayer and a brief pause, the presiding minister prays the first two lines, "We give you thanks . . . and raise them to eternal life," during which her or his hands may be uplifted in prayer. Then, without breaking the atmosphere of prayer, the presiding minister approaches each of the newly baptized, lays both hands on his or her head, and prays the remainder of the prayer for each of the newly baptized in turn, speaking each person's name. Even when a number of people are baptized, this portion of the prayer should not be broken up so that a few words are prayed over each person. Each person deserves undivided attention in both the laying on of hands and the prayer for the Spirit's gifts.

For the second portion of the prayer, those who are holding infants remain standing. Where it is possible, older children and adults who were just baptized may kneel. Alternatively, the presiding minister could remain in one place as each of the newly baptized steps forward and kneels for the laying on of hands and prayer. The sponsors (and parents) might also lay a hand on the head or shoulders of the person, and people in the assembly might extend a hand toward each of the newly baptized, palm down and fingers slightly cupped, in a gesture of blessing.

Sign of the Cross

The newly baptized are then marked with the cross of Christ, a sign that they are united with the Crucified forever. To be marked with the cross signifies that one belongs to God and is called to follow in the way of the cross. The Notes on the Services observe that the sign of the cross is "an integral part of the order of baptism." Other uses of the sign of the cross in worship—at the beginning of the service, at the announcement of forgiveness, and at the blessing—recall and confirm this original sign of baptism.

The presiding minister traces a cross on the forehead of each of the newly baptized. The presiding minister calls each of the newly baptized by name and says the accompanying words of declaration to each person, while marking the forehead with the cross. These powerful words of comfort and promise are said deliberately. The newly baptized (or the parent or guardian of those who cannot answer for themselves) respond, "Amen."

Oil may be used to accompany these words and the cross-marking as a further interpretive sign that baptism joins us to the Messiah or Anointed One, seals us with the Holy Spirit, anoints us for service in Christ's royal priesthood, and promises us wholeness and healing. Olive oil is normally used for this purpose. A very small amount of fragrance such as balsam or bergamot is sometimes added; however, those who prepare the oil should be sensitive to the possibility of allergic reactions.

The oil may be set out in a small glass bowl near the font. The oil may be applied with the thumb, or, if a more generous use of oil is desired, with the fingertips of the hand, held together. Also commonly used is a small screw-top container called an oil stock, into which the presiding minister dips the tip of the thumb used to trace the cross. A cotton ball soaked in the oil and placed in the stock will help control the amount of oil on the minister's fingers. A towel may also be set out, for use by the presiding minister after applying the oil.

Welcome

After the newly baptized are marked with the sign of the cross, a representative of the congregation may present each person (or the parents of infants and younger children) with a lighted candle. The order for baptism provides two scripture sentences that suggest the symbolic meaning of this gift. The first alternative is Jesus' declaration and promise, "I am the light of the world. Whoever follows me will have the light of life" (John 8:12). The second alternative (Matt. 5:16) is Jesus' teaching that, in the same way that we put a lamp on a stand so that it lights the whole house, so we allow the light of Christ or the gospel that is within us to shine in our lives as a witness of God's love to others. Both verses connect the gift of baptism with the daily lives of the baptized. The promise in the first alternative may be more appropriate for infants and young children, while the encouragement to let Christ's light shine in good works in the second alternative may be more fitting for older children and adults. The representative of the congregation might say one of these verses to the newly baptized as a group, and then present each with a candle. Alternatively, the congregational representative might say one of these verses to each person while presenting the candle.

The meaning of this symbol is enhanced when, as part of the presentation, each candle is lighted from the paschal candle and then given to the newly baptized. The sharing of the light of the paschal candle connects baptism and the resurrection of Christ, especially in congregations that make use of this candle during the Easter Vigil and the Easter season. Like the paschal candle, the candles presented to the newly baptized are white and may be decorated with a symbol of baptism or the Christian faith. The newly baptized extinguish their candles when they return to their places at the conclusion of the welcome. As part of baptismal preparation, they may be taught to save their candles and light them on the anniversary of their baptism.

The baptismal group and the ministers then turn to face the assembly. When they are in place, a representative of the congregation leads the assembly in the words of welcome. The assembly welcomes the newly baptized into the universal church, the body of Christ, and its mission. The assembly also invites the newly baptized to join its common life of thanking and praising God and bearing God's word to all the world. At this point, some congregations have additional customs of welcome such as applause or processions of the newly baptized. While these are not necessary, it is appropriate to offer a warm welcome to these new members of Christ's body in a style that suits this particular assembly.

The Service Continues

The baptismal party then returns to their places in the assembly. As they move, the assembly may again join in singing. Service music acclamations (#209–215) are suitable choices. Hymns or appropriate stanzas of hymns from the Holy Baptism section (#442–459) may be used. On occasion the hymn of the day may bracket the order of Holy Baptism. For example, the first four stanzas of "Dearest Jesus, we are here" (#443) may be sung before the order begins, and stanza 5 may be sung at its conclusion.

The order of service continues with the prayers of intercession, which will include petitions for the newly baptized, sponsors, and parents. Although the prayers of intercession were included within the order for baptism in *Lutheran Book of Worship,* a generation of experience revealed practical difficulties with this placement, especially when infants were being baptized. Placing the intercessions after the baptismal order, however, does not reduce the importance of including petitions for the newly baptized, sponsors, and parents. For example, the optional prayer in the baptismal service in *Lutheran Book of Worship* (p. 124) is a useful model for a petition to be included within the intercessory prayers on occasions when young children are baptized:

> O God, the giver of all life, look with kindness upon the *fathers* and *mothers* of *these children.* Let them ever rejoice in the gift you have given them. Make them teachers and examples of righteousness for their *children.* Strengthen them in their own baptism so they may share eternally with their *children* the salvation you have given them, through Jesus Christ our Lord.

When the order for Holy Baptism is part of the Gathering rite, the service may continue with gathering song. If the place of baptism is located near the entrance to the church, the baptismal party may enter in procession with the ministers during the singing and proceed to their places in the assembly. The service then continues with the greeting. Prayers of intercession later in the service will include the newly baptized, sponsors, and parents.

The essential connection between the sacraments of baptism and communion is richly revealed when baptism takes place within the service of Holy Communion and when the newly baptized participate in both sacraments at this service. Congregations are urged to consider the guidance of *The Use of the Means of Grace*:

> "Admission to the Sacrament [of Holy Communion] is by invitation of the Lord, presented through the Church to those who are baptized." (37)

> "When adults and older children are baptized, they may be communed for the first time in the service in which they are baptized. Baptismal preparation and continuing catechesis include instruction for Holy Communion." (37A)

> "Infants and children may be communed for the first time during the service in which they are baptized or they may be brought to the altar during communion to receive a blessing." (37D)

Although no special ceremony recognizing this participation is needed within the service, pre-baptismal preparation for this participation will be important for youth and adults and for the parents and sponsors of infants and children who will participate. After baptism, these children will also be "taught throughout their development" about the gift of the Lord's supper (37E).

Like baptism itself, the order for Holy Baptism overflows with grace and significance for the lives of the Christian and the assembly. Careful planning of a congregation's baptismal practice by its leaders and meaningful celebration within each assembly in which baptism takes place can transform the notion of baptism as the wellspring of Christian life from a useful metaphor for understanding the sacrament's significance to a lived experience of God's grace.

CHAPTER FOUR

Welcome to Baptism

In most Christian traditions where infant baptism has been the primary way that people have been received into the church, conversion is considered to be a gradual process. Faith is nurtured and developed over a period of years as a child matures into an adult who is able to make decisions and to articulate beliefs on her or his own. Much of congregational life, particularly in the Lutheran tradition, has focused on the faith development of children. Through generations of tradition, it is typical that parents seek to have their children baptized within a few months of their birth. Children are often encouraged to participate in Sunday school from the time they are three years old. Adolescents commonly attend weekly classes and other activities for two or three years in preparation for affirmation of baptism. And along the way there are usually first-communion programs, weeks at vacation Bible school or church camps, children's choirs, acolyte programs, retreats, and a variety of youth-group experiences, all designed to encourage young people to grow in their faith. By the time a young person is of high school age, a local congregation will have already offered a number of opportunities for religious instruction and faith development. Most of these activities are ways to support parents and sponsors in the responsibilities that they have undertaken as they bring young children to baptism.

The experiences of older youth and adults who enter the life of the church and who approach baptism at a later time in life is frequently much different. Typically, congregations do not offer much support to new members who come with little or no background in the Christian faith. Although several new-member sessions may seem sufficient for people who are transferring active membership from another congregation, whether of the same denominational tradition or not, such a practice is likely to be woefully inadequate for those who have not been exposed to several years' worth of hearing biblical stories, praying and singing together, and responding to the gospel by serving others in need. What do congregations offer older youth and adults who have not yet developed a basic vocabulary for the faith? Joining a high school or adult Bible study class, primarily made up of people who have been a part of the church for years, will probably not give the newcomer to the Christian community the experiences he or she needs to feel free to ask the basic questions about God.

Churches that approach coming to faith primarily from the perspective of working with children from families who have some grounding in the church's life often experience gaps in their approach to faith formation for youth and adults who do not have this grounding. The gaps between what many people need and what many congregations offer to adult newcomers seem to be widening ever further. As the twenty-first century unfolds, many church leaders have noticed a number of trends that have affected the ways adult newcomers are incorporated into the life of congregations.

Many communities have grown more diverse. Ethnic and racial groups that once provided social cohesion for many people within a community have been realigned. Though this may not be as surprising in older urban neighborhoods that have experienced waves of immigration over the decades, greater ethnic diversity has reached a number of rural and suburban areas within North America as well. Congregations that may have begun their life ministering primarily to a particular ethnic group have discovered that to meet the needs of their changing neighborhoods they have to welcome different languages and cultural traditions than they did in previous years.

Keeping a base of longtime congregational members while also reaching out to new groups of people creates the potential for conflict and raises questions about the fundamental mission of the church. In short, the increasing diversity of a neighborhood means that the local congregation needs to be more intentional about creating community and offering more opportunities for social interaction than it had to do in an era when most members knew one another through a variety of other relationships within the neighborhood or community.

Fewer people are fluent in the biblical tradition. Only a few decades ago it was often assumed that being a "well-educated person" meant, among other things, having a basic knowledge of the Bible. The Old and New Testaments were required reading not only to be a good church member but to understand a framework that was common in the works of great writers and in political rhetoric. The assumption that most people are at least roughly familiar with the major stories of the Bible now is clearly invalid as the wider culture becomes both more secular and more religiously pluralistic. Even people who have been reasonably active in the worship and educational ministries of the church tend to have a greater challenge recalling biblical stories than would have been the case only a generation or two ago.

Many people describe themselves as spiritual but not religious. While the interest many contemporary people have in spiritual matters may seem high, this seems not to correlate with higher levels of involvement in religious institutions. Robert D. Putnam chronicled how social organizations that were once the glue of civic and cultural life had waned in popularity in the late twentieth century.[1] If Putnam's analogy of bowling alone—people are not as interested in bowling in leagues as they are in bowling in informal groups that do not gather at regular times—holds true in the early twenty-first century, the church's existence—and the expectation that members gather regularly for worship, faith formation, and communal activities—will continue to be in contrast to the ways many people now interact. Considering the fragmentation also occurring in the ways that people get their news, consume entertainment, and communicate with one another, it is easy to see that several core activities that in past decades have been crucial to congregational life are not a part of the ordinary experience for many contemporary people.

People do not feel tied to neighborhoods and traditions of previous generations. As people become more mobile they often shop around for a church. Fewer people are tied to a specific denominational tradition. More people attend or are members of very large congregations, where connections between people and a congregational structure may be more fluid than was the case when people more often knew many of their fellow parishioners well. The decrease in close friendships has, in general, led to less stable interpersonal relationships among members of congregations.

All this is to say that newcomers to a congregation may not know much about a particular church's traditions and formal teachings, may have few personal bonds with others in that congregation, and may have less desire to attend a traditional Bible study class or commit to a lengthy or involved process of faith formation. Congregational leaders need to exercise creativity in adapting approaches to new-member integration so that they can better serve the needs of people who come from little or no faith background. But there are resources for ministering in a radically different cultural landscape.

Making Disciples, Forming Faith

As we move farther into what many are calling a post-Christian era, it is helpful to look back to the pre-Christian era. Prior to the official sanctioning of Christianity by the Emperor Constantine (d. 337), becoming a Christian was not the norm. In that era people in the church could not rely on other institutions to support the values and teachings of the Christian faith. Learning the scriptures, being formed in a life of prayer, and living out the faith through a variety of daily-life settings were all activities that had to occur deliberately within the context of the church. A process of education and formation leading to baptism and integration into the Christian community developed. It was commonly referred to as the *catechumenate* (kat-uh-CUE-men-ut), and those going through the process as *catechumens*. Those words come from the Greek, a word that in Galatians 6:6 is translated as "those who are taught."

After church and civic life became fused together from the fourth century onward, practices of the Christian faith were often taken for granted. Though it was a gradual transition, the occasion for entrance into the church was recognized as birth, since baptism often occurred within a few days after a child was born. For many individuals, living the faith was not really a conscious decision, since an array of civic and cultural institutions supported the Christian church, at least nominally. But an echo of the earlier catechumenate may be seen in the later development of *catechisms* (a word coming from the same root), which encapsulated basic Christian teachings in ways that could be understood by the young and the unlearned and thus could contribute to their fuller integration into the faith and life of the Christian community in which they had been baptized. Among Lutherans, the Small and Large Catechisms are the best-known examples of this development.

Renewed Interest in a Baptismal Process

Most people recognize that the overall cultural climate in North America has become less overtly Christian in recent decades. The reality of religious pluralism has meant that fewer people are automatically assumed to be Christian in many communities. More people have never had a connection with the church or may be "dechurched"—people whose parents or grandparents might once have been a part of the church, but who have not maintained those connections for themselves. In many communities, fewer parents of younger children now feel the need to involve their children in activities like Sunday school and regular worship. Likewise, when a number of people do express an interest in the church as older youth or adults, they come with little or no sustained exposure to the Christian faith and its teachings. Thus, many churches are seeking new or renewed ways of helping people enter the Christian community and forming them into conscious and active participants. These churches are recognizing the need to make a greater effort in developing the faith of newcomers. Loren Mead has described the need well in his book *The Once and Future Church*:

> Each [congregation] needs to understand the strategic importance of training for entry into the faith. Congregations in the church of the future will have to have strong entry processes, assuming very little previous knowledge or experience of religion or Christianity. Such congregations will have to set aside the time and energy to put first class attention on this need, year after year after year.[2]

In the last quarter of the twentieth century, a number of Christian denominations that had experienced infant baptism as the norm for centuries have produced liturgical and formational resources especially intended for use with the baptism of adults. *Occasional Services: A Companion to the Lutheran Book of Worship* (1982) included an order for the enrollment of candidates for baptism and some guidance as to how congregations might initiate a process of faith formation using elements of the catechumenal tradition. The most thorough-going and influential of the current generation of rites for adult baptism has been the Roman Catholic Church's *Rite of Christian Initiation of Adults* (usually referred to as RCIA). Other denominations that have produced similar resources in North America include the Episcopal Church, the United Methodist Church, and the Evangelical Lutheran Church in Canada (ELCIC). (See the bibliography for a list of resources from these churches.) The ELCIC's *Living Witnesses* was largely incorporated into an expanded set of provisional resources later produced in conjunction with the Evangelical Lutheran Church in America, with participation also from the Lutheran Church—Missouri Synod, and titled *Welcome to Christ*. The liturgical materials from this set were further revised and included in the provisional *Holy Baptism and Related Rites*, the third volume in the Renewing Worship series, which helped prepare the way for *Evangelical Lutheran Worship*.

At the time the core editions of *Evangelical Lutheran Worship* were published, the Lutheran churches in North America—and in particular the Evangelical Lutheran Church in America—were still in an exploratory phase regarding baptismal formation processes. The following description of recent Lutheran provisional resources is best understood as a snapshot in time while the church's exploration of these matters continues. It can be said, however, that across various denominations there is deep and ongoing interest in identifying contemporary ways of leading people into baptism, ways that are grounded in the Christian tradition and that suit today's contexts. This development has occurred together with renewal of worship, a profound awareness of the need for Christians to be grounded in word and sacrament, and a growing ecumenical convergence around these issues.

Shape of a Baptismal Process

The various denominationally produced versions of current resources for leading adults into baptism recognize that baptismal conversion is a process that occurs over some length of time, rather than being a single event. Most of the processes that have been developed describe a shape that recognizes several phases or periods. Each phase of the process is designed to nurture people in the Christian faith in ever-deepening ways. Related orders of worship, which occur both during and between phases, serve the purpose of drawing those inquiring into the Christian faith more closely into the life of a worshiping community.

Welcome to Christ: A Lutheran Introduction to the Catechumenate (1997), gives these names to four phases of a baptismal process:

- Inquiry
- Catechumenate
- Baptismal Preparation
- Baptismal Living

A chart describing this process was designed to interpret the overall shape of the process and how the various worship orders intersect with it (Fig. 4.1). Furthermore, in these resources terms commonly used to describe the people who are a part of this process were adopted: inquirers, catechumens, candidates, and the newly baptized. (Though it is possible to speak of a similar process or shape for people who have already been baptized but have not yet entered into active church life as adults, the terminology of today's baptismal processes generally does not refer to these people as catechumens, although that term has historically also been used for baptized people preparing for confirmation, especially among Lutherans.)

The period of *inquiry* is a constant ministry of reaching out to people and inviting them into life with Christ in and through the resources of the church. Typically a congregation will have a number of inquirers' classes or meetings, so that those who are interested in church membership may come to ask questions about God and the church and be invited into a process of faith formation. This time of formation includes getting to know more about the scriptures, becoming more familiar with patterns of prayer, and exploring ways of integrating the faith in service to others. When people are ready to continue in this exploration of the faith, they are invited to take part in an order of *welcome* that takes place within a regular worship service of the congregation. During the rite of welcome, these people are introduced to the congregation by name, and they pledge themselves to a process of exploring the faith more deeply. The congregation pledges its support and prays for those who are welcomed.

The second phase, sometimes called *catechumenate* or a more immediately descriptive term such as *training, education,* or *formation,* is a length of time that each congregation may define. Participants (sometimes called catechumens) meet regularly with sponsors and a leader (sometimes referred to as a catechist). In many churches the primary learning tool is the Bible, often as used within the context of Sunday worship. In some places, the pattern of the early church is followed, in which catechumens attend only the Word section of each weekly service of Holy Communion. After the readings and the sermon, they go to another location to reflect more deeply on the readings with their catechists and sponsors. The scripture readings—in effect, the weekly lectionary—serve as openings into learning about the Christian

THE CATECHUMENATE

Welcome of Inquirers to the Catechumenate	*Enrollment of Candidates for Baptism*	*Enrollment of Candidates at the Vigil of Easter*	

INQUIRY
Inquirers

Inquiry is an open-ended period of time during which *inquirers* make an initial exploration into Christian faith and life. This period of inquiry is shaped by the inquirer as well as parish leaders and the congregation.

Through a public *rite of welcome*, inquirers are received into the catechumenate. This welcome may be celebrated at any time during the church year.

CATECHUMENATE
Catechumens

The **Catechumenate** is an open-ended period of time during which *catechumens* explore more deeply the Christian faith through the reading of scripture, prayer, worship, and ministry in daily life. This period of reflection and study may last from several months to years.

Near the conclusion of the catechumenate, catechumens publicly express their desire to be baptized during a *rite of enrollment*. For persons who will be baptized at the Vigil of Easter, this enrollment normally occurs on the First Sunday in Lent.

BAPTISMAL PREPARATION
Candidates

Lent is a six-week period of final **Baptismal Preparation** for *candidates* who will be baptized at the Vigil of Easter.

Since the Vigil of Easter is the center of the church's year and life, it is an especially suitable time for candidates to receive *Holy Baptism* and partake of *Holy Communion* for the first time.

BAPTISMAL LIVING
Newly Baptized

Easter ushers in the lifetime of **Baptismal Living** for the *newly baptized*. This period extends throughout the Fifty Days of Easter and beyond.

Affirmation of Vocation of the Baptized

A *rite of baptismal affirmation* may be celebrated during which the newly baptized affirm their vocation in the world. For those who were baptized at the Vigil of Easter, it is particularly appropriate to celebrate this affirmation on the Day of Pentecost.

faith and the teachings of the church. The ten commandments are often introduced and interpreted during this time. In addition to providing a way to hear the scriptures, this second phase is also a time to learn a practice of prayer as it is modeled within a small group. Catechumens are also encouraged to consider forms of Christian service that put their faith into practice in daily life.

After catechumens have participated in such a time of formation involving worship, the scriptures, prayer, and some type of Christian service to others for a few months (or longer), they—with the support and counsel of their catechists and sponsors—may determine that they are ready to be baptized. Resources produced by many denominations offer a liturgical order intended for use with people who are ready for baptism and who are then *enrolled* as baptismal candidates (in the Roman Catholic Church this is referred to as the rite of *election*). Traditionally, the rite of enrollment occurs near the beginning of Lent.

Throughout the third phase, the period of *baptismal preparation*, the participants—now *candidates*—continue to meet together in the small faith-sharing groups that were established earlier in the process. The congregation's intercessory prayers mention the baptismal candidates by name regularly during this time. The congregation may also present or "hand over" copies of the Apostles' Creed and the Lord's Prayer during regular services of worship as a sign of the candidates' deepening understanding of the faith and life of prayer. These primary symbols of the faith (and major parts of the Small Catechism) are also significant touchstones in preparation for baptism. Baptismal candidates learn the Apostles' Creed as a summary of trinitarian faith, while committing the Lord's Prayer to memory is an important way to prepare for participating fully in the church's most commonly used prayer. When baptism is anticipated at the Vigil of Easter, the entire congregation may support the candidates as the church collectively experiences baptismal renewal during the season of Lent.

Following baptism, the *newly baptized* continue meeting for a few weeks to reflect on having received both of the sacraments. The early church called this the time of *mystagogy*—being led into a deeper appreciation of what it means to be joined through baptism to the death and resurrection of Jesus Christ—sometimes called the *paschal mystery*. Reflection on experience is a primary learning method throughout the phases of this process, and many people who have just been baptized and have received communion for the first time will be eager to talk about these experiences. The time immediately after baptism also provides an opportunity for the newly baptized to continue their commitment to a life of discipleship while considering the implications of their faith through their vocations as Christians and as ministers in daily life. Particular ministries within the congregation may be explored more fully during this time, but in the weeks immediately following baptism, it will be helpful to look at all the relationships that the newly baptized have in their lives. How does following Christ make a difference in the families, neighborhoods, and workplaces where a person lives most of his or her life? After a time of considering one's Christian vocation, together with the support of a catechist and sponsors, the newly baptized may join other members of a congregation in an Affirmation of Christian Vocation (AE p. 84). If baptism occurred at the Vigil of Easter, the vocation of the baptized might be celebrated at Pentecost.

Congregations that have begun using a baptismal formation process of some type have often adapted the resources prepared by their own and other denominations for use in their own settings. Even though there is a clear structure and shape to the process described above, the process invites and expects adaptation. Each person comes with a unique history and with a variety of faith experiences that need to be respected. The development of an individual's faith will never exactly follow particular timelines or course outlines. Even with a clear outline that can give shape to the process of coming to faith through baptism, the Holy Spirit's work requires some open breathing space. Congregations have often developed language to refer to such a process in their settings without using the word catechumenate, instead calling it "the way," "the journey," or some other language that is inviting to newcomers and leaders alike.

In their continuing exploration of ways to lead people into baptism, the churches will need to consider whether a single process is to be considered normative or whether there are multiple ways such integration may occur, and how best such approaches might be described. Furthermore, those called to administer the sacrament of baptism will also need to be prepared—and baptismal formation processes must be crafted to allow—for how to respond to a question like that posed to the apostle Philip by the Ethiopian traveler: "Look, here is water! What is to prevent me from being baptized?" (Acts 8:36).

Welcome to Baptism: Primary Uses

Welcome to Baptism (AE pp. 232–233; LE 592–595) is a helpful resource for a new era of making disciples and welcoming people into the church through baptism. As described earlier in this chapter, the order may be used as part of a more extensive process leading to baptism and into the baptismal life. It represents an approach to faith formation that has contemporary relevance as well as ancient roots.

Although the primary use of Welcome to Baptism may be for adults and older children who are involved in an instructional process leading toward baptism, this order may also be used with parents and sponsors of infants and younger children who are anticipating baptism. In the case of the parents and sponsors, the rite may be particularly helpful with nonmember inquirers who are seeking to have their children baptized. Children may be presented as candidates for baptism whose parents (and sponsors) will be involved in a series of pre-baptismal preparation sessions for their children. Pre-baptismal sessions may also be combined with membership sessions for baptized adults who have not recently been active members of another congregation.

Although Welcome to Baptism is not in any way a dedication ceremony for infants (such ceremonies are used primarily by faith traditions that do not observe infant baptism), in certain situations this rite may meet some immediate needs that are expressed by nonmember parents who are seeking baptism for their child. Welcome to Baptism may serve as a broadly inclusive invitation to baptismal preparation for nearly anyone, while baptism itself is planned for people who, or whose parents and sponsors, have demonstrated signs of willingness to commit to the responsibilities and promises made prior to baptism (LE 584). Welcome to Baptism is not intended for anyone who has already been baptized. Baptized people who are preparing for Affirmation of Baptism may be identified and welcomed as such, even if some of their preparation and instruction in the faith takes place along with unbaptized catechumens.

The title Welcome to Baptism has been intentionally chosen to convey the sense that, although the sacrament takes place on a single day, the journey to and from that day is rich and varied. Those who are welcomed to baptism within the assembly's worship are invited into a journey through which, we pray, "God may bring [them] to Christ in baptism" (LE 593). The service does not presume that a person's readiness for baptism has been fully determined, but it declares that the journey of baptism includes time for discernment about what it means to be baptized, and it affirms that the community welcomes to the baptismal journey all who inquire into Christian faith and life—whatever the outcome may be. Welcome to Baptism offers a time and a place where the journey of baptism may be publicly acknowledged. It presents an opportunity for those who participate to affirm their intention to continue a time of discernment and formation related to the Christian faith and life, and it calls upon the assembly to pledge its support and companionship to those who are making this journey. As the introductory paragraphs indicate (AE p. 232), the presentation section, the sign of the cross section, or both may be used.

Presentation

The notes introducing the presentation section of Welcome to Baptism (AE p. 232; LE 592) indicate that it may take place at the entrance to the church or in front of the assembly. One reason for using the entrance is that this rite is intended to welcome people into a community, much like a visitor to a home or a place of business might be greeted at the front door. If the congregation regularly begins its services with a preparatory rite (confession and forgiveness or thanksgiving for baptism) led from a baptismal font located near the entrance, such a spot could be ideal for beginning the Welcome to Baptism. The presentation may also begin in front of the assembly, with inquirers and their sponsors having been seated prior to the start of the service. When Welcome to Baptism is used, other preparatory rites may be omitted from that service. If the congregation also desires to use an order of confession and forgiveness, Welcome to Baptism may follow it. Normally, a service would not include both a thanksgiving for baptism and the Welcome to Baptism.

Welcome to Baptism is most suitably used when one or more inquiry sessions have occurred prior to this point so that the persons being welcomed have already indicated an interest in exploring what it means to follow Christ and become a part of the Christian community. When people have expressed such an interest, it is particularly helpful that the congregation select one or more persons to accompany each inquirer as a sponsor. Inquirers may already know people who have been responsible for bringing them into the congregation and who might be ideal sponsors. Sponsors will want to rehearse the rite to some degree with the worship leaders for the service so they know where it will take place and what their responsibilities will be.

Following the initial welcome by the presiding minister, a sponsor for each person being welcomed presents that person by name: "I present _name_ to be welcomed by this congregation" (LE 592). If the sponsors will not be heard easily by all worshipers without the use of a sound system, every attempt should be made to amplify the voices of the sponsors. Hearing the names is an important part of this rite, since it is a formal introduction to the entire assembly of those being welcomed.

The presiding minister asks questions of the persons being welcomed: "What do you ask of God's church?" and "What do you seek from God's word?" Prepared responses to these questions are provided in the leaders edition (LE 592–593) and may be rehearsed in advance with those being welcomed. In certain situations the presiding minister may work with those being welcomed to craft similar responses in the persons' own words and of similar length, while ensuring that the responses convey what is needed. In most cases, however, the responses provided ensure a common, confident reply from all who are being welcomed. Parents or sponsors of children who cannot answer for themselves also respond to the first two questions, as well as to a third: "For whom do you ask such faith?" The answer indicates the name of the child.

The presiding minister offers initial words of welcome, while asking if those being welcomed will be faithful in learning the way of Christ. The answer here, as in many other places within the church's life, is "I will, and I ask God to help me." The final question is asked of the assembly, and it is an important one since the primary responsibility affirmed in this service is really that of the baptized community in providing a welcome to those who wish to enter.

An assisting minister offers the final words of welcome in the presentation section of the liturgy—a welcome to gather with the community and to hear the word of God. If those being welcomed and their sponsors have gathered near the entrance, they may approach their seats (reserved if necessary) along with the worship leaders who will be entering for the service. If the presentation was conducted in front of the assembly, they may return to their seats as gathering song begins.

Sign of the Cross

Signing with the cross may be a part of Welcome to Baptism. After the hymn of the day, those being welcomed come to the front of the assembly, accompanied by their sponsors. The introductory statement by the presiding minister relates the actions that will follow to the liturgy of the word in which all have been participating. Note that a sponsor for each person being welcomed is invited to trace the sign of the cross on the person's forehead. This action anticipates the signing with the cross in the baptismal service (when oil may be used). Used here, the signing with the cross is more of an invitation to follow Christ, rather than a statement about the fullness of baptismal identity that happens later through the sacrament itself. Signing the forehead with the cross is a simple, clear action that declares "God's endless love and mercy" for the person being welcomed. In many circumstances, this signing is the only one needed when this section of Welcome to Baptism is used.

For use in some circumstances, especially where a congregation is deeply involved in a baptismal formation process, where the assembly is well prepared, and where leaders can ensure that those being welcomed are comfortable with the actions, additional signings of the various senses are provided as options (LE 594). If the additional signings are used, they have the effect of enveloping the whole person in the love of Christ and the Christian community.

The repeated signs on a person's ears, eyes, lips, heart, shoulders, hands, and feet are powerful ways of indicating that genuine Christian discipleship is not merely cognitive but involves our total beings. Furthermore, the embodiment of this uniquely Christian symbol, made by one or more sponsors, can have the effect of highlighting the closeness of the relationship between the person exploring baptism and her or his sponsor(s). All or only some of the additional signings may be used.

In making the sign of the cross, the sponsor may use the thumb or forefinger of one hand and trace a small cross on the forehead, or other part of the body that is named, while the presiding minister speaks the words provided. Each signing should be deliberate and not rushed. As a response to each signing, the assembly responds with the words "Praise to you, O Christ, the wisdom and power of God." This sentence, a reference to 1 Corinthians 1:24, is a way for the assembly itself to proclaim both the vulnerability and the victory involved in following Christ.

If the response is sung ("Praise to you, O Christ," #216), a cantor may sing the phrase through once, after which the assembly repeats it. The music is not difficult, but it is surprisingly powerful. If the assembly learns to sing this phrase well it can be a strong affirmation of faith. Because the Notes (LE 30) place the signing of the cross between the hymn of the day and the prayers of intercession so that the creed is omitted in this service, this response provides another way for the assembly to sing its faith. If the primary signing of the forehead is the only one used, the response may be repeated several times in succession, or it may be sung after each person receives the sign of the cross. If there are additional signings of those being welcomed, the musical response may be repeated once after each of the signings.

Next, a Bible may be presented to each person who is welcomed. It is best for the Bible to be presented by someone other than the presiding minister, perhaps one of the teachers (catechists) involved in the congregation's baptismal process or someone who has a particular responsibility for education in the congregation. The Bible may also be presented by someone whose love for the scriptures is well known within the congregation, even if that person does not have other leadership or teaching responsibilities. The Bible presented to each person should be a handsome, durable edition (not necessarily expensive, but likely hardbound), and should be in the translation most commonly used during the congregation's worship. The words that may be spoken at the time of the presentation of a Bible indicate its great value to the Christian community. Other, similar words may be used in place of those provided, but the intent should be the same.

Finally, the presiding minister blesses those being welcomed. Depending on the size of the group, the presiding minister may lay a hand on each person's head or shoulder during the prayer. When there are several participants, the presiding minister may extend both hands over all of them while sponsors for each participant may lay a hand on their heads or shoulders. If facilities for kneeling are available, they may be used during this prayer by the people being welcomed. A prayer of blessing is also provided for times when those being welcomed include infants and young children. Its rich biblical allusions are an invitation to open the scriptures just given and to—in the words of the presentation—

"learn and tell its stories." Again and again God has shown grace to children, who are fully welcomed into the household of faith.

Much like the dismissal spoken at the end of the Sunday service, the assisting minister offers the concluding words in the Welcome to Baptism: "God bring you in peace and joy to fullness of life in Christ and call you to the waters of baptism." This statement welcomes people to a continuing life of faith that is intended to culminate in baptism. The final response by the assembly adds a communal blessing to this order of welcome that is profoundly congregational in character: "May the God of all grace, who has called you to glory, support you and make you strong." Like the previous response, this one also may be sung (#217). It could be sung a number of times as those being welcomed return to their places, perhaps sung first by a cantor alone, then repeated as needed by the rest of the assembly.

As indicated in the section earlier in this chapter describing common patterns for a baptismal formation process, in some congregations those who have been welcomed (perhaps now called catechumens) go out from the worship space at this time (or after the peace) so that they may reflect more deeply on the scriptures in a location separate from the rest of the worshipers. If they leave at the conclusion of the Welcome to Baptism, and at subsequent services during the hymn of the day, it is best for them to leave as a group along with catechists and sponsors, so that their continued guidance in the scriptures may be seen as an extension of the worshiping community. A catechist may lead the catechumens out of the worship space while holding up a bound lectionary volume or a Bible.

Some congregations may choose to carry out the formation process at another time and not in conjunction with the Sunday assembly. In that case, those who have been welcomed remain in the assembly and may come to receive a blessing during the communion.

Other Services Related to Baptismal Formation

In addition to Welcome to Baptism as it appears in *Evangelical Lutheran Worship*, other worship resources can enrich the process of leading people into baptism. Some of these resources are explained in the first section of this chapter. A congregation that develops a significant ministry with adults inquiring into Christian faith and life may wish to examine the provisional orders in *Welcome to Christ*. As the family of *Evangelical Lutheran Worship* resources continues to be developed, congregations and their leaders are invited to be alert for additional worship resources related to processes of baptismal formation.

Whether or not specific orders of worship are used with those being welcomed into a deeper exploration of Christian faith and life, it is important for congregations to be mindful of the presence of these people and their need for support throughout the process of becoming a full part of the Christian community. The awareness and the ongoing prayers of the entire assembly are needed throughout a journey to baptism that may not always be easy. Such systematic recognition of the baptismal process within the Sunday assembly demonstrates the congregation's integral involvement in the tasks of evangelization and in faith formation.

Though the service at which a person is baptized lasts only a short time, the journey in faith that is prompted by the Holy Spirit's call ideally lasts a lifetime. Anything a congregation can do to support this growth in grace will likely be worth the effort.

CHAPTER FIVE

Affirmation of Baptism

In *Evangelical Lutheran Worship*, Affirmation of Baptism is a service designed to address a number of needs. First and foremost, this order of service relates to baptism, and it is intended for use only with people who have already been baptized. At various points in someone's life, it may be helpful to recognize a deepened or renewed commitment to follow Christ and for the assembly to pray for that person as he or she enters into a new relationship with the church. Affirmation of Baptism is therefore flexible enough to be used in a variety of circumstances, from adolescent confirmation to becoming a member of a congregation to indicating a renewal in the life of faith or to marking some other passage in one's life. This rite may also be used for an entire worshiping assembly to affirm baptism, particularly on a major baptismal festival such as the Baptism of Our Lord, the Vigil of Easter, the Day of Pentecost, and All Saints Day.

It is helpful to understand some of the historical roots of this order, especially what has been known as confirmation, since confirmation remains one of the primary uses of this rite in contemporary congregational life.

Historical Relationship of Confirmation to Baptism

Nowhere does the New Testament mention a rite or a process specifically called confirmation. There are, however, numerous scriptural accounts of the sending of the Spirit and the Spirit's presence among God's people. The presence of the Holy Spirit is especially significant at baptism, and it is in this sense that we can trace the origins of the rite of confirmation to the New Testament.

In the accounts of Jesus' baptism by John in the Jordan River (Matt. 3:13-17; Mark 1:9-11; Luke 3:21-22; and John 1:29-34), the Spirit plays a pivotal role in each. Following Jesus' baptism, the Spirit descended upon him like a dove. In the three synoptic gospels, a voice from heaven proclaimed Jesus to be the Son of God following the descent of the dove. According to these various accounts a structure emerges regarding the event of Jesus' own baptism: water-bath and descent of the Spirit.

Taking the view that various gospel accounts often provide evidence of what might have been ritual practice in at least part of the New Testament church, as well as documenting what was believed to have happened in the life and ministry of Christ, one could infer that the baptismal practice of the apostolic church naturally followed the several scriptural accounts of Jesus' own baptism by prescribing, first, the water-bath and then some kind of ritualization of the descent of the Spirit. Some scholars of the New Testament and of early church history claim that Christian initiation in the apostolic church consisted of *two* rites: baptism followed by an imposition of hands for the reception of the Spirit. But others note that there are pertinent documents that do not present this structure at all, most notably the Didache, a collection of teachings dating from the first centuries of the church.

Whatever patterns may have been common throughout the earliest decades of the church's life, no single, universal baptismal practice from that time has been firmly identified. Local assemblies may or may not have specifically ritualized the Spirit's sending at baptism. Yet if no single pattern for baptismal practice has emerged from the accounts in the New Testament and from the apostolic church, there is sufficient evidence to claim that the water-bath and the Spirit-gift are both important to the theological understanding of what happens in baptism.

Soon after the New Testament period it is possible to detect distinct actions in baptismal liturgies that accompany the water-bath. Though neither the Didache nor Justin's *Apology* (mid-second century) give detailed accounts of a baptismal ritual, by the time of Tertullian's *De Baptismo* (c. 200), a description is given of a water-bath occurring first, followed by post-baptismal anointing and an imposition of the hands with a prayer for the Holy Spirit.

Confirmation Is Separated from Baptism

A bishop was the ordinary minister for baptism in the pre-Nicene church. In the West, when it became impossible for the bishop to be present at all baptisms—both because of geographical expansion of the church and the association of baptism with birth rather than with Easter—those situations in which a bishop had not been present at baptism were to be completed by him at a subsequent time through the laying on of hands. Though it was a complex and seemingly unplanned development that can only be summarized briefly here, in the course of several centuries a second anointing and hand-laying by the bishop, removed in time from the actual occasion of baptism itself, became a standard custom in the West. This later anointing and hand-laying, regarded as a distinctly separate sacrament of confirmation, was interpreted as strengthening the Christian for battle and for preaching to others. The interval of time between baptism (in infancy) and a later anointing gradually grew from a period of several days to a number of years.

The actions of baptism, laying on of hands, and admission to the table, which had been kept together as a single event within the pre-Nicene church, were separated from one another and reordered in the West. Furthermore, with a greater concern over the care for the sacramental elements in the tenth through twelfth centuries, infants would in time no longer receive the sacrament of holy communion. Ultimately the Council of Trent was to decide that infants did not need to receive communion, since they were not able to lose their baptismal grace. What had been a united initiatory event—baptism, post-baptismal anointing, laying on of hands, and reception of communion—grew into a separation of those rites from one another. Rather than informing practice, the formal theology of the church appears to have followed what seem to have been some rather accidental developments. There appears to have been no intentional desire to separate baptism, post-baptismal anointing, the imposition of hands, and the reception of the eucharist; but in most cases there was no practical way to keep the bishop as the primary minister of anointing and imposition of hands without delaying these events from the celebration of baptism itself.

In the West the practice of confirmation seemed to be so far removed from baptism itself, and from any scriptural mandate, that it became one of many issues reformers in the sixteenth century faced as they attempted to steer the practices of the church into directions more in keeping with what they viewed to be the church's core beliefs and scriptural norms.

Early Lutheran History of Confirmation

Out of the already tangled history of confirmation, the Protestant reformers of the sixteenth century endeavored to reform the rite in keeping with its assumed origins and with the scriptures themselves. Most of the reformers could see no scriptural mandate for confirmation, thereby calling into question its status as a sacrament. Martin Luther had few kind words to say about this sacrament, calling it "monkey business," among other things (LW 45:24). In *The Babylonian Captivity of the Church*, however, Luther went on to suggest a fitting way to regard confirmation:

> It is sufficient to regard confirmation as a certain churchly rite or sacramental ceremony, similar to other ceremonies, such as the blessing of water and the like. For if every other creature is sanctified by the Word and by prayer [1 Tim. 4:4-5], why should not man much rather be sanctified by the same means? Still, these things cannot be called sacraments of faith, because they have no divine promise connected with them, neither do they save; but the sacraments do save those who believe the divine promise. [LW 36:92]

The Augsburg Confession does not regard confirmation as one of the sacraments. Furthermore, the Apology to the Augsburg Confession notes that confirmation lacks the command of God and a clear promise of God's grace—both necessary components for a sacrament, according to the Apology (BC 220).

Some early Lutheran attempts to reform confirmation concentrated primarily on its usefulness as a catechetical process, especially for the preparation of persons to receive holy communion. Arthur C. Repp, whose study of confirmation in the Lutheran church is perhaps the most comprehensive treatment still available, outlined six different forms of confirmation in the Lutheran church. Four originated in the sixteenth century, the earliest of which is a *catechetical type* of confirmation.[1] The early Lutheran church orders hesitated to call the process confirmation, preferring, said Repp, such titles as: "catechetical instruction . . . , confessional examination . . . , admission to the Lord's Supper, profession of Baptism, or some similar name . . ." (Repp 22–23). Little or no emphasis was placed on a liturgical rite to be associated with this chiefly educational program. Confirmation was simply a period of time in which the young or servants were to receive instruction in the catechism. When a child was thought to have learned enough for the reception of holy communion, he or she would be presented by the parents and sponsors to the pastor (and the congregation) for examination and eventual admission to the sacrament (22–24). Those who adhered to a catechetical type of confirmation did not understand *admission* to the sacrament of holy communion to have any sacramental underpinnings of its own. This was simply a functional preparation leading to the beginning of a person's communing.

Another form of confirmation in the Lutheran church comes from Martin Bucer (1491–1551) and is referred to by Repp as *hierarchical.* Bucer's use of confirmation was chiefly a reaction to the Anabaptists, who questioned the validity of infant baptism. The central development here is in the form of a vow that a person who had been baptized in infancy might make after the age of discretion and following a period of formal instruction (28–30). Initially cautious about implying that there was any kind of new covenantal relationship between God and a believer occurring in confirmation, Bucer nonetheless began to stress "the stronger and more concrete idea of commitment to the congregation, to obedience, and to discipline."[2] He also introduced a public rite that included a laying on of hands by the pastor, marking the conclusion of an educational period and the beginning of communing membership. Those who were "confirmed" submitted themselves to church discipline imposed by the pastor and the elders of the congregation (Repp, 32-35).

A third type of confirmation known in certain sixteenth-century Lutheran circles has been called the *sacramental type.* This view held that the Holy Spirit was not initially given at baptism but was imparted at a later time through the laying on of hands. Confirmation then conferred a more complete membership than had been given at baptism. The Cassel Church Order of 1539 is important to this understanding of confirmation, since it spoke of the church having "three sacramental ceremonies, the first of which was known as 'the order of confirmation and the laying on of hands'" (Repp, 37). This development also derived from Martin Bucer. Although those who employed the laying on of hands did not think of confirmation as a type of sacrament on a par with baptism and the Lord's supper, the definition of a sacrament at this time was not so narrow as to exclude it from being understood as a quasi-sacramental ceremony.

The fourth and final form of confirmation practiced in the early decades of the Lutheran church was a *traditional type* that retained some of the pre-Reformation practices of confirmation yet stayed unambiguously within the confines of Lutheran doctrine. One example of this type is from the Brandenburg Church Order of 1540, which retained the laying on of hands and was normally performed by a bishop or his substitute. This order was developed by Johannes Bugenhagen (1485–1558) and was approved by Luther. It was intended for already baptized children who had reached the age of understanding, even though those who were confirmed in this manner would not necessarily begin communing immediately (Repp, 44–46).

Martin Chemnitz (1522–1586), largely known for his role in co-authoring the *Formula of Concord*, attempted to harmonize some of the sixteenth-century developments regarding confirmation. He sought a form of confirmation that kept its baptismal focus while at the same time wanting a rite that incorporated the laying on of hands as a type of blessing. In his rite of confirmation, Chemnitz included six elements: remembrance of baptism; personal confession of faith; examination in the catechism; admonition to remain faithful; admonition to remain true to the baptismal covenant; and public prayer with the laying on of hands.[3] Perhaps this order has come to define a characteristically Lutheran form of confirmation more than any other has.

As should be obvious by now, the sixteenth-century reformers were not in complete agreement regarding the practice of confirmation. Perhaps the only thing that can be said definitively about the various Lutheran customs of confirmation in the sixteenth century is that the rite was not accorded the same importance that baptism and holy communion were given. While many customs associated with the pre-Reformation rite were retained, such practices as the anointing with chrism and the blow on the cheek were usually considered "too Roman" to be used. In some quarters even the laying on of hands was suspect. In virtually all of the early Lutheran forms of confirmation, instruction preceded the rite of confirmation (or a type of "first communion" rite). In Lutheranism's early years, while the pastor was involved in the examination of the candidates for confirmation, the parents (supplemented by the sponsors) were usually the primary instructors. The church could augment this instruction further through catechetical sermons and public reading from the catechism (Repp, 55–56).

Confirmation functioned basically as a bridge between the sacrament of baptism and admission to the sacrament of the altar. The examination assured the pastor that parents had done their part in raising their children in the faith of their baptism and that the children were ready to be admitted to the Lord's supper. Admission to the second sacrament could occur at a variety of ages. Evidence suggests that this happened anywhere from age six to age twelve during the sixteenth century (Repp, 56–57).

Confirmation under Pietism

In the seventeenth century, confirmation remained largely a catechetical experience, concerned foremost with cognitive development about the church's teachings and the Bible. Unfortunately, many of the teaching methodologies employed were quite unsuitable for catechization of the young. In some cases pastors and other catechists simply had a problem relating well to the children's level of understanding and interests. In other cases rote memorization of catechism texts mostly produced boredom. Catechetical sessions and sermons that might have been appropriate as a review for older church members were not generally helpful for young noncommunicant members.

Theophil Grossgebauer in the mid-seventeenth century offered the view that infants were baptized on the condition that they would later be converted through the word of God and the Holy Spirit. In this understanding, conversion happened through the process of catechization and pastoral work following baptism. His contemporary, the influential Justus Gesenius, spoke of confirmation as a renewal of the covenant of baptism rather than a remembrance of it.[4] Philipp Jakob Spener, a leading figure of Pietism, emphasized the confirmand's decision to take a vow. This added a more subjective element to confirmation than had been present before, since confirmation then became a time to experience a type of spiritual awakening or even a decision of faith.[5]

As Pietism took hold in the Lutheran church, a significant new twist was added to confirmation. It was during this period of Lutheran history that confirmation "became the occasion for the catechumen to ratify his baptismal covenant, to give witness of his personal faith or 'conversion,' and to accept the obligation to lead a Christian life" (Repp, 70).

With this new direction of confirmation's purpose in a solemn vow, the role of confirmation as primarily an educational process began to recede. Since the pastor had to ensure that the confirmands were now really Christians, Pietists also placed a greater emphasis on the pastor himself being the instructor, instead of delegating the task to someone else (Repp, 70–71). The subjective element of confirmation grew to such an extent that in at least one instance the catechist was to bring the confirmed to "holy tears" (Repp, 72).

The greater subjectivity in confirmation also caused confirmation to be practiced at a later age, emphasizing the life-turning point it came to represent. Whereas age twelve or before had been common for confirmation prior to the age of Pietism, it was now rarely practiced before age fourteen, sometimes even later (Repp, 75).

Confirmation under Rationalism

In valuing the intellect over traditional rituals, the period of church history known as Rationalism, particularly as it unfolded in Germany, also came to place greater emphasis upon confirmation than baptism. In this period there was a de-emphasis of sacraments in general, while greater stress was placed on understanding the faith and learning about Christian virtues. A detailed public examination of candidates came to be routine.[6] Confirmation was now seen as a time for the young person to take on more responsibility for leading a moral and ethical life.[7] While baptism was still viewed as the entrance into the Christian faith, confirmation was the occasion on which a person became a member of a particular congregation or church. Duties as a member of a congregation came not from one's status among the baptized but rather from one's status as a confirmed member (Repp, 77–78).

Confirmation came to be interpreted as the most important day of a young person's life. During this period an examination of the candidates for confirmation often began to take place at a separate event prior to the confirmation itself. Great emphasis was also placed on the vow of the confirmand—often referred to as an oath—and apparently made with a hand placed on the Bible (Repp, 78–80).

Confirmation became a great sentimental occasion. Children would go to their parents and ask for their forgiveness. A bell would ring at the precise moment of confirmation for each person. Special clothes and decorations would be used for the occasion. It became a time of great family festivity, ranking with a baptism or a wedding.

Repp concludes that "confirmation became more and more a part of the cultus rather than a part of the spiritual life of German Lutherans" (80–83).

Lutherans Bring Confirmation to the New World

Though Lutheran practices of confirmation in North America quite naturally followed many of the trends and developments that had been common in Europe, a remarkably different social climate existed in North America. Throughout the eighteenth century religious identity, religious education, and even education in general were quite minimal among the Lutheran immigrants along the mid-Atlantic seaboard. Whereas European Lutherans had grown accustomed to a society in which church, secular, and political life operated as a virtual unity, the situation in America was different. Faith formation, indeed basic education itself, was a great challenge in much of Pennsylvania throughout the eighteenth century. Schools were not well established and were nonexistent in many places. It often fell to pastors and other catechists to provide a rudimentary system of both religious education and general education in reading and writing skills.

It was to this environment that Henry Melchior Muhlenberg came in 1742, called from Germany by several united Lutheran congregations in Pennsylvania to serve as their pastor. While Muhlenberg's significance went far beyond providing a confirmation ministry for the many congregations he served, his journals give evidence to a particular pattern of faith formation and ritual process related to confirmation. Because of their detail, the journals offer valuable insights into the planting of a Lutheran form of confirmation on American soil. It is from those journals that the following description is drawn.

The process that led to the actual order for confirmation during Muhlenberg's ministry, whether for youth or adults, would ordinarily have begun some time before the day of confirmation itself. On that day an examination conducted by the pastor immediately before the service (or perhaps even during the service itself) served as a kind of review or summary of prior catechization.

While Muhlenberg's catechization was frequently for those who were preparing for confirmation and was therefore connected to preparation for the reception of communion for the first time, catechetical sessions were also frequently attended by those already confirmed and admitted to the celebration of the sacrament. Catechization took a variety of forms. Sometimes it was for children and adults together, while frequently it was for young people alone (called *Kinderlehre*). Catechization took place through sermons and often in a form of questioning about the sermon just delivered. Other times the teaching was based on a particular part of the catechism.

Though Muhlenberg believed that baptism was received passively as a gift from God, he also spoke of the need for later conversion in life. He stated the need for continual repentance this way:

Muhlenberg also spoke of confirmation as a strengthening of baptismal grace and that it was desirable between the ages of seven and fourteen. In his thought, this was a time when young persons had already received the gift of reason and were still developing their knowledge of good and evil. Confirmation was helpful in that it increased the grace needed to overcome temptation.

Confirmation in the Early Twentieth Century

The *Common Service Book* (CSB) of 1917–18, published by the United Lutheran Church in America, may be representative of a general pattern for confirmation that was known by a majority of Lutheran congregations in North America during the early half of the twentieth century. According to instructions preceding the Order for Confirmation in the *Common Service Book*, candidates were to have received instruction in the faith "as it is set forth in the *Small Catechism*, and be approved in such manner as may be deemed satisfactory by the Pastor and Church Council" (CSB 236). At this time confirmation also would have been regarded as an admission to participation in holy communion, though it would not by itself have allowed anyone to serve on a church council or to participate as a voting member at congregational meetings.

The *Common Service Book* liturgy regarded the seasons of Easter and Pentecost as most suited for confirmation, though it could occur at any time. Following an initial address, renunciation of evil, recitation of the Apostles' Creed, and a prayer spoken by the minister, there followed a prayer spoken individually over each of the candidates for confirmation, which was accompanied by a laying on of hands for the gifts of the Spirit. Following the prayer, the newly confirmed people were declared to be members of the congregation and were authorized to receive the Lord's supper "and to participate in all the spiritual privileges of the Church" (CSB 237).

The Order for Confirmation in the *Service Book and Hymnal* (SBH) of 1958 largely followed the order in the *Common Service Book*. One significant departure in the 1958 order was that confirmation was no longer referred to as the moment one became a member of the congregation. Presumably *membership* occurred through baptism when God was called upon to make the candidate "a living member of his holy Church." Confirmation in 1958 nevertheless still admitted people to participation in holy communion and to other spiritual privileges of the church.

The confirmation order of the Synodical Conference (most notably the Lutheran Church—Missouri Synod) published in *The Lutheran Agenda* had many similarities to the orders in the *Common Service Book* and the *Service Book and Hymnal*. The form for the affirmation of faith is noteworthy in *The Lutheran Agenda* rite. In addition to the standard renunciation of evil and affirmation of faith through recitation of the Apostles' Creed, several additional questions were asked of candidates for confirmation—including some arguably more appropriate for an ordination than for confirmation.

Following one of several possible prayers at the subsequent laying on of hands, the newly confirmed persons were welcomed as members of the Evangelical Lutheran Church and of the congregation, and to participate in all the rights and privileges of the Evangelical Lutheran Church.

We can summarize the practice of confirmation in the Lutheran church throughout the first seven or more decades of the twentieth century: First, confirmation was customarily considered to be a time when a person became a member of the Lutheran faith and a particular congregation, even while having been a member of Christ's church since baptism (though the *Service Book and Hymnal* departed from this in that membership was not specifically conferred at confirmation). Second, though persons were acknowledged as having received the Holy Spirit at baptism and would also have received the laying on of hands at baptism, confirmation was still the time at which the traditional prayer for the sevenfold gifts of the Spirit would have been used as a type of strengthening. Third, confirmation was the standard admission threshold for the reception of holy communion.

Confirmation in *Lutheran Book of Worship*

By the late 1960s many practices of the church were changing dramatically, including attitudes regarding confirmation. Prior to the 1970 *Report of the Joint Commission on the Theology and Practice of*

Confirmation (hereafter the 1970 Report), first communion in Lutheran congregations customarily happened only following adolescent confirmation. The 1970 Report recommended that first communion not be tied to confirmation.

> Admission to first Communion is an invitation of the Lord Jesus Christ to his Supper, presented through his church to the baptized child when he has been prepared and is ready to participate in the sacrament. This readiness involves the understanding, attitudes, and action patterns appropriate to his age level. The church will therefore invite to Holy Communion those baptized children who have been prepared and who then in the pastoral judgment of the congregation are ready to participate in the sacrament.

> Most persons reach this stage of maturity at the fifth-grade level. [585]

The same report also gave the following definition for confirmation ministry:

> Confirmation is a pastoral and educational ministry of the church which helps the baptized child through Word and Sacrament to identify more deeply with the Christian community and participate more fully in its mission. [582]

Meeting concurrently with the Joint Commission on Confirmation was a group known as the Inter-Lutheran Commission on Worship (ILCW). This group had been organized in 1966 for the purpose of planning for new Lutheran liturgical and hymnic resources (which became *Lutheran Book of Worship*).

In the process leading up to the publication of its provisional volumes, the ILCW (through its committees and subcommittees) discussed baptism, confirmation, and first communion for five years. At one point a single initiatory rite of baptism, confirmation, and first communion had been proposed for people of all ages. The various parts of that order were designed to be used whenever it was pastorally appropriate, functioning as an initiatory service to meet all occasions and needs. In the end, the commission produced two chief initiatory orders, one for baptism (persons of all ages), and one for affirmation of baptism (incorporating reception of members, confirmation, and restoration to membership).[8] Because confirmation would no longer be the general way in which persons would be admitted to communion, an order for first communion had been discussed in the ILCW's work. In the end, a rite was not provided for such a moment, primarily so as not to detract from the understanding of the role that baptism itself has in preparing persons for reception at the Lord's table.

If it could have had its own way, the ILCW's Liturgical Text Committee might have done away with the word "confirmation" entirely. Though it had always favored the development of an adolescent rite following a period of extended catechesis into the faith, it had long preferred simply to call such a rite an *affirmation* of baptism. Ultimately, *confirmation* seemed to be too important a tradition in the Lutheran church for it not to be mentioned at all, so a compromise was reached that created one rite of *affirmation*, into which was included a form for *confirmation*.

Ultimately the ILCW revised its groundbreaking rite of affirmation in *Contemporary Worship 8* to the form that was printed in *Lutheran Book of Worship,* to provide a service that would satisfy people's desire for confirmation. The *Lutheran Book of Worship* baptismal liturgy (Ministers Edition, 311) includes elements customarily associated with confirmation in its baptismal liturgy, where there is a prayer for the sevenfold gifts of the Spirit, together with the laying on of hands and anointing. *Lutheran Book of Worship* itself left open the question about the age for first communion. Notes on the liturgy in *Lutheran Book of Worship* indicate that older children and adults should commune at the liturgy during which they were baptized. Meanwhile, "infants may be brought to the altar and receive a blessing" (Ministers Edition, 30). *Lutheran Book of Worship* indicated in its notes on first communion that it is "the moment when a privilege granted in Baptism is first exercised. The gift of Communion is the birthright of the baptized" (Ministers Edition, 31). For this reason *Lutheran Book of Worship* did not encourage making an emphasis on first communion.

Affirmation of Baptism in *Lutheran Book of Worship* was intended for use on three distinct occasions: by persons who were baptized as infants or young children and who as adolescents or adults then wished to affirm their baptism (that is to be *confirmed*); by persons who had been members of other Christian denominations and desired to become members of the Lutheran church; and by persons who had previously been members of a Lutheran church and were seeking restoration of membership. (Ministers Edition, 324)

The service was nearly identical for each of these situations; however, a prayer was included for use "for confirmation only." This prayer for confirmation was intended for use only once following baptism, not repeatedly. Young children who could not answer the baptismal vows for themselves would be encouraged to affirm their baptism at a later point in life, and then become *confirmed* members.

Confirmation Ministry Task Force (1993)

Though a process for confirmation is not defined in the confessional or constitutional documents of the church, the Evangelical Lutheran Church in America did *receive* "The Report of the Study of the Confirmation Ministry Task Force" (hereafter the 1993 Report) at its Churchwide Assembly in 1993. The report of that five-year study would be the closest thing to an official policy or statement regarding the practice of confirmation throughout the ELCA.

The ELCA task force on confirmation based much of its initial work on the *1970 Report of the Joint Commission on the Theology and Practice of Confirmation*. The 1993 Report listed nine developments that had occurred since the 1970 Report:

- responsibility for confirmation ministry is more and more shared by both lay and clergy;
- catechetical instruction has broadened to include issues of the wider world;
- instruction in the Bible and the Small Catechism has recently returned to the fore;
- increased awareness of learning styles and contexts has generated a variety of approaches, strategies, and techniques;
- increased understanding regarding developmental stages in both faith and cognition affects both what is taught and how it is taught;
- though a large majority of congregations invite members to take part in communion before they are confirmed, the age for first communion varies;
- congregations continue to see confirmation as important even though the meaning remains ambiguous;
- the confirmation service is seen as an affirmation of baptism, not a completion of it or its competitor; and
- catechetical instruction has been a valued opportunity for experimentation.

The 1993 Report went on to emphasize that "Baptism is the basis for Christian education and nurture, including confirmation ministry" (585). Another paragraph clearly set forth the primacy of baptism: "Confirmation ministry does not *complete* Baptism, for Baptism is already complete through God's work of joining us to Christ and his body, the Church. In him is salvation. Moreover, confirmation ministry does not *compete* with Baptism, because confirmation ministry does not save anyone"(585).

The 1993 Report went further than other previous statements of the church toward suggesting that an affirmation of baptism could occur at various times throughout one's life. "While Baptism happens only once, affirmation of Baptism and prayer for the baptized can happen many times" (591). Rites of affirmation could be celebrated at significant life changes, such as the beginning of parenthood, changing occupations, or retirement, as well as at other times. The report imagined forms for affirmation that could occur both within the corporate worshiping assembly and in small-group situations. Even as it described these multiple possibilities for affirmation, the report still called specifically for a confirmation rite "preceded by years of instruction, relationship, and growth. Other rites of affirmation at other stages in people's lives also would involve preparation, perhaps in the form of pastoral conversation, in order to connect their faith with their transitions"(591).

In calling for additional opportunities for affirmation of baptism, the 1993 report went beyond what the Affirmation of Baptism service in *Lutheran Book of Worship* was able to do by calling for "a prayer for the stirring up of the Spirit's gifts; and laying on of hands for those affirming faith" (591). These two elements were clearly marked "for confirmation only" in the *Lutheran Book of Worship* affirmation service (Ministers Edition 327).

Sacramental Practices Statements

The statements on sacramental practices of the Evangelical Lutheran Church in America (*The Use of the Means of Grace,* 1997) and the Evangelical Lutheran Church in Canada (*Statement on Sacramental Practices,* 1991) do not devote much attention to orders for affirmation of baptism. *The Use of the Means of Grace* continues the emphasis seen in the 1993 Report on extending the use of rites of affirmation of baptism to other life passages (30A). It also includes this reference to confirmation:

The public rite of Affirmation of Baptism may be used at many times in the life of a baptized Christian. It is especially appropriate at Confirmation and at times of reception or restoration into membership. [30]

Confirmation as Baptismal Affirmation

In the preceding sections summarizing some of the historical developments of confirmation, we have seen how confirmation grew out of the liturgy of baptism. The chief reason for confirmation's existence as a separate rite (in the Middle Ages and beyond) was as a way to include bishops in the formal religious life of each Christian believer, although the rite also came to mark the culmination of a catechetical period, particularly for young people. In the Roman Catholic, Episcopal/Anglican, and other traditions where bishops continue to serve as the usual ministers of confirmation, part of the reason for maintaining the rite is the connection between each person and her or his local or diocesan bishop.

In the Lutheran tradition, the confirmation service has been experienced as primarily a congregational rite, led by a pastor of the local congregation. Here and in other traditions that do not practice episcopal confirmation, the order usually marks the conclusion of a chiefly catechetical period, and in some cases the occasion has taken on the character of graduation, complete with robes, flowers, gifts, photographs, and family celebrations.

Incorporating confirmation into a rite of baptismal affirmation has helped to underscore the primary importance of baptism. In one sense nothing is imparted in confirmation or in the affirmation of baptism that has not already occurred in baptism. Affirming baptism is something that may occur repeatedly throughout a person's lifetime. Nonetheless, it can be very desirable to have a moment during adolescence or young adulthood when a person may publicly affirm the baptismal covenant that oftentimes was made on his or her behalf by parents and sponsors. Youth have the opportunity to affirm and even challenge the faith in which they have been raised. In most congregational confirmation programs these days, youth also participate in some forms of service and ways of putting their faith into action, rather than merely undergoing a set of cognitive exercises that may have been the primary focus in generations past. To that end youth are often prepared to have some appreciation for what is asked of them during the Affirmation of Baptism:

Do you intend to continue in the covenant God made with you
   in holy baptism:
to live among God's faithful people,
to hear the word of God and share in the Lord's supper,
to proclaim the good news of God in Christ through word and deed,
to serve all people, following the example of Jesus,
and to strive for justice and peace in all the earth? [AE p. 236]

In many places, Lutheran constitutions and membership guidelines continue to make distinctions between those who have been baptized and those who have also been confirmed. Only people who have been confirmed may serve as voting members, officers, or council members in a congregation, synod, or the churchwide organization, even if confirmed membership itself is never specifically defined.[9] Confirmed membership is a privilege conferred on many baptized people enabling them to participate in many of the formal decisions and governance structures of the church. Only congregation councils may confer confirmed membership in the Evangelical Lutheran Church in America.[10]

People who are affirming their baptism by confirmation might do so at any time throughout the year. Though it was once common for confirmation to occur in the spring (along with graduations and similar rites of passage), a greater case can be made for scheduling Affirmation of Baptism in the fall of the year, when congregational and academic programming is gearing up for another year, precisely so that this moment does not seem like the end of anything but rather the beginning of new responsibilities in the life of the Christian faith. Congregations that have adopted this pattern have often scheduled confirmation on one of the Sundays nearest All Saints Day (with its baptismal resonance) or Reformation Day (with its focus on the ongoing renewal of the church and its members).

Using Affirmation of Baptism at Other Times

Introductory notes to the rite of Affirmation of Baptism indicate that in addition to being used "as part of a process of formation in faith in youth or adulthood (confirmation)," it may also be used "at the time of beginning one's participation in a community of faith, as a sign of renewed participation in the life of the church, or at the time of a significant life passage" (AE p. 234). The entire assembly may also use the order of Affirmation of Baptism. Even if Affirmation of

Baptism is understood by many people primarily as a rite of passage to be experienced in a person's teenage years, its intended purpose is far broader.

Apart from baptism itself, Affirmation of Baptism may be the form used to welcome all people into membership in the local congregation. Though Lutheran congregations typically welcome new members from other Lutheran congregations "by transfer," having one rite to welcome Lutherans and another to welcome people from other denominational traditions may seem cumbersome, and even insensitive, especially in this age of full communion relationships and greater ecumenical cooperation. The Notes on the Services seem to indicate precisely this with the suggestion that "Lutherans from other congregations may wish to mark the beginning of their participation in a new community of faith by making public affirmation of their baptism" (LE 31). In this manner, becoming a part of another community of faith is a moment for *all* people to affirm their baptism through recitation of the creed, indicate a desire to continue in the baptismal covenant, hear the support of the assembly, and to receive the blessing of the Holy Spirit.

People who have previously been members of the church but whose participation in the Christian community has been dormant for some time (in the congregation in which the affirmation is taking place or another congregation of any Christian tradition) may also be received as members of the congregation through Affirmation of Baptism. Although those who have never officially been removed from the church's roster would not need to be received in this manner, many people in such circumstances may express a desire to do so anyway. Baptized people who ask whether they can be rebaptized may be cared for with more than a "no" by directing them toward the possibility of affirming their baptism. They may experience a "reminder of baptism" (such as sprinkling with water or stepping forward to the baptismal font to dip their hands into the water and trace the sign of the cross on themselves) along with everyone else in the assembly.

When there are candidates for baptism and for affirmation of baptism who will be received into the congregation near the same time, worship planners may be tempted to combine the baptism and affirmation liturgies so that everyone's needs may be accommodated at once. While there is a certain logic to this notion, there are also reasons to refrain from combining the two orders. A single service combining baptism and affirmation of baptism may be lengthy and potentially chaotic for the worship leaders, the participants, and the assembly. More significantly, the celebration of baptism itself is both a reminder and an affirmation of baptism for those who are baptized.

A more workable solution may be to celebrate baptism one day, followed by affirmation of baptism the next week or at least during a different service the same week. For example, if there are a number of candidates who will be baptized at the Vigil of Easter (even a combination of infants and adults) and a number of candidates who have been prepared to affirm their baptism around the same time, it may be helpful to schedule affirmation for a later service on Easter Day or at a service the following week. Even if some of the pastoral and catechetical needs are similar between candidates for baptism and candidates for affirmation, those who have already been baptized need to be acknowledged as such. Keeping baptismal and affirmation liturgies at separate services will be a significant way to distinguish between the gifts received in baptism and the gifts received at affirmation. Note that the assembly has a different form for welcoming the newly baptized ("We welcome you into the body of Christ and into the mission we share . . .") and for greeting those who have affirmed their baptism ("We rejoice with you in the life of baptism . . .") (AE pp. 231, 236).

The introduction to Affirmation of Baptism also indicates that this order may be used to celebrate significant life passages, but it leaves these open for interpretation. It could be used with people who have had an intense exploration and renewal of their faith, even if they never were apart from congregational life. For example, people who have completed a lengthy Bible study course could renew their commitment to the church through an affirmation of baptism. The occasional services resources accompanying *Evangelical Lutheran Worship* offer additional guidance about how this order may be used in a variety of pastoral circumstances.

Although this service could also be used to acknowledge life transitions (movement to a new home, retirement, or entering a senior housing facility), other rites might seem more helpful on some of those occasions. The blessing of a home might be a more appropriate vehicle for celebrating a new stage of life, such as the adoption of a child or some kind of move. Similarly, Affirmation of Christian Vocation (AE p. 84) may be a better way to celebrate someone's new career or ministry within the church or in daily life. An order for Farewell and Godspeed would likely best serve the needs of people who are leaving the community in some way. Pastors and other leaders in the congregation should feel free to think about how best to honor and acknowledge the many transitions people make. Sometimes a mention in one of the prayers of intercession may be all that is needed to celebrate a significant milestone in someone's life. At other times, a ritual of some type may seem helpful, and Affirmation of Baptism is one of the services that could be used. Above all, keep in mind that not all people will want to have the same type of celebration.

Affirmation by the Assembly

The reasons for using Affirmation of Baptism by the entire assembly are varied. Particularly if a congregation observes baptismal festivals throughout the year (such as the Baptism of Our Lord, the Vigil of Easter, the Day of Pentecost, and All Saints Day), Affirmation of Baptism may be used on those occasions when no candidates for baptism will be presented. In this manner the congregation has a way to celebrate its own baptismal identity regularly, even if it does not have the opportunity to welcome many people through baptism. If there is some reluctance to scheduling baptisms mainly on the traditional baptismal festivals, using Affirmation of Baptism on those days may be a subtle way to encourage members of the congregation to think about having baptisms primarily on these festivals.

Affirmation of Baptism could be a way for a congregation to renew its collective commitment to one another, particularly after a period of loss or tragedy within the community, at the time of a congregational anniversary, or to celebrate the cooperation of two or more congregations (even those of various faith traditions) who have inaugurated a new relationship. In each of these instances the common thing celebrated is the unity that all Christians celebrate through baptism.

Affirmation of Baptism in *Evangelical Lutheran Worship*

Having explored many of the possible uses for the Affirmation of Baptism service, we will now examine each part of the rite and consider some of the options that might be used.

Presentation

Affirmation of Baptism ordinarily follows the hymn of the day in the service of Holy Communion. This placement in the service is logical, since much of the affirmation order is an expansion of the Apostles' Creed. This is also the primary place in the service where a baptism would be celebrated.

If possible, gather around the baptismal font. That location will reinforce the notion that this is a return to baptism, and centering this liturgy at the font should make it easier to use some type of reminder of baptism at the conclusion of the rite, if that is desired. Where gathering those making affirmation near the font is not possible, placing a large bowl of water near the place where they gather could be helpful.

If those who are affirming baptism are customarily clothed in a special way, the alb—with its strong connection to the baptismal garment and its use by leaders in the assembly—is more suitable clothing than a robe or cape (sometimes designed to be disposable) that suggests a kind of graduation ceremony.

Those who are making affirmation of baptism may be joined by others who have accompanied them throughout their faith development: parents and other family members, baptismal sponsors, mentors, small-group leaders, catechists, and others. On some occasions it may not be possible to have everyone in such a group gather at once since it could include nearly everyone in the assembly. If that is the case, gather only those who are making affirmation at the beginning of the order. Then, following the question to each about continuing in the covenant of baptism—and prior to the prayer during the laying on of hands ("We give you thanks, O God . . .")—most of those making affirmation could be seated as individuals or smaller groups of them come forward with their families, mentors, and sponsors.

Because the occasions for affirmation can vary considerably, it is helpful for the presiding minister to note to members of the assembly what the occasion is. If several young people are making public affirmation of baptism, that can be mentioned, along with some brief indication of what their process toward affirmation has entailed. Similarly, those making an affirmation as a way of participating more fully in the life of the congregation may be introduced in a way that speaks about their collective journey. It is important that someone other than the presiding minister presents those making affirmation by name.

When a catechist, a council member, or someone else who has a public responsibility presents the candidates for affirmation, it demonstrates that many people in the congregation are needed to form and welcome people in the Christian faith. This presenter should be heard clearly by all. Provision should be made for the person to use a microphone if worship leaders in the assembly normally use one.

As a conclusion to the presentation, the presiding minister gives thanks for those who will make this affirmation of their baptism. The words in italics will need to be altered accordingly if the affirmers do not constitute a group and if the group is not of both males and females. Though the prayer provided may be used for all occasions of affirmation, another prayer of thanksgiving might be more specific to the particular occasion of affirmation. Any newly composed prayer used instead could be modeled on the one provided and would probably not need to be any lengthier.

Profession of Faith

The assembly stands following the presentation and prayer of thanksgiving for those making affirmation. As at baptism, the profession of faith occurs in two parts, a renunciation of sin and a recitation of the Apostles' Creed. The responses to the renunciations may be spoken only by those making affirmation, or they may be spoken by the entire assembly. It may highlight the fact that these renunciations are part of the public witness by those affirming baptism if the rest of the assembly simply listens to that witness. In any case, it will be helpful to determine in advance exactly who will be joining in the renunciations and to cue them accordingly.

Regardless of the number of people who may have joined in the renunciations, the entire assembly answers the creedal questions as prompted by the presiding minister. The presiding minister should look to members of the assembly collectively while asking the creedal questions.

Affirmation in the Presence of the Assembly

The presiding minister asks those making affirmation—as a group, not individually—if they intend to continue in the covenant of baptism. Each phrase of the question speaks of a specific action of God's people, and it needs to be spoken deliberately and clearly. In many ways the baptismal covenant is simply a mission statement of the whole church that is also asked of all its members. The response is in the first-person singular. It can make for a powerful witness if each person speaks the response individually, as the rubrics indicate: "I do, and I ask God to help and guide me." Or, all those making this affirmation of baptism may speak the response in unison.

The assembly plays an important role in the affirmation of baptism as well, since all members are needed to support one another. After responding to the question regarding their support, members of the assembly may be seated.

If the worship space has a communion rail, that may be the most logical space for those making affirmation to use in kneeling for prayer. Another way to allow affirmers to kneel would be by having available a small kneeling stand (a *prie dieu*), often used by couples during marriage ceremonies or by presiding or assisting ministers. Or oversized decorator pillows could provide a place to kneel (though if these are used people may need a hand to help them up). The prayer along with the laying on of hands may also be spoken with each participant standing, though in that case it may be easier for the presiding minister to be standing a step higher than the participants. The first portion of the prayer ("We give you thanks . . . and raise us to eternal life.") needs to be spoken only once, regardless of the number making affirmation. The prayer that follows is to be spoken for each person separately. The prayer provided on the left side is for general use with people making affirmation of baptism, while the prayer printed on the right side is more specific to those who have been preparing for confirmed membership in the congregation.

While the presiding minister speaks the prayer and lays both hands on the head of each person making affirmation, other people may surround the person in a variety of ways. One or more teachers (catechists) or pastors could stand to either side of the presiding minister and join in laying one of their hands on the head of each person. Family members, mentors, and sponsors of each person affirming baptism could stand behind the person and place their hands on one of his or her shoulders (if the number of such participants is large, consider using a human chain, rather than having each person place a hand directly on the one affirming baptism). Involving people in addition to the presiding minister in this part of the service can be especially meaningful and powerful. Even if that adds time to the service, it gives a visible sign of the wider guidance and support that each person affirming baptism receives through the Christian community. When the number of participants is particularly large, it might be helpful to have two or more stations set up, with groups of those affirming baptism assigned to different stations. Then, as the presiding minister is praying at a station with one person, people at the other station(s) could leave or approach as needed. The presiding minister could alternate stations until a prayer has been spoken for each person, or a congregation with more than one pastor might designate a station for each pastor.

Unless the presiding minister is able to memorize the prayer that will be used during the laying on of hands, and unless the presiding minister is certain not to draw a blank on the name of each person, it will be important to have an assisting minister or acolyte hold a book with the prayer and a self-stick note or slip of paper with the names of each person. Alternatively, each person making affirmation could be wearing a nametag visible to the presiding minister—which would also be useful as others in the assembly greet them after the service. Presiding ministers need not be apologetic for having names written down; prompt articulation and accurate pronunciation of names will help ensure that equal respect is given to all at this important moment.

After those making affirmation stand and face the assembly, a representative of the congregation (perhaps the same person who presented the candidates at the beginning of the order) introduces the assembly's response of thanksgiving that culminates the affirmation. Members of the assembly may also stand at this time. Note that the statement spoken by the assembly does not "welcome" per se, since that is what occurs in the sacrament of baptism; the assembly's function now is joining together with those who have affirmed their baptism. A representative of the congregation may also lead the assembly in honoring those making affirmation with applause, after which they may return to their places within the assembly.

Affirmation by the Assembly

As mentioned in a preceding section of this chapter, Affirmation by the Assembly might be planned for a number of occasions. If the worship space allows all members of the assembly to gather in a large circle, that may be desirable since everyone will be affirming their baptism in one another's presence. Whatever physical arrangement of the assembly is possible for the affirmation liturgy might also remain through the prayers of intercession that follow; then members of the assembly may more easily exchange the greeting of peace, while also proceeding to the places they will use for the remainder of the service.

Affirmation by the Assembly may be led entirely by the presiding minister, although the question "People of God, do you promise to support and pray for one another in your life in Christ?" could be asked by an assisting minister.

Conclusion

A celebrative hymn, song, or psalm may conclude Affirmation of Baptism (several selections in the section of hymns on Holy Baptism, #442–459, would be fitting). A hymn may serve several functions at this point: first, it provides the assembly with another way to voice its response; second, the hymn or song may serve to bridge the return of those who have made affirmation of baptism to their places within the assembly; third, the singing may accompany a tangible reminder of baptism; and finally, it may allow worship leaders to reset the chancel area as needed and prepare for the prayers of intercession.

A reminder of baptism is suggested as a part of the conclusion of Affirmation of Baptism. Such a reminder could include the presiding minister and one or more worship leaders sprinkling members of the assembly with water. Alternatively, members of the assembly could approach the baptismal font or other container filled with water, dip their hands into the water and trace the sign of the cross upon themselves. Or, those who have made affirmation of baptism could make their way back to their places in the assembly by way of the font, where they could touch the baptismal water and make the sign of the cross upon themselves or upon one another, or they could receive such a sign from one of the worship leaders.

Prayers of intercession that follow will give thanks for the people affirming baptism and for those who accompanied and supported them on their journey. The prayers of intercession may also include more general thanksgivings and concerns appropriate for the current time in the life of the congregation, the community, the world, and all creation.

Following the liturgy, if it is customary for the pastor(s) to greet worshipers as they leave, those who have made public affirmation of their baptism in the service may also stand in places where they can be greeted and congratulated by members of the assembly.

CHAPTER SIX

Corporate and Individual Confession and Forgiveness

The primary form of confession and forgiveness experienced by a majority of North American Lutherans for the past several decades has been a brief preparatory order performed immediately prior to a service of holy communion or another primary worship service of the congregation. Most modern-day Lutherans would not be familiar with a confessional service that stood entirely on its own, though this provision has existed in several generations of Lutheran worship books. In previous centuries of Lutheran experience, corporate confession was commonly used for members of congregations to "announce" themselves or register a day or more in advance for a service of holy communion. This practice was more prevalent when communion was observed only a few times throughout the year.

The practice of holding a brief order for confession and forgiveness as the holy communion service begins seems to meet the pastoral needs that many people have for confession. As the frequency of communion has gone from quarterly, to monthly, and to weekly in a number of congregations (in approximately a century or less), there is little desire within most worshiping communities for people to gather regularly for a separate confessional liturgy in preparation for holy communion. Yet the longer order for corporate confession and forgiveness remains, even if it does not seem to fulfill the type of need it once did.

Even more curious to many people would be the existence of an order for individual confession and forgiveness. Many Lutherans would be surprised to know that individual confession was a possibility for them, since its association has been thoroughly identified with the Roman Catholic Church in references through popular culture. Yet individual or "private" forms for confession were provided in previous generations of Lutheran worship resources, though most members of congregations might not have been aware of them. Though there are many ways to experience confession and forgiveness, most people in the Lutheran church—lay and clergy alike—may only be familiar with the brief general order of confession and forgiveness that is a part of the service of Holy Communion.

The uses for both the corporate and the individual orders of confession and forgiveness will be explored separately below. However, both orders are rooted in the grace of baptism that constitutes the Christian assembly. People of faith live out that grace daily as they remember God's promises and are renewed in the covenant of baptism. Ultimately, confession and forgiveness is about restoring the bonds of human community, particularly following experiences of hurt or mistrust. Confession and forgiveness is one way in which Christians are invited to examine their lives, return to the grace of baptism, and be restored in their relationships with one another and the world.

Not only Christians, however, but also those who are not baptized may receive the grace of God through orders for confession and forgiveness. The gospels record the stories of a number of people who approached Jesus with the cry "Have mercy on me" and received the gift of forgiveness. The orders for confession and forgiveness may be one way in which those inquiring into Christian faith and life begin to experience the grace of God through the acknowledgment of their guilt and brokenness and the declaration of God's full and free forgiveness.

Historical Understandings

Prior to the Middle Ages, confession and forgiveness—or the sacrament of penance—inaugurated a formal return to the life of the community for those who had been under the discipline of the church for a serious sin and had been excluded from full participation in the sacrament of the altar. Upon completion of a process of satisfaction for a particular grievance, the penitent was able to confess sinful behavior to the gathered congregation and be reconciled to God and to the church. Such an act of penance could happen only once in a person's lifetime. The rite of reconciliation included a laying on of hands by the bishop. The reconciliation was made complete by participation again in holy communion.

The transition from a publicly administered process for reconciliation to an almost exclusively private penitential practice was a lengthy one. By the sixth century a system for assigning tariffs or fines for particular offenses had been established in Ireland. Forgiveness for sins could be obtained by doing penance: acts of contrition, making a confession, and performing satisfaction for the offense for some duration of time. Unlike the earliest centuries of the church, this form of confession was repeatable and possible even for small offenses. Private confession to a priest became the standard practice by which persons were absolved and reconciled to full communion with the church. Then at the Fourth Lateran Council, in 1215, every Christian was required to make a confession of sin to a priest at least once a year.

For Protestants in the sixteenth century, and certainly for Lutherans, the emphasis in the process of reconciliation was in the absolution with its declaration of God's grace. Satisfaction and contrition for one's sins was thought by the reformers to place too much emphasis upon human works. Still, individual confession and absolution was retained by the reformers as an option to be used in ministering to troubled consciences. The Lutheran reformers were not of one mind as to whether confession and forgiveness should be numbered as one of the sacraments, though the Apology of the Augsburg Confession (Article XIII) named it as one.

As preparation for the reception of holy communion, Luther instructed that people should announce an intention to commune to the pastor, who then examined prospective communicants about the meaning of holy communion. Communicants were also expected to have committed the words of institution to memory. At times the examination with the pastor also included individual confession and forgiveness. Catechetical examination was removed as a prerequisite for reception of communion in the eighteenth century.[1] According to Dietrich Bonhoeffer, Luther held to three different modes of confession: daily confession to God directly through prayer; public and general confession of sin; and personal confession of specific sins before another Christian, with a personally addressed absolution. Luther advocated that the first two forms of confession were mandatory, while the third, though optional, was nonetheless important.[2]

Corporate Confession and Forgiveness

Corporate Confession and Forgiveness is a service that might be used on a number of occasions, as the second paragraph of the introduction to this service describes:

> Corporate Confession and Forgiveness may be used on penitential days, such as the final days of Lent, or as part of the regular schedule of the congregation. Occasions suggesting its use include

the reconciliation of those estranged from one another; the confession of sharing in corporate wrongs; and a time of lament in the life of the congregation, the community, the nation, or the world. Selected portions may be used when a fuller order for confession and forgiveness within another service is desired. [AE p. 238]

While other worship resources for Lent provide for an intensified experience of confession and forgiveness (in particular the services on Ash Wednesday and Maundy Thursday), it is possible that certain midweek services during Lent—perhaps some of those scheduled for Wednesdays or Fridays—could make use of Corporate Confession and Forgiveness. Over a period of weeks, a series of biblical stories which deal with appropriate themes (confession, contrition, making restitution, experiencing forgiveness, and being restored to right relationships with God and with others) could be used at confession and forgiveness services.

The corporate order for confession and forgiveness could also be arranged to meet a specific need within the life of the congregation, an extended family, or even other people within the community at large. The service could be announced following a time of intense conflict and misunderstanding among a group of people. Of course, when to schedule the service could be a matter of some delicacy. If such a service were scheduled too soon, in the midst of severe problems where sides are clearly drawn or where people are actively engaged in blaming one another, it is possible that people would not be ready for such a service or that they would view it as manipulative. But once considerable efforts have gone into addressing problems and people from various vantage points of an issue are ready to move on, corporate confession and forgiveness could serve an important function in effecting a formal reconciliation among people, and the service could help to move relationships forward in positive ways.

The use of Corporate Confession and Forgiveness as a communal lament liturgy may provide a possibility for those occasions when leaders within a congregation or community feel the need to respond to a local or national tragedy. This service may also be helpful during a time of war, especially if citizens have questioned the reasons for going into war and feel some responsibility for its difficult outcomes.

Gathering

Suggested psalms for the gathering rite serve to anchor corporate confession and forgiveness in the scriptures. The indicated psalms may provide a more meditative way to begin this service. Alternatively, a number of hymns, especially those from the confession and forgiveness section (#599–609) in *Evangelical Lutheran Worship*, might have a similar effect. Care should be exercised in selecting hymns that are relatively well known by the assembly that will gather for this service. Since the actions of confessing and receiving forgiveness may be harder work than usual, it will be helpful if worshipers don't need to be concerned about too many of the mechanics of the service.

The invocation spoken by the presiding minister is a reminder of the triune name and the sign of the cross marked at baptism. The prayer of preparation serves as a prayer of the day for this liturgy, in addition to preparing for the confession that will follow after the scripture readings. Both prayers are repeated from the order of confession and forgiveness that is a part of the gathering rite of Holy Communion in *Evangelical Lutheran Worship*. The prayer on the right side (AE p. 239) is one that has been used for many generations by English-speaking Christians. It may be especially useful in connection with situations where the keeping of secrets has been a significant component in the breach of community. The newer prayer on the left side, an adaptation of a prayer in the parallel order within *Lutheran Book of Worship*, is suitable for general use and serves as a summary of the actions that will unfold during the service.

Word

Scripture readings that proclaim God's love and forgiveness will be helpful at this time. Lists of readings for days of penitence, mourning, and peace are provided in the Propers section of *Evangelical Lutheran Worship* (AE pp. 62–63), and these selections may be useful for various occasions when Corporate Confession and Forgiveness is scheduled, although they are only some of the possible scripture readings that could be used. As it is likely that many people gathering for this service already have some understanding of their sinful condition, the readings need not be chosen to convince people of their failures and misdeeds. Some of the more helpful readings might be those in which people can identify empathetically with the persons in the biblical stories who have also failed and stood in need of forgiveness. Here are some additional possibilities for readings (related days when these texts appear in the Revised Common Lectionary are given for preachers interested in finding biblical commentaries):

Genesis 50:15-21 (Lectionary 24A)
Exodus 32:7-14 (Lectionary 24C)
Jeremiah 31:31-34 (5 Lent B, Reformation)

Psalm 65 (Thanksgiving A)
Psalm 130 (Lectionary 10B, Vigil of Pentecost)

Colossians 3:12-17 (1 Christmas C)
1 John 1:1—2:2 (2 Easter B)

Matthew 18:21-35 (Lectionary 24A)
Luke 6:27-38 (7 Epiphany C)
John 20:19-23 (Day of Pentecost A)

Preaching or conversation that follows the readings might be led or begun by the presiding minister—or perhaps by another trusted leader from the community, with pastoral oversight—who can describe the things needing to be confessed. For a smaller group, meeting in a space where chairs can be arranged in a circle may be most effective. A less structured time of conversation may occur after the scripture readings. People who wish to confess their own failures and misdeeds to one another may do so at this time.

If there is a particular pain or trauma that the group has experienced, it can likely be named without attempting to find fault with anyone. This is not a time for blaming in any form. Participants should have arrived at the point of being able to own up to their own complicity in the problems that have led to broken relationships, without needing to point out the faults of others.

Confession

Following preaching that may occur, or following an opportunity for mutual conversation, the presiding minister continues with a formal invitation to confession, either as provided at the bottom of page 239 (AE), or in similar words. The invitation to confession in the right-hand column is drawn from 1 John 1 and, like the prayer above it on the page, has been used as part of confessional orders among English-speaking Christians for many generations. In the left-hand column, an invitation to confession new to *Evangelical Lutheran Worship* quotes Romans 5:8.

The litany that follows (AE p. 240) is an opportunity to hear of the many ways in which human beings have fallen short of God's intention for our lives. While the magnitude of sinfulness is obvious in this prayer, the naming of many aspects of human shortcomings may help those who have been focused only on a single difficulty in their lives. Although this form is inspired by the historic list of the "seven deadly sins," this adaptation focuses especially on the ways in which these sins are communal in nature. For that reason this form of confession may cause people to look beyond their own personal faults and failures into seeing how organizations, governments, and systems in which they participate may also stand in need of correction.

In situations that are not fundamentally moments of confession (national grief or mourning for example), it may be helpful to substitute for this litany something that seems more appropriate for the occasion—for example, one of the more general confessions used at the beginning of the Holy Communion liturgy on page 95, or the Great Litany (service music #238).

Forgiveness

Both forms of the declaration of forgiveness provided in this rite are strongly trinitarian. The form on the left side of the page includes an overtly declarative form ("As a called and ordained minister of the church of Christ, and by his authority, I therefore declare to you the entire forgiveness of all your sins . . ."), reflecting a theological accent deeply ingrained in some Lutheran traditions in North America. The form on the right side of the page announces forgiveness more simply ("In the name of Jesus Christ, your sins are forgiven"), reflecting a theological accent deeply valued within other Lutheran traditions in North America. The form on the left recalls baptism directly through the naming of the triune God, Father, Son, and Holy Spirit. The form on the right ("Almighty God strengthen you with power through the Holy Spirit, that Christ may live in your hearts through faith") is a compilation of biblical texts (Eph. 2:4-5; Acts 3:6, 10:43; Eph. 3:16-17) and concludes with a declarative blessing rather than a direct baptismal connection.

Laying On of Hands

Two forms for pronouncing an individual absolution are provided in this rite. The form on the left is customarily used on Maundy Thursday and could be spoken whenever this service is used. One advantage in using this form is that the sentence may be more easily committed to memory. Though the address printed on the right-hand side is longer, the second sentence is a blessing that also provides hope and encouragement for the future. Whichever form is used, it is helpful that the presiding minister have hands and eyes free of the need to be using a book at this moment so that the words may be addressed to each person coming forward and both hands can be placed on each worshiper's head.

Assembly song may accompany the laying on of hands (see hymns suggested in the gathering section above), or this could also be a time for silence or subdued instrumental music. The peace that follows the laying on of hands may be more heartfelt than usual, especially if people who have come together for corporate confession have experienced genuine hurts with one another. In some smaller gatherings especially, each person may be able to extend a greeting of peace to everyone else present.

If the first portion of this liturgy was subdued, everything following the announcement of forgiveness and the exchange of peace might well have a more joyful tone. Such a transition is not so different from many psalms of thanksgiving where beginning verses confess problems and difficulties, while concluding verses are ones of praise (see for example Psalms 18, 30, 41). Many hymns of praise and thanksgiving could be helpful here, but especially these or others that speak of having endured challenges:

The Peace of the Lord / La paz del Señor (#646)
Amazing Grace, How Sweet the Sound (#779)
Come, Thou Fount of Every Blessing (#807)
Lift Every Voice and Sing (#841)
Praise the One Who Breaks the Darkness (#843)
I'm So Glad Jesus Lifted Me (#860)
When Long before Time (#861)
Praise, My Soul, the God of Heaven (#864)
In Thee Is Gladness (#867)
We Praise You, O God (#870)
Sing Praise to God, the Highest Good (#871)

Prayers

In keeping with the spirit of thanksgiving that comes from experiencing God's forgiving power, the prayers at the conclusion of Corporate Confession and Forgiveness could be ones primarily of thanksgiving as well as praying for the needs of others. At this point in the service brevity may be especially desirable. Prayers of intercession in forms that may be common to other services of the congregation may be used. Either the prayer for general thanksgiving (AE p. 74) or the prayer of Julian of Norwich (AE p. 87) may also be useful here. The Lord's Prayer appropriately concludes the prayers of the assembly.

Sending

Both forms of blessing are standard forms that many presiding ministers will have committed to memory. Other forms of blessing may also be fitting for this occasion, such as the third option at the conclusion of Holy Communion or the Service of the Word ("The God of steadfastness and encouragement . . . ," AE pp. 115, 221). The concluding blessing in the thanksgiving for baptism at the end of Morning Prayer ("Almighty God, who gives us a new birth by water and the Holy Spirit and forgives us all our sins . . . ," AE p. 307) may also be an appropriate blessing for Corporate Confession and Forgiveness. In either case, the dismissal is a fine way to depart in a spirit of forgiveness ("Go in peace. Christ has made you free"). The implication of this dismissal is that members of the assembly, having been freed from their own burdens, are now able to serve others.

Although the notes within the service do not specifically indicate it, Corporate Confession and Forgiveness might include holy communion. If such is desired, the Meal and Sending sections of the Holy Communion service might follow the exchange of peace (AE p. 241). The service might then conclude with the dismissal from Corporate Confession and Forgiveness (AE p. 242).

Individual Confession and Forgiveness

A popular misconception is that only Roman Catholic believers have the opportunity to go to an ordained person and confess their sins individually. In fact Lutherans—along with believers in a number of other Protestant traditions—never formally abandoned individual confession; it just has not been viewed as a requirement for people to confess their sins privately to a pastor with any degree of regularity in order to remain as church members in good standing. Many Protestant clergy—Lutherans among them—no doubt speak with parishioners who have troubled consciences within pastoral counseling sessions, but the same pastors may not commonly think to offer individual confession and forgiveness as a part of their ministry of pastoral care. This worship form is worth a look, if only to be aware of all possible tools to help people who are burdened by their consciences and misdeeds.

Insights from the Practice of Pastoral Counseling

It is generally believed that modern pastoral counseling began as an outgrowth of depth psychology. Techniques in pastoral counseling have varied as developments in the field of psychology have occurred.[3] While clergy did not initially apply the fruits of the psychiatric field to their work of pastoral counseling, since at least the 1950s, many clergy have embraced psychological methods to varying degrees. It is common now for clergy to use psychological labels in describing the situations their parishioners face. The ancient practice of confession and forgiveness of sin has largely been replaced in favor of a more psychotherapeutic model of pastoral care.

Even though pastoral care and conversation may often be based primarily in therapeutic categories, forgiveness is a gift that alone can address the needs of people to be reconciled to God. Lyman Lundeen has stated it this way:

> We fight to justify ourselves and look to find someone to verify our status. Forgiveness offers another route. It takes guilt and loss seriously and opens up the future to new possibilities. Even if only one person forgives another, the power of change is far greater than all attempts at self-justification and mutual admiration. By taking loss or guilt seriously, forgiveness shares in the suffering of the other person, making risk bearable and the future hopeful.[4]

If genuine reconciliation and forgiveness is to occur for people, it is helpful for at least one dimension of the pastoral counseling process to have some visible relationship with the worship of the faith community. By simply using the physical space belonging to the worshiping community for a private act of reconciliation, much can be done to convey the public nature of genuine pastoral care. Even where this is not possible, the use of words and symbolic actions that are connected to a communal activity is in itself a powerful sign (for example, the laying on of hands, words of forgiveness often used in public worship, or water that symbolically represents baptism).

The Communal Dimension of Individual Confession

The communal dimension of individual confession can be highlighted even though the content of the confession is private. In the order for Individual Confession and Forgiveness in *Evangelical Lutheran Worship*, the pastor indicates that he or she is a pastor in the church of Christ (AE p. 243). This statement helps to underscore the public dimension of this ministry of reconciliation. Notes for the rite indicate that the church's worship space—perhaps near the baptismal font or the altar—may be an appropriate place for the service, that there might be regular times when the pastor is available for this ministry, and that it is appropriate for the pastor to be vested in alb and stole (LE 34). All of these things help to underscore that even the work of individual confession and forgiveness relates to the worshiping community.

Dietrich Bonhoeffer, in his book *Spiritual Care*, addressed the communal dimension of confession:

> Genuine community is not established before confession takes place. The whole community is contained in those two people who stand next to one another in confession. If anyone remains alone in his evil, he is completely alone despite camaraderie and friendship. If he has confessed, however, he will nevermore be alone. He is borne by Christ on whom he has laid his sin, and by the community which belongs to Christ and in which Christ is present with us. In the community of Christ no one needs to be alone.[5]

The pastor who presides within the Sunday assembly and who provides care to people in one-on-one situations stands in a unique role. A pastor is called to lead a faith community in the most important and holiest treasures it owns: God's word and sacraments. When someone seeks out a pastor for a personal or confidential matter, it is as if that individual is seeking the most direct way of being reconciled to God. Though it may be argued that the pastor is not the only one who can hear a person's confession and pronounce words of comfort, the pastor is the one who most clearly acts in response to Christ's command to forgive sins (Matt. 16:19; John 20:23). Thomas Oden's definition of soul care bears out a relationship to the Christian community:

> Soul care occurs within a caring community whose primary corporate act is the praise of God's care. It is not incidental that the same pastor who meets persons in one-on-one conversation concerning the health of their souls, also leads the service of worship where life is received with thanksgiving, sins are confessed, divine pardon received, and life consecrated to God. Since the life of prayer holds up before God all dimensions of the nurture of the soul, it is a crucial activity of care of souls. Guidance of the service of common prayer is an indispensable aspect of pastoral guidance.[6]

The pastor carries the unique privilege of being able to represent an entire community—indeed the whole church throughout all times and places. When a pastor ministers to someone, even in a private situation, it can represent very public dimensions. The pastor is called to act on behalf of the whole church.

When a pastoral conversation leads to an issue in which the parishioner has spoken about the pain of sin or separation, the proper role of the pastor is to proclaim God's reconciliation and forgiveness. This reconciliation may happen through the use of an order for confession and forgiveness, or it may be done in another way that gives witness to the fact that God's will is to restore all people to harmony with the whole of creation and to its creator. However it is expressed, the news of God's reconciliation is a unique gift that the church—and especially those who are publicly ordained to its ministry—can genuinely offer.

Pastors who are sensitive to others' feelings of isolation or alienation may come to understand that a part of what people may be seeking in a return to the ministry of the church or in a pastoral care relationship is forgiveness, even if this is not always voiced as a need that people face. Those who have been absent from a congregation or from any Christian community for an extended period of time may have a need to confess and to experience God's forgiveness in a particular way. For example:

- People who have spent a long time caring for a terminally ill family member or grieving that person's absence may have felt isolated and may express some guilt about limitations they faced regarding their relationships with others and their participation in the church.

- People who have remained away from the church as a result of a difficult incident or strained relationship may have a need to experience forgiveness to enter into Christian community again.
- Those who have been absent from the church for a time during young adulthood may need to reflect on some of their experiences before they are ready to reenter the life of the Christian community.
- Military personnel returning from war and other conflicts may feel ambivalence about their experiences, even if they feel that their service was honorable.

In addition to hearing forgiveness for himself or herself, a person harboring resentments, hostilities, or anger may also need to express forgiveness to someone else. A full dimension of pastoral care provides not only experiences for conversation and therapeutic assistance but also the opportunity to confess and hear God's forgiveness.

In every situation in which individuals confess sins and receive the forgiveness of God, the reminder in the introduction to this order bears reinforcing: "There is a confidential nature to this order, in keeping with the discipline and practice of the Lutheran church." Participants must be assured that the pastor's commitment to confidentiality enables them to be "free to confess . . . sins of which you are aware and which trouble you." At the same time, as part of her or his professional responsibility, the pastor must be aware of any legal or circumstantial limitations to the "seal of the confessional" that may apply in a particular situation.

Suggestions for the Setting

As stated in the notes in the leaders edition (LE 34), this worship form may be conducted in a worship space, perhaps near a baptismal font or altar. Provision for kneeling may also be made. The pastoral leader may be vested in an alb and a stole in the color of the season.

One possible way to encourage people to take advantage of this opportunity on a regular basis would be to have a regular time during which one or more pastors would be available for confession and forgiveness, perhaps for an hour or more before the start of one of the congregation's weekly services (concluding a few minutes prior to the service). In this manner parishioners may more easily come unannounced to a period of confession, simply arriving in advance of most other worshipers. Some congregations may wish to schedule this rite seasonally, perhaps during Advent and Lent.

Care should be taken to ensure a certain amount of privacy (especially auditory), while at the same time promoting a safe environment for people who wish to confess. In some cases a corner of a gathering area or a small chapel would be an ideal location for individual confession and forgiveness. Having a small screen behind which a penitent may sit or kneel for confession could be helpful, while at the same time the pastor could be more visible to others who may be arriving or waiting for confession in the same space.

This form for confession and forgiveness may also be used to conclude a pastoral counseling session and could simply occur in the same space where that conversation has occurred, or the time for confession and forgiveness may be moved to a worship space.

The penitent (as well as the pastor) may kneel for the confession, or both may remain seated facing one another.

Confession

Either of the two trinitarian invocations may be spoken by a pastor in beginning the confession (AE p. 243). The form on the left uses the triune name of God, more directly recalling baptism; the form on the right speaks expansively of God's love, using imagery from the psalms. The brief statement made by the pastor ("You have come to make confession before God . . .") simply sets the purpose for the conversation that will follow.

The pastor may invite the penitent to pray in a way that confesses things that trouble her or him, using either the words provided in the worship book or words from the heart. Even if the printed text is used, there is also provision for the penitent to speak specifically of certain burdens and sins.

Following the penitent's prayer, the pastor may speak more specifically to the penitent's situation. According to the service notes, the conversation may be in the form of admonition, counsel, and comfort from the scriptures. Very likely the penitent will be mindful enough of sins and challenges that have led to confessing them before the pastor and seeking God's forgiveness. Pastoral counsel might include conversation about ways that the penitent could work to restore broken relationships and live in ways that are harmonious with the gospel.

Passages from the scriptures that might be useful are mentioned above in the section on Corporate Confession and Forgiveness. As indicated in the rubrics, the penitent and the pastor may speak Psalm 51 or Psalm 103 together.

Forgiveness

Two forms of the declaration of forgiveness are provided. The form of forgiveness printed on the left is traditionally used in the Maundy Thursday liturgy as an individual absolution and may be desirable for its familiarity both to penitent and pastor. The form on the right is especially fitting if the order takes place near a baptismal font.

Placing both hands on the penitent's head is a powerful gesture in announcing the forgiveness, though the pastor should be sensitive to someone who is not comfortable being touched in this manner. The order ends simply with an announcement of God's peace. Both pastor and penitent may exchange a sign of God's peace at this time (by a handshake, for example). If the baptismal font is nearby, the penitent and the pastor could each make the sign of the cross upon themselves after dipping a hand into the water.

2

Life Passages:
Healing, Funeral, Marriage

CHAPTER SEVEN

Healing

Worship resources for healing, funeral, and marriage were brought together for Lutheran use under the heading Life Passages in *This Far by Faith: An African American Worship Resource* (1999). Again in the provisional Renewing Worship resources this linkage was made, and now in *Evangelical Lutheran Worship* these three ministry rites are part of a major section titled Life Passages. As the name implies, these present opportunities for the church's ministry in times that are common to many people and that are frequently observed within a gathered assembly in public worship.

The three services are appropriately considered in the present volume since, as the introduction (AE p. 273) makes clear, they can be viewed as echoes of the great life passage for Christians, the baptismal transition into a saving relationship with God. Additional resources for ministry with people in a variety of transitions and life circumstances are part of the occasional services that accompany *Evangelical Lutheran Worship*. In this and the following two chapters, however, we will examine more closely the orders of service that appear in the core editions of *Evangelical Lutheran Worship*.

A Brief History of Healing Rites

People of faith have ministered to the sick and dying at least since biblical times. Prayers asking God to heal people abound in the Hebrew scriptures. Gospel accounts in the New Testament provide many examples of Jesus and the disciples laying hands on the sick and curing them of disease. A number of passages in the book of Acts describe the healing work of the apostles. The book of James notes a healing ministry of the church where elders prayed over the sick and anointed them with oil (Jas. 5:14). Simply stated, providing support and comfort to people who are sick has been one of the central activities and missions of the church from its beginning, and it has continued to be so to our own day.

The widespread use of the ministry of healing can also be inferred from the many mentions of oil in the Bible. As one of the symbols associated with strength and health, it has a varied and rich use within the biblical witness. In Psalm 133, oil is mentioned in conjunction with its use for anointing chief priests in Israel, in this case Aaron. Oil was also used in the Hebrew scriptures to anoint kings and prophets. In Psalm 23:5, oil is a sign of rich and abundant blessing. Isaiah 1:6 and Luke 10:34 mention the use of oil in order to promote physical healing.

There are numerous indications that in the early centuries of the church a ministry of healing was considered an important part of the church's life. Laying on of hands and anointing with oil are actions associated as much with baptism as they might be with healing. Connections between holy communion and the practice of setting apart oil for a ministry of healing are evident in the *Apostolic Tradition,* attributed to Hippolytus in the third century:

> If anyone offers oil, [the bishop] shall render thanks in the same way as for the offering of bread and wine, not saying it word for word, but to similar effect, saying: O God, sanctifier of this oil, as you give health to those who are anointed and receive that with which you anointed kings, priests, and prophets, so may it give strength to all those who taste it, and health to all that are anointed with it.[1]

This text offers a clue that oil could have been brought by nearly anyone in attendance to the gathered assembly so that it might be blessed for their own use later. Furthermore, this prayer indicates that the oil was consumed internally as well as applied externally. That the bishop was the usual presider on an occasion at which the oil was blessed suggests how central this element was to the wider faith community's mission.

Beginning in the Middle Ages, rites for healing seem to have been focused primarily on those near death, and thus were experienced not so much as offering a sense of well-being for the sick as about enabling people to be forgiven for their sins in order to be reconciled finally to the full sacramental ministry of the church, especially in the eucharist. Many Protestant reformers of the sixteenth-century abandoned a sacramental understanding of ministry to the sick—largely dispensing with the laying on of hands and anointing—although prayers for the sick were retained.

In general, ministry to the sick in the Lutheran tradition has been through pastoral acts performed privately by ordained ministers for people who are acutely sick or near death. Liturgical books used for such occasions until recent decades provided scriptural readings, prayers, and an opportunity for confession and forgiveness, as well as communion. In 1982, *Occasional Services*, a companion to *Lutheran Book of Worship*, provided both a public liturgy of healing as well as resources to be used privately. That resource was also instrumental in reintroducing Lutherans to the laying on of hands and anointing in their ministry with the sick.

Leading the Service of Healing

The order for Healing in *Evangelical Lutheran Worship* is a form of prayers and ministry with the sick that is primarily designed for a public gathering of the Christian community in a place where a worshiping assembly ordinarily gathers. The order is flexible enough, however, that it may also take place in homes or hospitals, or nearly anywhere that ministers to the sick may need to go. This order of worship encourages a ministry with the sick that draws upon the full word and sacrament ministry of the church. Connections to baptism are plentiful in this rite—in the prayers of intercession, in the suggestion that the order be led near the baptismal font (LE 42), and in the use of the laying on of hands and the (optional) use of anointing with oil. The rite is designed for use primarily within the context of either Holy Communion or Service of the Word, following the hymn of the day.

Introduction

The words of introduction clearly set forth the purpose of this service, without the expectation that those who are sick may experience a cure as a result of their participation. This ministry is grounded in the biblical accounts of Jesus' own ministry of healing. Even without a miraculous outcome, the church's ministry of healing is transformative in its own right because it proclaims gifts of wholeness, well-being, and peace that can endure through any disease, clinical diagnosis, or death itself.

Particularly if this service of healing is held in a special location or season of the year, a reference to these contexts may also be spoken aloud by the presiding minister as part of the introduction.

Prayers of Intercession

The prayers of intercession may be the general intercessions included in the assembly's concerns for the given week and the time of the year. Petitions may also include other prayers for healing, encouragement for those who work and minister in special ways with those who are sick, as well as for families of the sick. Two forms for prayers of intercession are provided in the leaders edition (661–663). Other prayers that could be used at this time are in the Additional Prayers section (AE pp. 84–85, LE 155–157). Still other prayers for specific times and circumstances are in the *Evangelical Lutheran Worship* occasional services resources.

Laying On of Hands

The presiding minister may invite worshipers to receive a sign of healing. If a communion rail or other provision for kneeling is available, worshipers may kneel if they are able to do so. Worshipers may also stand or remain seated to receive the laying on of hands. The laying on of hands is a powerful symbol. Its use here echoes its use in baptism. It is also used in affirmation of baptism, ordination, and other rites. A brief silence after placing hands on the person's head may be kept until the minister begins speaking the address or prayer that follows, allowing the gesture itself to communicate the care and concern about each person's well-being.

Several options are provided for prayer or blessing accompanying the laying on of hands. It will be helpful if those who are praying and laying on hands have memorized the prayer or if an assisting minister is able to hold a book opened to the text that will be used. Note that two forms of the prayers mention each person by name. Provision will need to be made for obtaining the person's name, either from memory or asking each person to state his or her name so that the minister can repeat it. The rubrics do not specifically state that the laying on of hands is to be performed solely by presiding ministers or ordained clergy. Especially when the number of people who are to receive the laying on of hands is large, assisting ministers may join the presiding minister in the laying on of hands (if this will be the case, keep in mind that assisting ministers will require some additional instructions and practice for this role).

Each form of the prayer may also be accompanied or followed by anointing the individual's forehead with oil in the sign of the cross, even though only one of the prayers provided specifically mentions oil. The oil used for this liturgy (traditionally olive oil, sometimes with a scented oil such as bergamot or balsam added) might be prepared in a small glass bowl or shell that can be held with one hand while enabling a thumb or fingertips from the other hand to be dipped into the oil. An oil stock may also be used. (An oil stock is a small metal container with a securely fitting lid that is easily kept in one hand by an attached ring.) Placing a small cotton ball soaked with oil within the container that will be used by presiding and assisting ministers might facilitate distribution, though using larger quantities of oil may better convey the generous intention of this sign. When oil is used along with the laying on of hands, it will be helpful to have a small table nearby so that any containers of oil may be prepared ahead of the service, and so that those containers of oil may be set down while both hands of each minister are free to be used in the laying on of hands. Towels for ministers to use in wiping the oil from their hands should also be available.

Oil might be set apart at a service for blessing oil sponsored by the local synod, at which the bishop or bishop's representative presides (these services are usually scheduled during Holy Week or a few days before it). The point of such a blessing is not that it adds anything to the efficacy of the rite but rather to help communicate that this is a ministry of the whole church, not just one congregation. Even if the amount of oil distributed from such a joint service is small in quantity, it may be added to a larger amount of oil that the congregation could keep on hand for a healing ministry as well as for baptism. Congregations may keep the oil that is intended for healing in an attractive, clear glass bottle. Some congregations display oils in a glass-fronted cabinet mounted near a baptismal font. Oil used for healing of the sick as well as following baptism may be kept in a single container or divided into separate bottles for each of these uses.

Assembly song or instrumental music may accompany the laying on of hands. Four pieces in the service music section of *Evangelical Lutheran Worship* (#218–221) are designed for use with this order, and each might be sung as an ostinato (that is, repeated) throughout much or all of this part of the service. Other congregational songs having repeated refrains may also work well for this liturgy. Instrumental music could be used during the laying on of hands too, although care should be exercised in selecting music that will reflect the character of this service, which may be relatively quiet or subdued.

The prayer concluding the laying on of hands portion of this liturgy extends the intentions of the assembly to all who are in need.

Blessing

The blessing within this order stands as a powerful reminder of God's presence in everyone's life, and that this is the source of genuine healing.

Peace

The order for healing itself culminates in the sharing of the peace of Christ with one another, which becomes the point of transition to the remainder of the service of Holy Communion or the Service of the Word. The service then continues with the offering.

If holy communion follows, Prayer V (AE pp. 65–66) may be especially appropriate for use as a thanksgiving at the table. For the prayer after communion, the prayer beginning "We give you thanks, almighty God, that you have refreshed us through the healing power . . ." is particularly fitting. Also note the prayer after communion, final blessing, and sending that are provided in the order of Healing in the leaders edition (665).

Planning for a Service of Healing

The order for Healing in *Evangelical Lutheran Worship* assumes that people with various illnesses will be able to attend public worship, at least upon occasion. To ensure the participation of people who are ill (though likely not everyone in a congregation who may be seriously ill), some things to consider when planning a healing service are location, the length of the service, and time of day. Having a portion of the service (particularly the laying on of hands and anointing with oil) led from the area surrounding a baptismal font could be especially helpful in drawing connections to that sacrament. Having a service held in a place close to an accessible entrance and with convenient restroom facilities nearby may be important considerations for some people who are ill.

Keeping a service of healing shorter than is typical for most of the congregation's services could help people who have difficulty being away from home or another comfortable environment for a long period of time. A service that is neither very early nor very late in the day may be helpful to people who require a considerable amount of time readying themselves to leave home or get ready for bed. Finally, perhaps more than at most other occasions of worship, it will be helpful to plan healing services together with some participants who would be most interested in attending, to determine what their special needs might be and how worship planners might best accommodate them.

Because many people who are ill require assistance in moving from one location to another, having volunteers available who could transport participants in appropriate vehicles may be helpful for services of healing. Ushers and other ministers of hospitality should be alert to special needs that participants might have and how those needs could be accommodated with dignity and grace. In order to be sensitive to people who may require help in standing or kneeling, consider having all participants remain seated throughout this liturgy. If holy communion is planned, think about having the elements distributed by worship leaders to the locations where the participants are seated throughout the service. This provision may require more ministers of communion than is customary.

Keep in mind that even the most ambitious attempts to provide support for people who are homebound in various ways may not be adequate to enable all people who are ill to attend a service outside of their usual environments. In such situations the church extends ministries of healing through its pastors, ministers of communion, and other worship leaders into homes, hospitals, nursing-care facilities, and nearly anywhere that a need might be.

When to Use the Service of Healing

Many congregations that have used healing services for laying on of hands and anointing have scheduled them periodically throughout the year. Some congregations may have designated a certain day in the liturgical year for having a service of healing, particularly on or near the day of Luke, Evangelist (October 18), who according to tradition was a physician. Still other congregations have scheduled healing services monthly or even weekly.

Congregations that have particularly close relationships with specific hospitals or nursing homes might consider scheduling healing services in a chapel or common room of such a facility on a regular basis, perhaps with the involvement and support of a chaplain or an on-site activities coordinator. Family members of those who are ill, as well as their caregivers, may also have a special interest in services of healing, and such a liturgy may prove to be a form of outreach to them, particularly if attending other regularly scheduled worship services is a challenge for them because of the need to be constantly close to a person who is ill.

Using Elements from the Order for Healing

The laying on of hands in this service could also be used separately or within the context of other services. One alternative to experiencing a healing service as it is presented here might be to have one or more healing stations set up immediately following a regular worship service of the congregation, or possibly during communion distribution. A corner of the worship space or an area near the baptismal font could be set up as a special place for prayer, including provision for kneeling or small seating groups. Ministers of healing could be appointed to pray for healing or for other special concerns worshipers might mention.

The laying on of hands section of this liturgy could also be used within a general ministry to the sick and homebound provided by pastors or communion ministers in various settings apart from designated worship spaces.

Scripture Readings and Other Propers for Healing

Congregations scheduling an order for healing during a principal weekly service may use the appointed propers of the day, including scripture readings drawn from the three-year lectionary. If the healing service will occur on a weekday, the readings might be from the daily lectionary (AE pp. 1121–1153), which are related to the Sunday readings. When services of healing are held less frequently than every week, scripture readings specific to the theme of healing might be selected. Hymns to consider using with this service include #610–617, as well as those listed in the topical index under healing (AE p. 1182). Appendix C, Propers and Hymns for Life Passages, includes a list of suggested readings and hymns for services of healing.

CHAPTER EIGHT

Funeral

The Funeral service in *Evangelical Lutheran Worship* (AE pp. 274, 279–285, LE 658, 666–674) follows the pattern for worship of the Sunday assembly, including provision for celebrating the Lord's supper. Common elements of Christian funeral practice have been identified as washing, anointing, and dressing the body (actions reminiscent of baptism); a communal vigil followed by a service of word and possibly meal (rites expressing the baptismal community); and a final commendation with a procession to the place of entombment while hymns or psalms are sung (rites expressing the completion of baptism).[1] Some of these elements are not fully represented in the assembly and leaders editions of *Evangelical Lutheran Worship* but are part of the accompanying occasional services. Even within the funeral service itself, however, attention is given to actions reminiscent of baptism (in the Gathering), the provision for word and possibly meal, and a sending that includes both commendation and committal, which many consider the distinctive features of the Christian funeral rite.

The service is intended primarily for use when the body (or cremated remains) of a baptized Christian is present and the funeral takes place in a church. However, the rite is easily adapted for use as a memorial service or with an unbaptized person, and the pattern is appropriate for services held at funeral homes and other locations. The service is flexible enough to accommodate customs of the culture and desires of the family that are appropriate to the gospel and bear witness to the resurrection of Christ.

The service in *Evangelical Lutheran Worship* "extends the work of *Lutheran Book of Worship* by immersing the funeral even more intensely in the promise of baptism and thereby grounding the funeral itself in Luther's own baptismal emphasis."[2] For example, a thanksgiving for baptism may be included as part of the gathering rite. A pall may be placed over the coffin or urn as a symbol of being clothed with Christ in baptism. The notes include an additional option for sprinkling the coffin or urn with water from the baptismal font (LE 44). Other provisions enable the rite more explicitly to reflect the Christian community, itself a gift of baptism.

The Notes on the Services (LE 43–45) make clear that the Christian funeral is an action of the entire assembly. All who gather share in the grief of those that mourn, remember the brevity of life on earth, thank God for a loved one, and entrust a companion into God's hands. The notes also describe the funeral service as one of a number of occasions for pastoral care and worship, both in smaller groups and the larger Christian assembly, as the congregation ministers at the time of death. Those who plan funerals and work with families to plan them consider the baptismal and communal nature of the funeral service and its place in the congregation's ministry to people who are dying and grieving. They also specifically address the ways death is ritualized in the culture, how the gospel will be preached, and whether to include holy communion in the service.

The Completion of Baptism

Joined to Christ's death and resurrection in the baptismal waters, our death becomes birth into eternal life. In Luther's words, the death of sin is not fulfilled completely in this life, but only happens when the Christian "passes through bodily death and completely decays to dust. . . . [T]he spiritual baptism, the drowning of sin, which [baptism] signifies, lasts as long as we live and is completed only in death. Then it is that a person is completely sunk in baptism, and that which baptism signifies comes to pass." The Christian life, then, "from baptism to the grave, is nothing else than the beginning of a blessed death. For at the Last Day God will make [the Christian] altogether new" (LW 35:30-31). Paraphrasing Luther, on that day God will raise us from death, from sin, and from all evil. God will make us pure in body and spirit. We will be completely born, put on the true baptismal garment of immortal life in heaven, and live eternally with God.

Because death is the completion or fulfillment of God's promise of eternal life given in baptism, when death comes to us and to those we love, we do not need to be afraid. The Christian community certainly does not worship in ways that suggest we need to fear either death itself or God as we face death. Rather, the Christian community witnesses to, proclaims, and clings to the good news of Christ's resurrection. The Christian funeral, then, is a remembrance and celebration of baptism. In its grief and loss, the Christian community gathers with those who mourn to hear God's promise read in scripture and proclaimed in the assembly, to pray, and to share in the Lord's supper as a foretaste of the resurrection and a participation in the communion of saints. Trusting in the promise God made in baptism, the church commends the deceased to God's care and commits the body to its resting place.

Death also marks a new baptismal vocation for those who grieve, as they must continue their baptismal journey without the one they love. The Christian funeral is one way the church accompanies those whose lives are forever changed by the death of someone they love and who are confronting their own mortality. Even when they are assured of the promise of the resurrection, these brothers and sisters grieve as they face the difficult task of letting go of one who is precious to them and then beginning a life without that person. The Christian community helps these brothers and sisters embrace their grief as holy, since it is an indication of how God has loved and blessed them in this life. The community also helps those who grieve to trust that God will raise them to new life in this world as surely as God will raise their loved one to new life in the world to come. The funeral service proclaims the baptismal promise of rising from death to new life as much for the lives of those who grieve as for the deceased.

Those who plan funerals within the Christian community seek to proclaim the promise of baptism as the source of meaning amid all changes and crises, and our baptismal identity as our most important status as we face death. The assembly celebrates the meaning of baptism by including symbols and actions of baptismal remembrance in the service. The coffin or urn might be placed by the baptismal font and covered with a white pall, which proclaims again that in baptism we have been clothed with the righteousness of Christ forever. The paschal candle, with its associations to baptism and Jesus' resurrection, might be lighted and placed near the body. During the committal, three shovelfuls of dirt might symbolically be thrown on the casket, recalling the threefold washing of baptism. The assembly celebrates the communal dimension of baptism by holding the funeral in the midst of the congregation. Sharing holy communion in the funeral service helps underscore that it is the meal of the communion of saints. Those who plan funerals intentionally use these and other signs in ways that are as intelligible as possible to those who have not learned their meaning and significance. The assembly also celebrates the promise of baptism when the proclamation of God's word is the central message. In these ways, the Christian funeral in a ritual way concludes the passage from this world to God (John 3:5), which began at baptism, and provides a way for the Christian community to accompany the bereaved in the time of loss with the comforting words of scripture and the support of the Christian community.

The Funeral in Culture

The funeral, which from a Christian perspective marks the completion of baptism, is also a universal rite of passage that North Americans increasingly celebrate in diverse ways, often unrelated to the Christian faith. In many places, the church is losing, or ceding, its determinative role in shaping both formal and informal ritual actions surrounding death. Families are increasingly guided by the desire to avoid death, the need to honor the deceased, and economic realities. Our death-denying culture is undeniable. Rather than confront death honestly, families might minimize and even eliminate the funeral. More often, as families plan funerals according to the wishes of the deceased and the desires of individual mourners; they may find the elements of the church's worship at the time of death either unfamiliar or just additional options to be considered. While the church views the funeral service as a celebration of the resurrection, those close to the deceased desire to pay tribute to the person they have lost. Perhaps the most important factor that families consider in funeral planning is the amount of money they are willing and able to spend. As they weigh these considerations, many families regard both the church and the funeral home as consultants and providers of services, rather than as participants in planning the service.

The funeral service might be either a service where the body is present or a memorial service, which takes place after cremation or burial. The complexity of bringing people together from great distances on minimal notice has resulted in memorial services becoming more common. The service is most often held at a church, a funeral home, or at the graveside; however, it might be held at other, often less formal, locations. Burial may take place at sea, on a beach, or in a forest, as well as in a cemetery or mausoleum.

Some families choose to have a family member, friend, or member of the funeral home staff lead the service, rather than a pastor. For many families, a eulogy—an address recounting significant relationships, events, and achievements in the life of the deceased—is an expected part of the service. The service or the preceding vigil (wake) may also include a video presentation of the life of the deceased, with favorite music playing in the background. The family often selects music for the service according to whether it holds special meaning for the deceased or the family, and they might invite a friend or a family member to perform as vocalist or instrumentalist rather than invite the congregation to sing. Other symbols and rituals, which hold special meaning for the family, sometimes replace Christian symbols and rituals.

In addition to the ways that the general North American culture has shaped funeral practices, specific cultural heritages can also play a role. Funeral services within the African American community are often long and dramatic, freely expressing both the pain of loss and celebrating the hope of resurrection. Open caskets are common both before and after the service. The casket, closed during the service, is reopened afterward so that the assembly can file past the deceased and the family, who form a receiving line. The funeral service often reflects specific ancestral roots in West Africa and the Americas. For example, funeral rites of the Caribbean tend to be elaborate, steeped in religious ceremony, and grounded by cultural heritage because they are considered the final rite of passage for those whose elders passed down specific customs from the West Indies. These funerals are communal affairs in which each person has explicit duties to perform. There can be a period of more than a week from the time of death to the burial. The lowering of the casket and covering of the grave are considered mandatory. The few cremations that are requested by African Americans of Caribbean descent take place only after the same traditional viewing and funeral service associated with burial. African Americans whose heritage is intertwined with Southern tradition follow many Caribbean practices. However, cremations have increased, often because of the desire of the deceased to have their remains spread in the land of their birth or with their ancestors.

Commonly, African migrants to the United States hold on to their ancestral rituals in their funeral rites. In such cases, the entire community contributes to the expenses, food, and necessities of the family. The wake is spread over many days. The funeral begins and ends with ritualistic drumming, singing, and dancing. The priest speaks in the language specific to the common ancestry or geographic location of the family in Africa. Following the service, the assembly processes from the funeral site to the final resting place or to the airport when the deceased will return to Africa for burial with the ancestors. This procession is marked by continued drumming, singing, and dancing.

Funeral rites are also most often communal events within Latin American cultures. Family members, as well as church and community members, donate whatever is necessary to give the deceased a "proper" burial. Wakes frequently last a minimum of two days, with an open casket for viewing. The service is often a full funeral mass and burial in a cemetery. A distinctive custom in some Latin American cultures is the use of photography of the deceased during parts of the funeral rite. The pictures taken at the funeral service preserve the death as an important historical event in the heritage of the family. Children are significantly included in the entire funeral service, since reverence for the dead from one generation to another is held in high esteem. In general, Latin Americans show no particular interest in the adaptation of contemporary or secular rituals during the funeral rite.

Many other symbolic actions and expectations for the time of the funeral, representing various communal expressions and interests from motorcycle clubs to fraternal societies, are encountered by worship leaders in the course of planning the liturgy. For example, it will be important for many presiding ministers to address questions that arise when the deceased is an active member of the military or a military veteran. Will there be expected actions regarding the flag or a form of salute, and where will these be located around the complex of liturgical actions that are part of the funeral?

As in its early centuries, the church again finds itself needing to evaluate cultural messages and practices. The church will use some practices as they are found. The church will adapt others. The church will reject still others. The question before those who plan funerals is how will we draw upon the customs, narratives, and images of our time to proclaim the good news of Christ's resurrection while recognizing that these tools may also have the power to undermine and reshape the countercultural message of the gospel. The early church seems to have asked whether a given practice is life-giving or whether it leads to death.

Texts, gestures, music, and symbols that contradict the foundational Christian faith in the resurrection are not included in the Christian funeral. In particular, the church avoids practices that emphasize the earthly class or status of the deceased or the family, such as overly expensive coffins and an inordinate amount of flowers, because they undermine baptismal equality.

Other cultural practices surrounding death are adapted by finding ways to instill them with baptismal and paschal dimensions. For example, families who wish to cover the coffin with flowers—or a flag—may be helped to see instead the value of the pall, which represents a universal baptismal identity of the Christian rather than a particular cultural or national identity. Planners creatively incorporate still other cultural symbols and actions, which may not support but do not undermine the gospel, into the service because they comfort the mourners. In so doing, they are careful to ensure that these cultural expressions do not overshadow the service's proclamation of the gospel and witness to the resurrection. Sometimes, making these determinations is difficult. Even when the possibility exists that something done or said in the funeral might be interpreted as challenging the claims of the gospel, pastoral considerations may lead to its inclusion in the service. By weighing the claims of the gospel, the meaning of cultural words and practices at the time of death, and the needs of those who mourn, those responsible for planning make the funeral a true witness to and proclamation of the gospel, and an authentic rite of passage for the family, while incorporating the best values and ritual acts of the culture.

Part of a Larger Ministry

Those who plan funerals are also concerned with how the service fits in the congregation's overall ministry at the time of death. As we have seen, the celebration of baptism, as the central event in the life of a Christian, is surrounded by other significant moments and events, which the church observes with rites of passage. So also the Christian funeral, though the chief expression of the completion of baptism in the life of the deceased and a change in the baptismal vocation of those who mourn, is one of several opportunities for the Christian community to proclaim the gospel and witness to the hope of resurrection during the time of death. The notes in *Evangelical Lutheran Worship* accurately describe the church's ministry during the time of death as a continuum that ranges from care for the dying to care for those who mourn at significant anniversaries of the death. The congregation's ministry includes both pastoral care and worship by small groups and the entire assembly.

Sharing scripture and praying together are key elements of Christian worship at the time of death. In some moments individuals worship together informally; in other moments the bereaved may gather more formally with the pastor and representatives of the congregation. Ancient Christian practices, including laying on of hands and anointing, confession and forgiveness, and celebrating holy communion, provide deep assurance to both the one who is dying and the family. Some people find singing hymns and hearing scripture read aloud particularly comforting. The congregation will surely remember the dying and the mourning in the prayers of intercession in the Sunday assembly. The *Evangelical Lutheran Worship* pastoral care occasional services include prayers and scripture readings for a variety of circumstances leading up to and following the time of death, as well as several worship orders. One of these, a commendation for the dying, may be used with the dying person and those who surround that person as death nears. Another service, for comforting the bereaved, could be used at the place of death, the home of the deceased, or a funeral home. Such a service of comfort is most appropriate for use at the vigil (visitation, wake) the night before the funeral or on the morning of the funeral, with the coffin or urn present. Additional services include prayer for when life-sustaining care is to be discontinued and a rite of observing the anniversary of a death. The pastoral care of a Christian community encompasses much more than the care provided by the pastor. Prayers, visits, meals, sympathy cards and calls, as well as the meal following the funeral, are all ways the congregation expresses Christian care and the hope of the resurrection.

The way the congregation's ministry unfolds at the time of death informs the planning of the funeral. The funeral service guides the congregation's subsequent care of those who mourn. Congregations might consider discovering and developing resources and establishing a defined-but-flexible pattern for their ministry to the dying and their families. Over time the entire assembly will come to know the funeral service as the centerpiece of this ministry rather than an isolated event.

A Communal Act

As an expression of baptism, the funeral service is a communal act that calls for the participation of the entire assembly. Those who plan funerals give serious consideration to the nature of the assembly that will gather, the appropriate ways for that assembly to participate, and the type of participation to be expected. These factors greatly influence the form, content, and location of the service.

The congregation that gathers for the funeral is different from the Sunday assembly. Many people, both inside and outside the congregation, are present to lead or provide some aspect of the funeral. They may include the funeral-home staff; the family, friends, and neighbors of the deceased; the congregation's musicians, altar guild, custodian or sexton, secretary, pastor; the people responsible for the meal following the committal; and the employees at the cemetery or crematorium. Some in the assembly will be people of deep faith. Others may be skeptical of religion, uncomfortable inside a church, and desiring only to honor the deceased and comfort the family. Many will claim a Christian identity and even church membership. Some will be familiar and comfortable with the congregation's worship, while others will not.

Everyone who gathers for the funeral brings real needs—for space to express their grief, for hope, for consolation, for making sense of what seems senseless. Even those of deep faith may experience uneasiness as they confront the irretrievable loss of a loved one and come face-to-face with their own mortality and the uncertainty of life. The assembly is united by the needs that people bring, as all who gather look to the church to provide comfort and hope, whether for themselves or for those around them. This desire makes the assembly particularly receptive to the words and actions with which the church proclaims the gospel and expresses its faith.

Though the assembly that gathers often includes many people who are not part of the congregation and who may not believe in Jesus Christ, these people may experience an outright call to faith or invitation to church membership as manipulative and self-serving. On these occasions, the most compelling invitation the church can make is providing an experience that takes people's needs seriously and bears witness to the hope of God's promise of eternal life. Such a witness calls for worship that is rich, faithful in all its parts to the core values of the Christian faith, and appropriate to those gathered. When funerals are held in a church, the Christian message and symbols are central and explicit. They are also presented in ways that are sensitive to all who gather. When the Christian message and symbols will be more disquieting than comforting, and divide rather than unite the assembly, or when the family desires that the funeral be conducted without a Christian perspective, those who plan funerals might advise holding an observance at the funeral home or other location.

Regardless of where the funeral is held, singing psalms and hymns is encouraged because of music's power to create community, increase the assembly's participation in the service, help the assembly express emotions, and create an atmosphere of comfort. All music used at Christian funerals reflects the Christian faith in both text and music. Appropriate themes include the promise and hope of Christ's resurrection, baptism, the presence of the Holy Spirit, the communion of saints, and Christian comfort. Hymns are chosen with the expectation that everyone will sing. Therefore, preference may well be given to hymns that the majority of the people are likely to know. Singing these hymns often profoundly connects the members of the assembly with those who have gone before them in faith. Similarly, singing hymns from other parts of the world joins the assembly with the church in those places. Those who plan funerals should resist the temptation to limit music exclusively to performances by instrumentalists and vocalists and recorded music. Rather than simply honoring a favorite song of the deceased or the family, music proclaims the promises of God and creates comfort and hope in a way that includes the entire assembly.

Holy Communion

In holy communion the members of the assembly participate in the forgiveness, life, and salvation that are the fruits of Jesus' death and resurrection; they are united with one another and the communion of saints as the body of Christ. Depending on the nature of the assembly, celebrating the Lord's supper as part of the funeral service is a powerful way for all who gather to accompany the deceased and those who mourn, and to bear witness to and participate in new life in Christ. Receiving the bread and cup is also a way the entire assembly proclaims the gospel. This proclamation is especially fitting in situations when words alone may sound hollow or empty. Under these circumstances, the embodied word of the sacramental meal and the actions of the assembly embracing in the peace of Christ and sharing Christ's body and blood together, in silence or in song, are particularly helpful ways to profess their hope that Christ brings life out of death. The assembly celebrating communion together may be the best way for the church to show God's power to heal, unite, and triumph over death to those who have not experienced this grace for themselves.

Like baptism, the Lord's supper is itself a passage from death to new life. More than the new life that results when our sins are forgiven through the gift of Christ's body and blood, the communion banquet is a foretaste of and a participation in that day when God "will make for all peoples a feast of rich food, a feast of well-aged wines . . . [and] will swallow up death forever. Then the Lord GOD will wipe away the tears from all faces" (Isa. 25:6-8). We not only share this new life with those physically at the table with us. Holy communion in the context of a funeral is a tangible expression of the communion of all the saints, uniting us with the whole church, Christ's body in heaven and on earth. Many Christians report that, as they prepare to commend a loved one to God, it is a powerful experience to share the holy meal one last time in the presence of the body of the deceased. As they receive communion, they think of their loved one feasting forever with Christ. They are aware that, united with Christ, they are also united with their loved one, the assembly, and the whole church. In the holy supper they receive the grace to commend their loved one into God's hands.

Like the cake that the angel of the Lord gave to Elijah as the prophet journeyed to Mount Horeb and the bread that the risen Christ broke and gave to two disciples in Emmaus, the bread and cup strengthen the members of the assembly to continue their life journey in faith. The Lord's supper reminds the assembly of God's providence. The gifts of Christ's body and blood help the assembly rejoice over all God's blessings, especially when we are most acutely aware of what we lack. Both the Lord's supper and the meal that traditionally follows the committal (or the funeral if the committal will occur later) are ways the members of the assembly declare, by eating and drinking both heavenly food and earthly nourishment, that they want to remain alive, to continue living despite the pain of the moment. Approaching the Lord's supper as God's strength and nourishment for the journey through grief and all the changes that lie ahead may be the most compelling reason for deciding to celebrate holy communion in the context of the Christian funeral.

Since the Lord's supper is such a precious gift, those who plan funerals should consider whether including the sacrament in the service is appropriate for the assembly that will gather. Holy communion may not be appropriate when the number of unbaptized persons who will attend the funeral is significant. The sacrament may not be appropriate when an inaccurate and even harmful rationale for celebrating the sacrament at a funeral is pervasive—for example, that the eucharist is a good work that will help the deceased enter heaven. Including communion may not be appropriate if the chances are good that it will be more divisive than unifying, more exclusive than inviting, as people cannot or will not come to the table. In making this determination, those who plan funerals are sensitive to both the wisdom of the family and the sacramental practices of churches from which friends and relatives may come.

Above all, those who plan funerals are guided by the assurance that Jesus extends the invitation to the table. "Admission to the Sacrament is by invitation of the Lord, presented through the Church to those who are baptized" (UMG 37). Baptism, as God's promise, is intended to assure believers that they are welcome, whatever their status and despite any other reality in their lives, and not as a way to exclude. Recalling the ministry of Jesus, who ate with outcasts and sinners, the assembly celebrates the Lord's supper trusting Jesus to invite people to the table. "Believing in the real presence of Christ, this church practices eucharistic hospitality. All baptized persons are welcome to Communion when they are visiting in the congregations of this church" (UMG 49). As a sign of hospitality, the inclusion of a brief statement in the worship folder that teaches Christ's presence in the sacrament helps people to decide whether to participate in holy communion. Under no circumstances is the sacrament received only by the family of the deceased and not the congregation. When communion is celebrated as part of a funeral service, communion is offered to all the baptized (UMG 49B).

Preaching for the Occasion

The notes for the funeral observe that a sermon by the presiding minister will normally be part of the service. However sermons are crafted, preaching at funerals demands a clear, bold, and meaningful proclamation of the gospel.

Ideally, the sermon serves four purposes. First, and most important, when we are confronted by the chaos, loss, doubt, and permanence of death, the preached word is where we encounter the risen Christ, who has transformed the gates of death into the gateway to eternal life. We need to hear God's word of grace in a way that gives us hope. Second, the comfort and assurance of the gospel help the sermon address death honestly. Third, the sermon makes the occasion personal, so that the funeral is the proclamation of the gospel in and through a particular life. Finally, the sermon can facilitate participation in the funeral liturgy by reflecting on its ritual words and actions, including the sacraments, and making their meaning and significance more accessible to the assembly.

Since death marks the completion of baptism, the funeral sermon is a proclamation of God's faithfulness and covenant relationship. The funeral sermon speaks of God's love and eternal life in the face of this particular, painfully real death. The preacher proclaims God's grace in and through this life transition in such a way that the assembly hears God's good news, even as they confront the death of one of God's own children and commend a loved one to God's care. The goal is that the assembly experiences God's presence, grace, and power in this moment, so that they also trust in, turn to, and rely upon God's presence, grace, and power as they face the future. This is the goal for everyone present.

Helping the assembly face death honestly is an essential part of preaching the gospel. Society and even the church rarely engage in serious conversation about death and mortality. Our society is largely numb to violence. Yet Jesus commanded the mourners to take away the stone from Lazarus's tomb, where the stench of death was already present (John 11:39). The preacher speaks of death as the enemy and of violence as contrary to God. The preacher does not present death as a problem to be solved, a subject to be avoided, or a reality to be denied, but as the painful truth of life. Yet in Christ the enemy that is death becomes release from suffering, the completion of the baptismal life, the fulfillment of God's baptismal promise, and the gate to eternal life.

In order that the sermon may be an experience of grace for this assembly, the message is particular, relevant, even personal. A generalized message, which takes no account of the deceased or of the needs of the mourners and the gathered assembly, will not suffice. Nor will an account of the character and significant achievements of the deceased, or an overview of the stages of grief. Eulogies and prolonged reminiscences look backward on an earthly life, not forward to the completion of that life with God. Instruction or advice on grieving confuses preaching with counseling. Counseling surely has its place at the time of death, but that place is not the sermon. Funeral sermons declare Christ's victory over death, the participation of the deceased in that victory, and God's continuing presence, love, and power for the deceased and for all who mourn in a way that speaks directly to both the universal and the unique experiences of death and dying. The way the sermon speaks to those who mourn varies, depending on theological and cultural tradition, the perspective of the preacher, and the makeup of the assembly.

Regardless of how the life of the deceased is included in the sermon, the preacher is sensitive to personal and family history, neither publicly airing difficulties nor denying or negating them in the sermon. Most important, the preacher incorporates the life of the deceased into the sermon in ways that lift up God's faithfulness. The preacher relates the life and death of this particular deceased person and the grief of these particular mourners to the universal hope revealed in Christ's death and resurrection. In so doing, the preacher guards against delivering words from the pulpit that ought to be said in private. Giving overly personal details about the life of the deceased and the state of the family singles out those who are most vulnerable for public examination and often causes them to feel self-conscious and embarrassed. The members of the assembly may feel uncomfortable, because they know too much about the deceased and family, and empty, because they have not experienced God's presence, grace, and power.

Like all preaching, the funeral sermon is a response to and proclamation of God's promise recorded in scripture. The preacher brings scripture, the deceased and those who grieve, and the church through its liturgy and teachings into mutual conversation and reflection. The hope is that the assembly, and in particular those who mourn, will recognize God's grace in the particular life of the deceased and in their own lives as good news in the face of this particular death. The preacher might explore some feature of our common humanity illuminated in the text, as well as a particular characteristic of the deceased, to witness to God's grace at work in a human life. The preacher might approach scripture as a mirror into which the assembly can look and see Christ reflected in the life of the deceased. Scripture might provide the language and images with which the preacher proclaims God's promised future, both the future in which we continue living without the deceased and that future when God's promise of resurrection will be fulfilled.

In crafting the sermon, the preacher carefully weighs the balance of theological content and pastoral sensitivity. The funeral is not the time for catechesis. The funeral sermon does not attempt to argue or prove Christian doctrine. It does not deal in the realm of abstractions. Instead, the funeral sermon attempts to clarify how and where the living God has been and is continually working to comfort and assure, and to bring healing and new life. Because people are less likely to objectively "think" on these occasions, scripture must speak to the heart, not only to the head. Images and narratives work better than explanations and concepts.

As in all preaching, the way the sermon is crafted is also shaped by the preacher, the assembly, and the mood of the service. The sermon is influenced by how the preacher understands the church's role at the time of death. How can the church and the pastor best witness to Christ's resurrection and to commend to God the deceased and those who mourn? The sermon is also shaped by how preachers regard the funeral sermon. For example, some preachers argue that people do not hear or even listen on these occasions, so the gospel is really proclaimed through the presence of the assembly, the actions of the liturgy, and music. Others feel that funeral sermons possess a certain urgency because confrontation with death makes people receptive to the gospel in ways they otherwise are not. Still others regard funeral sermons as among a congregation's best opportunities to attract members.

The assembly also shapes the sermon in several ways. The funeral sermon differs, depending on whether the assembly includes members of the congregation, baptized Christians, people of other faith traditions, or people who claim no relationship with God. The location of the funeral is often a good indication of the people who will attend, as are the choices desired and the decisions made about the funeral. The preacher might consider how the family understands God's involvement in their lives and in the service. People often have definite but often unspoken expectations of what should be included in a funeral sermon. Family members tend to think of including a eulogy or words about the deceased written and spoken by relatives and loved ones. The preacher must decide how to respond to these expectations.

Finally, the mood of the assembly will also influence the sermon. The strong emotions that charge these special days are often complex and conflicting. Members of the assembly might feel both grief over their loss and joy in the resurrection, as well as anger and relief. The preacher honors all these emotions without making them the focus or content of the sermon. The mood of the assembly is reflected in the sermon's tone and delivery.

Leading the Funeral Service: Preparation

Every Christian funeral is a unique celebration of Christ's resurrection. The individual life that the assembly remembers and commends to God, as well as the needs and wishes of the family and those who mourn, shape the content of the funeral service in many ways. The choices made about the service also depend on whether the deceased is a baptized Christian, whether the body or cremated remains are present, whether the funeral is held in the church, and whether holy communion is celebrated as part of the service. The Funeral service in *Evangelical Lutheran Worship* is intended primarily for use with the body or cremated remains of a baptized Christian present, and the service presumes a location in the congregation's worship space (without precluding other locations). However, the notes include ways to adapt the service for use as a memorial service or with an unbaptized person. When the liturgy is a memorial service, the texts may be used without the accompanying actions. When the deceased was not baptized, the thanksgiving for baptism is omitted and the second prayer of the day may be used. The references to the coffin in the liturgy also include possibilities of an urn or other smaller container, in which the ashes of the deceased are placed after cremation. Other adaptations of the service for particular circumstances are a natural part of pastoral ministry at the time of death.

The manner in which the funeral is conducted is determined in many ways by the realities of the worship space. Therefore, those who plan funerals attend to the placement of the coffin or urn, the procession and seating of the family and other mourners, and the movement of those who will lead the assembly. The worship space itself can proclaim death as the completion of baptism in numerous ways. At a minimum, the cover of the baptismal font could be removed and the font filled with water. Similarly, if a paschal candle is present, lighting it and placing it where the head of the coffin or the urn will be located for most of the service testifies to the presence of Christ and the deceased's participation in the resurrection. If space permits, both the coffin (or urn) and the paschal candle might be located near the baptismal font. When holy communion is a part of the service, the placement of the coffin should be planned not only to facilitate movement by the assembly but also so that there is some sign that the whole communion of saints, those who "are the Lord's" both in life and in death (Rom. 14:8), are gathered around the table of Christ.

The coffin is closed throughout the service. When the funeral is held in a funeral home the coffin is closed and in place before the service begins. Other items necessary for the service are put in their appropriate places. These items may include a small table for the urn, a funeral pall (or a pall or similar cloth suitable for covering an urn), processional cross and torches, the lectionary or Bible, and an evergreen branch (or another suitable means for sprinkling water from the font) for the thanksgiving for baptism. When communion is part of the service, the table and elements are prepared according to the congregation's practice. The ministers vest in albs; the presiding minister wears the appropriate vestments in the color of the season.

Those who will participate in leading the service are identified and their responsibilities are explained to them. These persons may include pallbearers, ushers, and those who will place the pall; participants in the procession; family and friends who will offer comment or make a vocal or instrumental offering of music; those who will read scripture, lead the prayers of intercession, bring forward the bread and wine, and distribute communion; and any other assisting ministers necessary. These leaders generally find it helpful to walk through the service in the worship space, when that is possible.

Gathering

The Gathering section may include an introductory address by the presiding minister; thanksgiving for baptism; placing a pall on the coffin and other symbols of baptism; a procession with a hymn, song, or anthem; and the greeting and prayer of the day. As suggested above, the specific elements used in the Gathering rite, as well as the order in which they are used, depend on the space where the service takes place and the particular circumstances of the deceased and the family.

The ministers may meet the coffin and the bereaved, usually the immediate family, at the entrance of the church and lead them into the assembly, or may escort them from the place they have been waiting. Alternatively, the coffin might be in place, and the family seated with the assembly prior to the start of the service. When the baptismal font is located near the church door, the ministers lead the coffin and family to the font for the start of the service. Otherwise, the ministers and family may remain at a place near the door where the assembly can hear what is said. When, prior to the beginning of the service, the coffin is in place at the front and the family is seated, the ministers might begin the service from the front of the church.

The assembly stands and faces the presiding minister. The presiding minister addresses the family (and the assembly), using one or both of the paragraphs provided or similar words. This address is intended to introduce the service and extend a gracious welcome to the assembly. The first alternative describes the purposes of the gathering as worship: proclamation, remembrance, commendation, and mutual comfort. The second alternative (from 2 Corinthians 1) praises God as the source of mercy and consolation, and describes God's activity at the time of death as comforting us and empowering us to comfort others. When the name of the deceased is inserted in the liturgy, as in the first choice of address, it is appropriate to use only the given (Christian) name, as a way of recalling baptism and assuring that, as God's child, the deceased is known to God. One of the two paragraphs might be used, or they might be combined.

Thanksgiving for Baptism

When the deceased is a baptized Christian, a thanksgiving for baptism may follow. Either the presiding minister or a representative of the congregation declares the significance of God's gift of baptism using one of the two options provided. The first, a paraphrase of Romans 6:3-5, celebrates baptism as participation in Christ's death and resurrection and the promise of new life. The second, based on Galatians 3:27, describes baptism as putting on Christ and declares that the baptized will be clothed with glory in the day of Christ's coming. An assisting minister might hold the book as the presiding minister or representative of the congregation speaks the declaration, possibly dipping a hand in the water and letting the water fall back into the font in order to visibly connect the words and baptism.

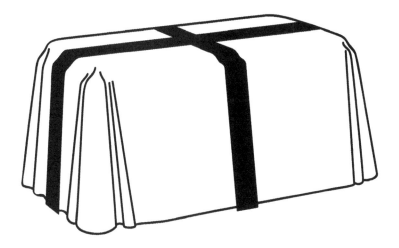

Fig. 8.1. Pall for a coffin. *The pall is a reminder of being clothed with Christ at baptism. It also signifies the dignity and equality of baptism by making simple and costly coffins appear alike.*

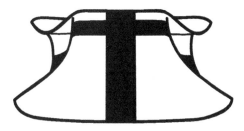

Fig. 8.2. Pall for an urn. *Like a pall for a coffin, the pall for an urn symbolizes Christ's righteousness with which we are clothed at baptism.*

As a sign of being clothed with Christ in baptism, family members, pallbearers, or other assisting ministers may place a pall over the coffin or a smaller but similar cloth over the urn. The white cloth placed over the coffin or urn is a reminder of the robe of Christ's righteousness with which the baptized are clothed, and which may have been symbolized earlier in life by the white robe given at baptism. The pall also signifies the dignity and equality of baptism by covering both costly and simple coffins and making them the same. Regardless of whether a pall is used, other decorations, including floral arrangements, flags, and other insignia that distinguish the deceased and suggest that salvation depends on something other than Christ, are removed from the coffin prior to the service. It may also be possible to place the pall in silence—before, after, or in place of the spoken words—and thus allow the symbol to speak for itself.

When the pall is in place, the presiding minister may lead the acclamation, which recalls the profession of faith in the order of Holy Baptism. Here as in the profession of faith, each person of the triune God is named and proclaimed. Rather than the presiding minister asking questions and the assembly responding, the presiding minister names each person of the triune God, and the assembly offers glory, praise, and worship. As a visible sign recalling the gift of baptism, the presiding minister may use an evergreen branch, or one of various liturgical implements designed for this purpose, to sprinkle the coffin three times, once while naming each person of the Trinity. When the coffin cannot be placed near the font, a basin of water may be used from which to draw water to sprinkle the coffin.

At the conclusion of the thanksgiving for baptism, or when the thanksgiving for baptism is omitted, a hymn, song, or anthem may be sung. Congregational song provides a way for the rest of the assembly

Fig. 8.3. Remembering baptism. *The gift of baptism may be recalled at funerals by dipping an evergreen branch into the font and sprinkling the coffin three times, each time naming a person of the Trinity.*

to gather in the Spirit and with the bereaved, and it is also practical in accompanying a procession that may take place at this point. When the first part of the Gathering rite takes place near the door of the church, or when the baptismal font is a distance from the altar, the worship leaders, pallbearers, and the bereaved form a procession and, led by the ministers, enter the assembly. Typically, the procession includes (in order) assisting minister(s), presiding minister, pallbearers with the coffin, and the bereaved. It may be led by the processional cross, torches (or the paschal candle), and perhaps a book bearer. The procession provides a meaningful way of involving children in the service. In the context of the funeral liturgy, processions recall the Exodus, when God's people passed through the water from slavery to freedom and from death to new life.

Where space permits, the coffin may be placed before the altar. In some places, it is customary to position the casket with the head toward the altar if the deceased was a pastor and with the feet toward the altar if the deceased was not. The custom is said to reflect the accustomed place of the deceased in worship—facing the altar as part of the assembly or facing the people as the presiding minister. Like all other signs of status within the funeral liturgy, though, this practice may be seen to conflict with baptismal equality by honoring a dignity other than that of baptism, and perhaps should be allowed to fall into disuse. If a paschal candle is not present and torches are included in the procession, they may be placed at the head and foot of the casket. The processional cross is put in its accustomed place and the lectionary or Bible on the reading stand.

Greeting and Prayer of the Day

The ministers go to their places, either at the chairs or the center of the chancel, for the greeting and prayer of the day. Facing the assembly, the presiding minister uses the words of the apostle Paul (2 Cor. 13:13) to greet the people in the name of the triune God, and the assembly greets the presiding minister in return. The presiding minister's traditional gesture is to open the hands while speaking the apostolic greeting, bringing them together again as the assembly responds, "And also with you."

The presiding minister invites the assembly to pray ("Let us pray"). After a brief silence in which the assembly enters into common prayer,

Fig. 8.4. Funeral procession. *In the context of the funeral liturgy, the procession recalls the Exodus—from slavery to freedom and from death to new life. It may be led by a processional cross, torches, and a book bearer, followed, in order, by assisting minister(s), presiding minister, pallbearers and coffin, and the bereaved.*

the presiding minister prays the prayer of the day, possibly lifting the hands in a posture of prayer (see Fig. 3.3, p. 66). Three alternative prayers of the day are included in the rite. The first prayer names the deceased as a brother or sister in Christ, a gift from God, and a companion on the pilgrimage of faith. This description of the deceased, together with the explicit reference to "faith . . . in the victory of our Lord Jesus Christ," commends this prayer for use when the deceased is baptized. The second prayer, which describes God as the source of all mercy and is expressly for those who mourn, is more appropriate if the deceased was not baptized or lived outside the covenant of baptism. The third prayer is for use when the deceased is a child.

The assembly sits after the prayer of the day. The gathering may conclude with a time when relatives or associates of the deceased comment briefly in thanksgiving for and remembrance of their loved one. If the inclusion of a eulogy in the service is desired, this

Fig. 8.5. Apostolic greeting. *The presiding minister may communicate the mutuality of the greeting by extending open arms toward the assembly. The assembly responds, "And also with you."*

is the appropriate time for it. Those who will speak are identified in advance of the funeral so that they might prepare their remarks. If the family desires a longer time of sharing, in which people can speak spontaneously, it is more appropriately included in the meal after the service. Locating a brief eulogy, if used, at this point in the service helps the assembly, after looking backward in thanksgiving to a completed life on earth, now look forward in hope to the consummation of that life with God, as it listens to the proclamation of God's word.

Word

The fullest expression of the Word section of the service includes scripture readings, sermon, hymn of the day, the Apostles' Creed, and prayers of intercession. When holy communion is not celebrated, the Lord's Prayer concludes the intercessions. Two or three scripture readings are proclaimed. In the service of Holy Communion, the established pattern is a reading from the Old Testament, a reading from the New Testament letters, and a reading from one of the gospels. Whether two or three readings are included, the last should be from the gospels. The readings chosen may well reflect the season of the church year. The readings selected should also express the heart of the Christian faith, the unconditional love of God and the hope of the resurrection. Including family members in selecting the readings and inviting them to proclaim the readings in the service is a significant way of involving the family. It is helpful to provide the family with a list of appropriate readings from which to choose. (See Appendix C, p. 232.)

The last reading, from the gospels, may be preceded by a sung acclamation and be proclaimed by the minister who is preaching. When a psalm is selected as a response to a reading from the Old Testament, particularly Psalm 23, many people find it comforting and meaningful for the assembly to say or sing it together. The assembly might also sing appropriate hymns and songs in response to the readings.

The readings are followed by a sermon, which is preached by the presiding minister or another pastor. The funeral sermon is a proclamation of the promise of the gospel that empowers the assembly to honestly face this particular death in the hope of Christ's resurrection. The sermon takes the needs and concerns of those who are bereaved very seriously. It recalls and gives thanks for the life of the deceased in ways that lift up God's grace and point to the hope of the resurrection for everyone present. (See pages 164–168 for additional comments on the objectives and possibilities for the funeral sermon.) A period of silence for reflection follows the sermon. Only under rare circumstances might it be acceptable to omit the sermon, trusting scripture to proclaim God's comfort and hope.

In response to the sermon, the assembly stands and professes its faith and proclaims the gospel by singing the hymn of the day and confessing the creed. The notes describe the hymn of the day as "the principal opportunity for the assembly to express grief and proclaim hope in song." This description provides helpful guidance for selecting the hymn of the day. The hymn is one the assembly can and will sing, and that helps them express grief. For this to be true, the hymn is one the assembly knows and probably loves. The hymn of the day is also one that enables the assembly to proclaim hope, which means that the hymn's theme or message is Jesus Christ.

The Apostles' Creed, which is used at baptism, may follow the hymn of the day. The assembly professing the faith together can provide a powerful experience of the communion of saints. Thus, the presiding minister may introduce the creed by saying, "With the whole church, let us confess our faith." Since the creed is a confession of faith that unites the whole church, it is appropriately omitted when the deceased was not baptized or the assembly is not predominantly Christian.

The Word portion of the service concludes with the prayers of intercession. A model for appropriate prayers is included in the leaders edition (670). These prayers may be adapted or other prayers prepared for the occasion. When an assisting minister prepares the intercessions, petitions may be included that ask God to grant peace to the church, to bring all the baptized and all people to the fulfillment of God's promise, for strength and courage to live by faith, for grace to meet the days ahead, and for the communion of saints, as well as prayers specifically for the deceased and those who mourn. Short petitions better involve the assembly. Prayers that ask God to do something, as opposed to asking God to help the assembly to do something, reinforce God's ongoing presence and participation. The assembly is not bargaining with or persuading God but trusting in and depending on God's love, faithfulness, and goodwill. Using biblical images and language reinforces the proclamation of God's word. As in so much of the funeral service, the precise form and content of the prayers of intercession depend on the circumstances surrounding the funeral and the character of the assembly. Particularly if the assembly is following the service from the pew edition, it will be helpful if each petition concludes "God of mercy" so that the assembly might voice its assent using the words given in the assembly edition, "hear our prayer."

The prayers of intercession are best led by someone other than the presiding minister to indicate that the prayers are an action of the assembly in response to God's word. To visibly connect the prayers and God's word, the intercessions might be led from a reading desk or lectern. The prayers may also be led by the assisting minister standing at his or her chair, or as the ministers stand before the assembly. The presiding minister typically prays the concluding prayer to the prayers of intercession ("God of all grace . . ." or another suitable prayer), and the assembly responds, "Amen."

A service without communion continues with the Lord's Prayer. The presiding minister may introduce the Lord's Prayer using one of the two options provided (LE 671). The choice of which form of the Lord's Prayer will be used depends upon the practice of the congregation and the nature of the assembly. The Lord's Prayer is perhaps the part of the service in which most people can most comfortably participate. The choice of versions may honor this consideration. It cannot be assumed, however, that people know either of the two versions of the Lord's Prayer from memory; the text should be provided to the assembly either by referring to the book or by including it in a worship aid.

Meal

As discussed above (pages 162–164), the decision about including holy communion in the funeral service depends upon the nature of the assembly. When communion is celebrated, the service continues immediately following the prayers of intercession with the exchange of peace. Following the peace, family members or friends of the deceased may bring the bread and wine forward as an offering hymn is sung; this is another excellent way to involve children in the service. Among the thanksgivings at the table, fitting choices may include thanksgiving I, which includes the promise of John 3:16; thanksgiving VI, which asks God to give us our portion with all the saints in light and refers to the prayers of the saints of every time and every place; and thanksgiving X, which declares that God has entered our sorrows to grant us life. Family and friends of the deceased may assist in distributing communion. All who are baptized are welcome at the table; to restrict the bread and wine to the family of the deceased is contrary to God's gift of the sacrament. Appropriate music, especially congregational singing, enhances the sense of community. The meal concludes with the prayer after communion, which is led by an assisting minister.

Sending

If we understand that different parts of the pattern of worship are more prominent in some services than in others, we might think of the Sending as especially prominent in the funeral liturgy. Everything the assembly has done in the service to this point—giving thanks for baptism, proclaiming and hearing the gospel, and receiving Christ's body and blood—prepares the assembly to be sent to live in the hope and peace of Christ, even as they symbolically take leave of the deceased and "send" her or him into God's all-embracing hands. In addition to the blessing and dismissal, the sending portion of the funeral service includes the commendation, in which the assembly entrusts the deceased to God's care, and the committal, in which the assembly places the remains of the deceased in their final resting place.

Commendation

The ministers go from the table or their chairs to the coffin for the commendation. In some places, it is customary for the immediate family to surround the coffin as a visible expression of the great cloud of witnesses (Heb. 12:1). At a memorial service, the presiding minister may go to the place where the prayers were led. The presiding minister invites the assembly into the commendation, saying, "Let us commend. . . ." Only the given name is used in these words of invitation and in the prayer itself. After a suitable period of silence, the presiding minister may lay a hand on the coffin while praying the prayer of commendation. If family members have gathered at the coffin, they may place hands there as well.

The prayer of commendation recalls Jesus' last prayer from the cross (Luke 23:46, quoting Psalm 31:5). It is the assembly's way of entrusting a loved one into the arms of God's mercy. Through this prayer, the assembly acknowledges that it is now separated from the deceased and that its relationship with the deceased has changed. Melinda Quivik observes that the prayer of commendation allows the assembly to put into words all the deepest things that can be said of a person:

> (1) You and I belong to God. We are, more precisely, lambs—young and needy all our lives. (2) We are sinners—unable to achieve perfection and unworthy of even the crumbs that fall from the Lord's table. (3) We are redeemed by the Shepherd's own work—made worthy, made righteous, made able to stand before the Lord along with the other saints. All of these things can be said of both the deceased and the mourners. . . . Finally, the commendation (4) names the bond that still exists between the mourners and the deceased. The prayer asks God to receive into God's arms this one who has died.[3]

The commendation is understood as an expression of faith and hope. These words are what the assembly would say if it were present at the moment of death. The assembly prays that God will give the deceased eternal life, the joys of heaven, and companionship with the saints because the assembly trusts the promise of baptism and hopes in the promise of resurrection. The assembly does not pray to persuade God or change God's mind. The church follows Jesus' example when it commends its beloved dead to God, remembering God's unbreakable promise, given when they were joined to Christ's death and resurrection in baptism. Trusting in God's grace and mercy, the church commends its loved ones to God.

Following the commendation, a farewell hymn may be sung. A setting of "Now, Lord, you let your servant go in peace" (AE p. 113 or 135, #200–203, 313) or an acclamation (#222–223) is suggested. The first acclamation ("Into paradise") uses biblical images and allusions to poetically entrust the deceased to God's care. This acclamation is addressed to the deceased and complements the prayer of commendation. The second acclamation ("All of us go down to the dust") anticipates the committal and sings of hope even at the grave.

During the singing, a procession may form in the same order as before: cross, torches, the ministers, pallbearers with the coffin, the bereaved. An assisting minister dismisses the assembly, using the words provided, either before or after the farewell hymn. When the dismissal comes before the sung farewell, the assembly may join the procession behind the bereaved. In this case it may be preferable to have the ministers follow the coffin. The pall is removed from the coffin in the narthex of the church, and symbols removed from the coffin before the service may be put in place. The processional cross may be taken to the cemetery or place of interment, if there will be a procession.

One possible alternative within the commendation may be especially appropriate when interment will not take place immediately after the funeral, when the place of interment is a great distance from the location of the funeral, or in the case of a memorial service. The presiding minister may say the verse from the committal, "Rest eternal grant *her/him*, O Lord . . . " after the prayer of commendation, or the verse may be sung as the response to the prayer of commendation. The minister may then bless the assembly using one of the blessings provided in the committal service. A sending hymn or song may then be sung, particularly if there is to be a procession. The assisting minister then dismisses the assembly.

Committal

The committal is the most ancient and universal part of the funeral service. The family and community process with the body to the grave or place of interment with accompanying ritual. The gospel of Luke recounts one such procession, when the people of Nain accompanied a widow and the body of her only son (Luke 7:11-17). While the church does not expect Jesus to interrupt and stop its funeral processions, the church lays its dead to rest in the confidence that Jesus will raise them to new life. Although there are pressures in a sometimes death-denying culture to minimize or avoid this part of the community's ritual, it continues to be important both theologically and psychologically, and leaders should counsel against downplaying it for the sake of convenience or to avoid discomfort.

The committal service in *Evangelical Lutheran Worship* is intended to follow immediately at the conclusion of the funeral service. However, the committal may take place at a later time. This arrangement may be especially appropriate when the body is cremated. Under certain circumstances, such as when the body is interred immediately after death and a memorial service is held later or when the body is donated to medical science, the committal may precede the funeral. The prayers and readings in the committal service are helpful resources for family members and friends who scatter ashes in a location where it is not possible for the assembly to gather. Regardless of how the committal rite is used, printed materials are normally not provided to participants in this service; the leader may therefore need to prompt the responses of the assembly.

The leaders edition (672) provides a number of scripture passages that may be read as the assembly gathers at the cemetery. (The pastoral

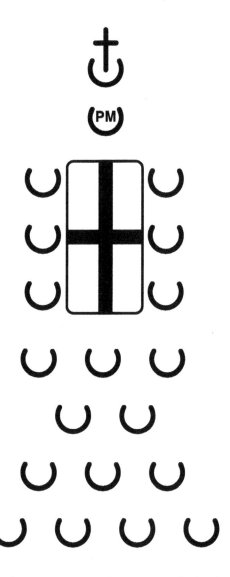

Fig. 8.6. Gathering at the grave or resting place. *The cross, if used, and presiding minister may lead the coffin to the resting place, followed by the mourners.*

care volume includes the texts of these passages.) Ideally, the assembly gathers at the hearse, and the presiding minister (following the processional cross, if present) leads the coffin to the grave or place of interment, followed by the people. The scripture passages may then be read by the presiding minister, an assisting minister, or people in the procession as the assembly walks to the grave. Alternatively, or in addition, a cantor may sing one or more of the suggested psalms. The entire assembly might recite Psalm 23 together. The procession might conclude with the reading of John 11:25-26a, in which Jesus declares himself to be the resurrection and the life.

When those who have gathered are settled at the grave or resting place, the presiding minister greets the assembly. (If a military, fraternal, civic, or other ceremony is to take place, it is perhaps best to include it before or just after this greeting.) The presiding minister then prays the appointed or another suitable prayer. It may be appropriate to omit this prayer or to substitute another prayer when the deceased is not baptized.

The proclamation of God's word from scripture follows. When the committal occurs immediately after the funeral service, a single reading may be sufficient. When the committal takes place at another time, several readings are appropriate. Particularly in such a case, the readings may be followed by a brief homily and words remembering the deceased.

The committal follows. The words of committal declare our hope in the resurrection to eternal life as the power by which the assembly commends the deceased to God and commits the body to its resting places. Four alternatives ("the ground, the deep . . .") for the place of interment are provided. The committal continues with words reminiscent of both the words that God spoke to Adam (Gen. 3:19) and the words the church speaks on Ash Wednesday. The deceased is now included in this common human experience. The words of committal conclude with the Aaronic blessing (Num. 6:24-26). Circumstances may require that the words and actions of the committal be adapted.

Whenever it is possible, the coffin is lowered into the ground or the urn is put in its resting place in the presence of those gathered. (A prior request to the funeral director may be necessary for this to occur.) Pastoral-care providers advise that it is upsetting to the family to leave the body resting on top of the device by which it will later be lowered into the grave after they have departed; some mourners even question whether their loved one is where she or he is supposed to be. When the body can be placed in the ground prior to the words of committal, casting and even shoveling dirt is a powerful gesture. One approach is to put three shovelfuls of dirt on the casket in remembrance of being buried with Christ in baptism. Another approach is to allow everyone present to participate in the burial by putting a shovelful or handful of dirt on the grave. Similarly, everyone present might participate in scattering cremated ashes. When the words of committal precede burial or when ashes are placed in a mausoleum, the presiding minister might lay a hand on the coffin or the urn while speaking the words of committal. In some places, it is customary for the presiding minister to use sand to sprinkle the coffin as a symbolic burial or to make the sign of the cross on the coffin at the words "earth to earth, ashes to ashes, dust to dust." In this approach, the presiding minister then lays a hand on the coffin for the blessing that concludes the words of committal.

The response, "Rest eternal grant *her/him*, O Lord, . . ." may be sung by a cantor or spoken by the minister. The assembly may join the minister in saying, ". . . and let light perpetual shine upon *her/him*." With these words, the action of commending the deceased to God and committing the body to its resting place is complete.

The presiding minister then leads the assembly in prayer for those who mourn. Two prayers are included in the service. Both ask for support in this life and participation in the life to come. The first speaks to the human condition and may be more appropriate when the death had been anticipated for some time. The second alternative, which speaks of the brokenhearted and describes the assembly as weak, troubled, fearful, and doubting, may be the appropriate choice when death is shocking, unexpected, or seemingly unfair or unnecessary. Though named in the second prayer, the deceased is referred to rather than prayed for because the deceased rests secure in God's care. The Lord's Prayer may be prayed, especially if the committal is separated in time from the rest of the funeral service. The minister then blesses the people with words from Hebrews 13:20-21 or a trinitarian blessing, and either the presiding minister or an assisting minister sends them forth in peace.

Like the baptismal life, the funeral liturgy is a journey, a vigil recalling that of Easter. Proclaiming God's unconditional promise of new life and commending a loved one to both God's unfailing care and a community of saints—the heart of the church's journey at the time of death—is the same thing the Christian assembly does at the font. Reflecting both sadness and hope, the mood of the funeral liturgy is itself a way of dying and rising with Christ. Those who work with families to plan the funerals of their loved ones are privileged to bring this perspective and gift to particular circumstances of life and death in ways that embody the gospel and celebrate death as the completion of baptism.

CHAPTER NINE

Marriage

Lutheran Christians understand marriage in two ways. On the one hand, marriage is God's gift. God intends to bring strength and joy to those who enter into marriage and, through marriage, to promote the well-being of the whole human family. On the other hand, marriage is a human estate. Two people make vows to each other, which are publicly witnessed, and society recognizes their status as legally married. In the order of Marriage in *Evangelical Lutheran Worship* (AE pp. 275, 286–291; LE 659, 675–686), the Christian assembly surrounds those who enter into this human estate with the gifts of the presence and support of the Christian community, the promise of God's word proclaimed from scripture, and prayers of blessing and intercession.

The Christian practice of surrounding the institution of marriage with God's promise is evident in the pattern for worship for Marriage in *Evangelical Lutheran Worship* (AE p. 275), where the words and actions associated with marriage are encircled by the pattern of the Sunday assembly. For example, the declaration of intention, which is included in the Gathering rite and can be celebrated at the font, recalls the questions addressed both to those about to be baptized and the assembly when candidates are presented for holy baptism. The other ritual acts of marriage (vows, giving of rings, acclamation, and marriage blessing) are located between the hymn of the day and the prayers of intercession, the same place that the baptism of adults is celebrated in the Sunday assembly. Just as provision is made for the newly baptized to begin their life in Christ by going to the table to receive the Lord's supper, provision is made for the couple to begin their married life by receiving the body and blood of Christ together with the assembly. In all these ways, the rite in *Evangelical Lutheran Worship* celebrates the human estate of marriage as God's gift. The couple responds to God's gift by approaching their marriage as a baptismal vocation.

The notes (LE 45–46) include helpful suggestions for adapting the service, depending on location and circumstance; these options are discussed in this chapter. Yet before attending to these details, those who plan weddings—their own or weddings within the congregation—are well advised to think about matters such as marriage as a baptismal vocation, the influence of cultural values on marriage and marriage rites, how the gospel will be proclaimed in the service, and the appropriateness of the couple beginning married life by receiving holy communion with the assembly. Each of these topics is specifically addressed in this chapter.

A Baptismal Vocation

Baptism is the source of our most basic dignity and vocation. As an expression of baptism, marriage is one kind of baptismal call. Marriage is one way that Christians participate in the priesthood of all believers in response to the promise God made to them by water and God's word. In marriage, one particular human being can become an embodied expression of God's unconditional love, revealed in Jesus Christ, for another particular human being. A particular marriage can be seen by others as one way God's love is expressed. When the baptismal vocation of marriage is marked by faithfulness that unfolds in service for the sake of the life of the world, it is an expression of Jesus' self-giving love. Reflecting on marriage as a baptismal vocation yields important implications for the relationship of partners in marriage and for how marriage is celebrated in the church.

First, God's baptismal promise of lifelong faithfulness and daily forgiveness is both the source and the model of marriage. Jesus remained faithful to God and to us, to the point of giving his life on a cross. In baptism God joins us to Christ's death and resurrection and promises to remain faithful to us, even when we are not faithful to God. Trusting in God's faithfulness, the partners in marriage pledge lifelong faithfulness to each other. Relying on God's forgiveness, they are empowered to forgive one another. Marriage, like baptism, is daily dying to sin and rising to new life as the partners in marriage respond to God's love by loving each other as God loves them. From a Christian perspective, couples can only promise lifelong faithfulness in the marriage rite by trusting in and responding to God's promise of lifelong faithfulness in baptism. Human love is not enough. The promises couples make in the Christian marriage rite reflect this reality.

Second, in baptism we become children of God and equal members of the body of Christ. Baptismal equality calls us to live with each other the way Christ lived with us. Paul reminds us, "As many of you as were baptized into Christ have clothed yourselves with Christ. There is no longer Jew or Greek, there is no longer slave or free, there is no longer male and female; for all of you are one in Christ Jesus" (Gal. 3:27-28). The equality we receive in baptism applies to all human relationships—partners in marriage; parents and children; employers and employees. All are to live toward the other as Christ lives toward them.

Since all Christians are equal by virtue of their baptism into Christ, the church does not consider marriage as either higher or lower, better or worse than any other baptismal vocation. During the Reformation, when the church thought in terms of a hierarchy of callings, rather than a coequal priesthood of all the baptized, Martin Luther and the reformers considered marriage and parenthood to be Christian vocations more honorable than that of monks and nuns.[1] In our day, the church may need to take care so as not to elevate those who are married over those who are not.

Since all the baptized and all baptismal vocations are equal before God, all members of the body of Christ are treated equally in the life and worship of the church. Within marriage, partners live together as equals. The church interprets directions such as "be subject to . . ." in Ephesians 5:22, as well as promises to obey in some marriage rites, in the context of Christ's relationship with the church. Partners in marriage willingly are subject to and obey each other within the context of self-giving love for each other, "just as Christ loved the church and gave himself up for her" (Eph. 5:25). Biblical instructions to "be subject to" and marriage promises to obey presume a relationship grounded in and modeled on Christ's relationship with the church. In assemblies where this is not explicitly understood, such words are best avoided altogether, so that they are not interpreted in ways that undermine baptismal equality. Everything in the marriage rite ought to express and maintain the baptismal dignity of those joining their lives in marriage. For example, the couple freely assents to being married. Wedding rites or customs that suggest that the partners in marriage are not equal before God, or that either the bride or the groom is property, such as a father giving his daughter to her husband, undermine baptismal equality, and their appropriateness within a Christian marriage service must be questioned.

Finally, marriage is one way the baptized participate in the life of the Christian community and share its mission of bearing God's creative and redeeming word to all the world. Christian marriage is missional when it points to and is a sign of Christ's marriage to the church and, through the church, to the world. Christian marriage helps people, both inside and outside the Christian community, to glimpse the love with which Christ gave himself up for the world. To support marriage as a response to and proclamation of Christ's self-giving love, the church celebrates marriage within the gathered Christian community and seeks the participation of the entire assembly in the service. Everything in the service attests to and celebrates God's unconditional love for the whole world.

Couples who appreciate marriage as their baptismal vocation will most often choose to be married in church, surrounded by the Christian community. These couples plan their weddings so that God's word is central and baptismal images are rich and vivid. These weddings may well include the sacramental meal so that the couple can join the assembly in participating in God's promised marriage feast and be strengthened to bear witness to the marriage of Christ and the world.

One way that marriage as a baptismal vocation can be vividly demonstrated is by celebrating the order of marriage in the principal service of the Sunday assembly, rather than as a separate service. This arrangement gives God rather than the couple, central place. In a sense, the couple is even subordinate to the assembly, which gathers primarily to worship God rather than to witness the bride and groom exchange their vows. The assembly exercises its baptismal role and responsibility to support and nurture the couple in their life together through the preaching of the word and the administration of the sacraments. Though part of the assembly, the couple is also the assembly's guest, rather than the host of a wedding. As we will see, in North America, celebrating marriage in the context of Sunday worship makes a powerful, countercultural statement.

A Worldly Estate

For many couples, thinking of marriage as a baptismal vocation is new and unfamiliar. This is understandable, since marriage rites and even marriage itself are only secondarily Christian in nature; marriage and marriage rites originate in society rather than in church. Jesus indicates that marriage existed since creation (Matt. 19:4-6). A process of transition in which a couple moves from being unmarried to socially recognized as married is part of every culture. These processes possess deep cultural connections. The way the couple becomes engaged and the partners express their consent to marry, as well as the way the society gathers around and supports them, differs from culture to culture. In the long history of marriage, Christian meanings, including baptismal vocation, and explicitly Christian practices are relatively late additions.

Though Luther and the reformers considered marriage and parenthood to be baptismal vocations surpassing those of monks and nuns, they regarded marriage as a "worldly estate" instituted by God, rather than as a sacrament instituted by Christist.[2] Yet, though a worldly estate, marriage has a scriptural foundation and is a divine creation and command. Luther nevertheless held that marriage should be regulated by the state and that getting married before a civil magistrate is as valid as marriage in the church. So, for example, when a civil marriage has taken place and the couple comes to the Christian community asking for God's blessing, the consent and marriage vows need not be repeated but may be affirmed. (The *Evangelical Lutheran Worship* pastoral-care occasional services provide an order for prayer and blessing after a civil marriage.) Yet to honor marriage as a Christian vocation equal in ceremony to that of monks and nuns, and to provide pastoral care to those entering into marriage, Luther recommended that marriage be celebrated in a church.

Luther understood the influence that cultural practices exert on marriage rites and was not concerned with these customs as long as common prayer and God's blessing are prominent. "Since marriage and the married estate are worldly matters," Luther wrote, "it behooves us pastors or ministers of the church not to attempt to order or govern anything connected with it, but to permit every city and land to continue its own use and custom in this connection" (LW 53:111-112). Luther's marriage rite was a simple exchange of vows and rings and the pronouncement of marriage, followed by scripture readings (and probably a sermon) and a blessing.

The proclamation of the word of God and the prayer for God's blessing on the couple and their household are considered the universal Christian additions to the human process of marriage. By this nuptial blessing, the church acknowledges the union "in Christ" of husband and wife. The church's essential role in marriage is defined by this blessing. The church neither marries people nor determines whether they can be married; these are functions of the state, though often carried out by representatives of the church. The church proclaims God's unconditional love and faithfulness and asks God to bless this couple in their life together.

Christian Ideals Meet Cultural Realities

Though adding the proclamation of God's word and God's blessing to the culture's marriage rites theoretically balances the Christian and societal aspects of marriage, many weddings are characterized by the collision of faith and culture. Marriage has always been the most difficult rite of passage for the church to negotiate. In the case of funerals, for example, concern over the fate of the deceased, coupled with the grief of the family, gave the church greater control over funeral rites. People are less willing to defer to the church when it comes to marriage. The collision of conflicting notions of marriage is evident in the enormous influence that the values of the broader cultures in which Christians live exercise over Christian marriage rites. Some of our most cherished wedding practices, including the bride wearing white and processing down the aisle as the center of attention, the father giving the bride away, choices of music, and ceremonial innovations like the unity candle reflect the values of the culture rather than the church.

In the United States, marriage is a civil matter regulated by the states, which may be celebrated in the church. Since most weddings take place in churches and are conducted by religious leaders according to ecclesial rites, people assume marriage is primarily a church ceremony. In reality, in the formal and legal making of the marriage, the pastor or other identified religious leader functions as a magistrate for the state. Today, the most prominent cultural value with regard to marriage is that the wedding is considered the pivotal experience in people's lives and marital love the principal focus of their emotions, obligations, and satisfactions.[3] Marriage rites are viewed as expressions of couples' love and intimacy; fidelity and community are secondary concerns. Since our culture celebrates marriage as being primarily about the lives of the bride and groom, the ceremony is often expected to reflect the couple's personal tastes and is designed to make a unique statement about them.

Moreover, since the wedding is concerned with the bride and groom, those who gather function like an audience at a performance rather than as participants in a worship service.

The notion of marriage as an individual expression and choice is reinforced by changing sexual norms, greater acceptance of divorce and children born outside of marriage, and self-fulfillment as a priority. This view of marriage is a change from understanding the wedding as a political or economic arrangement, which were dominant values well into the nineteenth century. But understanding marriage as two individuals directing their lives toward each other to the exclusion of others is very different from marriage as a baptismal vocation. As a response to God's gift and promise, marriage as a baptismal vocation is directed toward God, a witness to God's faithfulness, and a way of serving the world. Weddings, then, are frequently the scene of conflict between church and culture as the church's understanding of marriage, grounded in the gospel, collides with a cultural understanding of marriage based on economic and political realities or, in our time, romantic love.

Balancing competing values when planning a wedding is frequently a matter of negotiation. The church responds differently, depending on what the couple desires. In some instances those who plan weddings will incorporate or adopt the desired practices in ways that make them appropriate to the gospel and the church's understanding of marriage. In other instances, the congregation will choose to make a countercultural statement by resisting practices that communicate marriage-related values that may be contrary to the gospel, such as individualism, consumerism, and an understanding of love that is limited to romance. Occasionally, couples are so intent on practices that communicate values contrary to the Christian faith that they render a church wedding undesirable and even inappropriate. In these instances, the church's response is to sincerely help the couple discover an appropriate location and ceremony for their wedding.

Celebrating Holy Communion as a Marriage Feast

Almost universally across cultures, when a couple joins their lives in marriage the celebration includes a meal, a banquet, or a feast, which is characterized by joy and relative extravagance. Holy communion is the church's feast in celebration of the marriage between Christ, the bridegroom, and Christ's bride, the church. Here we receive a foretaste of "the marriage supper of the Lamb" (Rev. 19:7-9), which we will share with Christ and all the saints in the fullness of the reign of God. The church has long used the marriage feast as a metaphor to proclaim the gospel and illustrate the relationship between Christ and the church in holy communion. The New Testament writers love the image of the wedding banquet. In John's gospel, Jesus reveals his glory for the first time during a marriage feast at Cana in Galilee. In Matthew, Jesus compares the reign of God with a wedding banquet at which the host's chief concern is that the hall be filled. The image of Christ as bridegroom and the church as Christ's bride is found in all four gospels, in Paul, and in Revelation.

Writing in the fourth century, St. Ambrose used lush sensual images drawn from the Song of Solomon to describe the relationship between Christ and the church in the sacramental meal. When we receive the bread and the cup, we receive Christ's love for us, which is as passionate and intimate as love between a bridegroom and a bride. Christ, the bridegroom, gives his body and blood, his very life, for his bride. We become one with Christ as we receive and return Christ's intimate and abiding love. "Just as I have loved you," Jesus commands, "you also should love one another" (John 13:34). More than giving us an example, Jesus' intimate love is the source of our love. Receiving Christ's body and blood strengthens the bride and groom, partners in marriage, and every member of the assembly to love one another as Jesus loves us.

Since we share so intimately in Christ's love when we receive the Lord's supper, those who plan weddings may carefully consider whether including that sacrament in the service is appropriate for the assembly that will gather. Both *The Use of the Means of Grace* (49B) and the notes for the marriage service clearly state that when communion is part of the service, the sacrament is celebrated with the whole assembly. The gift of holy communion is not limited to the couple or the wedding party. If circumstances prevent including the assembly in the meal, a service without communion is used. One circumstance that prevents including the assembly in the meal is that a significant number of those attending the wedding are not baptized or are not practicing members of a church community. Another circumstance might be that celebrating holy communion will be more divisive than unifying, more exclusive than inviting, as people from differing religious traditions determine that they cannot or will not come to the table. In determining whether holy communion will be part of the marriage rite, those who plan are sensitive to both the wisdom of the family and the sacramental practices of churches from which friends and relatives may come.

Even as those who plan weddings are alert to circumstances that make inclusion of the meal ill-advised, they are mindful that Jesus is the bridegroom and extends the invitation to the feast. "Admission to the Sacrament is by invitation of the Lord, presented through the Church to those who are baptized" (UMG 37). The promise of baptism is a way the church assures believers that Jesus welcomes them to the marriage feast, regardless of any other status and despite whatever is happening in their lives. As a sign of hospitality, the congregation might include a brief statement in the worship folder, reflecting the guidance of *The Use of the Means of Grace* (49): "Believing in the real presence of Christ, [the Evangelical Lutheran Church in America] practices eucharistic hospitality. All baptized persons are welcome to Communion when they are visiting in the congregations of this church." This statement is intended to help visitors decide whether to participate in holy communion, not keep them away.

Preaching for the Occasion

The marriage rite includes a sermon as part of the Word portion of the service. Yet, except when the marriage rite is included in the Sunday assembly, few people attend weddings for the sermon. Under certain circumstances, it is wise to allow scripture to speak for itself and to trust the rites associated with marriage to convey the meaning and significance of the occasion. On the other hand, understanding marriage as a baptismal vocation demands that the promise of the gospel be proclaimed into the lives of the couple and the assembly. This is the task of preaching at weddings.

The wedding sermon calls for a bold, clear, relevant proclamation of the gospel. The gospel proclamation is bold to compete with all the other values represented at the wedding, which make their own claim on the couple and the assembly. The gospel proclamation makes clear that God delights in the bride and groom, whom God claimed as children in baptism, and blesses them in their life together. The preacher might enumerate God's baptismal gifts—unconditional love, lifelong faithfulness, daily forgiveness, the guidance and support of the Holy Spirit and the Christian community, and baptismal dignity and equality. These gifts are more than examples for the couple to follow. They are God's assurance that the Holy Spirit leads and empowers the assembly, and the couple in particular, to live toward others as Christ lives toward them. The gospel proclamation is relevant in that it aims to help the assembly experience God's presence, joy, grace, and blessing in and through the marriage liturgy so that the people respond by trusting in, turning to, and relying on God's faithfulness and love as the source and foundation of marriage and all loving relationships. In this way, lifelong faithfulness and self-giving love, which characterize marriage as a baptismal vocation, is a response to God's love and faithfulness. Witnessing to Christ and serving the world is the natural consequence of responding to God—not a burden imposed on the couple.

The preacher might effectively use the words and actions of the marriage rite, including the sacraments, to point to God's presence, participation, and blessing in marriage. One helpful approach is to consider the ways the order for Holy Baptism relates to the marriage rite. For example, the exchange of rings, which is a pledge of lifelong faithfulness and the sign that identifies people as married, can be interpreted as a response to being marked with the cross of Christ forever and identified as God's children. By making the words and actions of the marriage rite an integral part of the wedding sermon, the preacher can make elements of the marriage service accessible to the entire assembly in engaging ways. This approach also clearly states that Christian marriage is grounded in God rather than the couple.

At weddings, it is not enough to preach about God's unconditional love and promise of faithfulness in general terms. The wedding sermon speaks to both the shared experience of the assembly and the unique experience of the couple. Wedding sermons are an opportunity to relate the gospel to individual lives. We preach God's grace in and through the life transition that a particular couple is making. The way the couple is included in the sermon varies. Sometimes the preacher speaks directly to the couple. At other times, the preacher speaks to the assembly about the couple. In either case, the purpose is not to honor, instruct, or embarrass the couple. Sermons that treat marriage as a baptismal vocation will incorporate the couple into the sermon in ways that lift up God's unconditional love and faithfulness.

The wedding sermon is not the place to disclose personal information about the couple, such as premarital counseling revelations, or to offer last-minute advice on a successful marriage. This approach embarrasses the couple and causes them to feel scrutinized. It also overwhelms and embarrasses the assembly, who now know things about the couple they may not care to know. More troubling, the hearers go away from the sermon empty because the message was about the bride and groom rather than God.

When talking about the couple, the preacher might say something truthful about the couple, something truthful about God, and then reflect on how these truths intersect. For example, the preacher might bring scripture and the couple into mutual conversation and reflection by pointing to a characteristic of the couple that scripture identifies as a gift of or a witness to God's grace. The preacher might use scripture as a mirror to help the assembly see authentic love in Christ. The preacher might use images from scripture to assure the assembly that God will be part of the future. Scripture surely provides the preacher with language and images with which to speak of human love as a response to God's love, and marriage as a baptismal vocation. In all these approaches, the couple provides a fresh perspective on the grace of God, and the grace of God provides a new vision of and orientation to both the couple and marriage.

The preacher certainly speaks truthfully about marriage, particularly since it is reasonable to assume that some in the assembly are struggling in troubled marriages and even engaged in infidelity. Yet the wedding sermon is not the place to instruct, exhort, or persuade. Concerns about the bride and groom are addressed in premarital counseling; concerns about other couples are addressed in pastoral visitation. Concern about the state of marriage is reserved for another occasion. Weddings are the time for pastoral sensitivity. It is better to name God as the source and power of love, describe how God's love empowers human love, assure God's blessing and the Spirit's guidance, and appeal to people's best selves.

The sermon seeks to be as appropriate to the assembly as it is to the couple. While the proclamation of the gospel remains unchanged, the content and language of the sermon differ, depending on whether the assembly consists of members of the congregation, baptized Christians, people of other faith traditions, or people that claim no faith tradition. In preparing the sermon, the preacher does well to reflect upon the reason the couple is being married in the church and the assembly's reason for gathering, as well as how the couple and assembly understand God's involvement in the wedding and in marriage. The preacher might consider what understanding of marriage governs the choices the couple desires and the decisions they make, as well as who is actually making those decisions. Whose day do the couple and the assembly understand the wedding to be? Is it God's or the church's or the couple's or the family's? Who is the primary audience for this sermon? Is it the couple, the family, or the entire assembly? If the couple, what will this sermon communicate to those who will "overhear" it? For example, while the couple may be excited about marriage, others present may regard the gift of the family as a burden. The preacher is sensitive to the personal and family history that is always played out at weddings and to all the futures marriage makes possible. The sermon does not disclose personal and family secrets or deny or negate personal and family realities. For example, the preacher cannot authentically talk about creating a new home when the couple has lived together for two years. Finally, the preacher is sensitive to the emotions and expectations operating in the assembly. While this is certainly a joyous day, it also marks an ending, which for some may be bittersweet.

Preachers are also attuned to their own biases and presuppositions. The sermon will be shaped by how preachers understand the church's (and their own) role in marriage. Proclaiming God's word and asking God's blessing is distinct from "officiating" at a wedding and ensuring that the couple has a successful marriage. The sermon will also be shaped by how preachers view the wedding sermon. As is the case with funerals, some preachers are convinced that the wedding sermon is perfunctory because people do not really listen, and that it is better to let scripture and the liturgy communicate the church's understanding of marriage. Others regard the wedding sermon as a unique opportunity to preach the gospel in a way that touches the heart of people's everyday lives. How the preacher views the wedding sermon depends, in part, on the couple, the assembly, and the order of marriage, as well as the preacher's own experience.

Leading the Marriage Service: Preparation

The flexibility and options provided in the *Evangelical Lutheran Worship* Marriage service invite advanced planning of the service and thoughtful preparation and rehearsal prior to the wedding. Providing couples with the congregation's wedding policy when they inquire about a wedding helps them to plan by answering many of their immediate questions. A wedding policy also helps prevent the negotiations that are part of every wedding from becoming overly personal. A congregational wedding policy typically explains how the congregation understands marriage and describes what is and is not permissible.

In addition to relying on a wedding policy, those in the congregation responsible for planning weddings use a combination of strategies when working with couples. First, the congregation intentionally prepares people for marriage in a manner reminiscent of baptismal preparation. The Notes on the Services (LE 45) observe that the celebration itself is preceded by a period of preparation, which normally begins at least six months prior to the wedding. Preparation for marriage usually includes one or more private conversations among a couple and a pastor and may also include group sessions involving a number of engaged couples and sometimes also married couples. Preparation for marriage includes counseling that explores the gifts and responsibilities of marriage and alerts couples to the fact that no single relationship can fulfill all their needs and expectations. Couples are also taught a Christian understanding of marriage (as a baptismal vocation) and the church's role in marriage (proclaiming the gospel and asking God's blessing on the couple in their life together). Most important, during the period of preparation, the congregation prays for and with the couple, and includes prayers for them in the worship of the Sunday assembly. To encourage the congregation's prayers, an announcement of the upcoming wedding might be communicated to the congregation during the time of preparation, using a form like that provided in the notes (LE 45).

Preparation for marriage also includes explaining the marriage service and planning the wedding. Just as in baptismal preparation, the order of marriage may itself be the best means for teaching about Christian marriage. Instruction includes the meaning of the words and actions contained in the rite, not merely the mechanics of the service. Those who work with couples will probe the depths of meaning in the rite and consider all the possibilities for emphasizing baptism, the centrality of God's word and blessing, the participation of the entire assembly, and the missional character of marriage. Regardless of the quality of premarital preparation, those who work with couples know that—even when couples understand and appreciate the meaning of the church's marriage service and the significance of cultural practices that are contrary to the gospel—sentiment, tradition, and family expectations often prevail in their decision-making.

The worship space so much determines what is and is not possible in a wedding service that couples have been known to pick the church where they will be married by the size and design of the worship space. The space influences what options are available and how they might be used. Those who plan weddings therefore determine the location for each part of the service and choreograph how the wedding party will move from place to place. This is most apparent in the procession and recession; however, consideration is also given to the service of the word, exchange of vows and rings, and the sharing of holy communion.

Planning the wedding also includes determining which family members and friends will help lead the service. In addition to attendants, these persons may include ushers; family and friends who will make a vocal or instrumental offering of music; people to read scripture, lead the prayers of intercession, bring forward the bread and wine, and distribute communion; and any other assisting ministers necessary for the service. Preparation for the service includes explaining their responsibilities to all who will help lead the service. These leaders generally find it helpful to walk through the service in the worship space as part of the wedding rehearsal.

Gathering

For many, the entrance or procession is among the most important parts of the service. The notes (LE 45) observe that "in the congregation's worship space, a procession with instrumental music or singing appropriate to the praise of God is fitting." Yet a procession is not necessary. In small weddings, the bride and groom, with their attendants, may simply gather at the front of the altar, facing the minister.

If an entrance procession is desired, the participants and order may vary, except that the couple is afforded the place of honor and enters the assembly last. The congregation stands for the entire procession. The procession might be led by those carrying the processional cross and torches. The ministers may lead the procession (following cross and torches if they are used). The parents of the bride and groom may enter in the procession, or they may be seated prior to the start of the procession. The bride and groom may be preceded by attendants. The couple may enter together at the conclusion of the procession, or the groom may enter accompanied by one or both parents, and the bride may follow accompanied by one or both parents. One possible order of procession, then, is the cross, torches, assisting ministers, presiding minister, attendants, parents, and bride and groom.

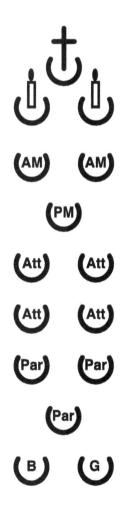

Fig. 9.1. Marriage procession. *A procession is not required. If used, the participants and their order may vary, except that the couple is given the place of honor and enters last. A possible order might be: cross, torches, assisting minister(s), presiding minister, attendants, parents, and bride and groom.*

The preceding description provides for forms of the procession that most clearly honor the sense of equality of bride and groom—a sense of equality that is not only proclaimed in baptism but is commonly held in modern Western society. However, many traditions surrounding the marriage procession are deeply entrenched, even though they reflect much older societal patterns of inequality among men and women and of marriage as the transfer of property. Those who preside at marriage will need to weigh how much energy they want to invest in persuading people to consider other patterns for the procession. But at least they should consider presenting a range of options and thinking about ways to adapt other societal traditions to a service of Christian worship in the local context.

The music that accompanies the procession, whether instrumental or singing, praises God's love and faithfulness. Music that expresses the couple's love for each other is best saved for the wedding reception.

When the baptismal font is located near the entrance of the church, the greeting, introduction, and declaration of intent may take place near the font, as a way of enacting marriage as a baptismal vocation. The bride and groom stand before the presiding minister at the baptismal font. An assisting minister may stand beside the presiding minister; those in the procession stand around and behind the bride and groom. The assembly stands facing the font. At the conclusion of the declaration of intent, the assembly sings a hymn as the procession forms and moves to a place before the altar for the prayer of the day. Most often, the presiding and assisting minister stand before the altar, facing the assembly. The bride and groom stand before the ministers, flanked by their attendants.

Greeting and Introduction

When the hymn is concluded and all are in place, the presiding minister and assembly greet one another using the apostolic greeting. The presiding minister's traditional gesture is to open the hands while speaking the apostolic greeting, bringing them together again as the assembly responds, "And also with you."

Following the pattern in Holy Baptism and other related rites, the greeting is followed by words of introduction, which may be spoken by the presiding minister or another minister. The service (LE 676) provides three alternatives, or the minister may use similar words. All three introductions explain the church's understanding of marriage and

Fig. 9.2. Apostolic greeting. *The presiding minister at a wedding may effectively communicate the mutuality of the greeting by extending open arms toward the assembly.*

sexuality as God's gift. They celebrate God's presence and blessing by proclaiming that God intends the gift of marriage as a sign of both the union of Christ and the church and the joy of the reign of God. The first and third alternatives also describe the assembly's role in the wedding as witnessing, surrounding the couple with prayer, sharing in their joy, and asking God to bless them. Those two alternatives include naming the bride and groom. In keeping with the baptismal nature of marriage, baptismal names rather than surnames are used in these places. The second alternative honestly recognizes sin's power to obscure the joy of marriage and transform God's gift of family into a burden. Yet God steadfastly strengthens and blesses married people in their life together. The assembly can therefore enter into the celebration with confidence and joy.

Declaration of Intent

The declaration of intent recalls the presentation in the order for Holy Baptism. In the presentation, candidates for baptism (or their parents) are asked if they desire to enter into the covenant of baptism. Here, as an expression of baptismal dignity and equality, the man and woman are asked if they freely desire to enter into the covenant of marriage together. Moreover, just as the family and assembly are asked to support the baptized in their life of faith, so family and assembly are asked to love, bless, support, and care for the couple in their life together. As in the order for Holy Baptism, the distinct questions for families and the assembly increase participation in the service and symbolically strengthen the assembly's commitment to the couple.

The minister questions the couple, using one of three alternatives provided in the rite (LE 677) or similar words. All three alternatives include the promise of lifelong faithfulness amid all the circumstances of life. The first and second ask each partner to *have* or *receive* the other and live together or bind themselves to each other in the covenant of marriage. The first alternative is the more traditional. The third includes an explicit reference to living in the promise of God and being joined to Christ in baptism and, in keeping with the image of Christ, asks each partner if they *give* themselves to the other in marriage. Baptismal names are used in all three alternatives. Each partner is questioned in turn, and responds, "I will."

When it is pastorally appropriate, the minister then addresses the families, using the question provided or similar words. When doubt exists as to whether the families bless and support the couple in their marriage, this question might best be omitted. The notes suggest that parents might stand behind their children and place a hand on their children's shoulders while responding to the question addressed to families. The families respond, "We will." As part of their response, parents or others may speak additional words of blessing, support, and encouragement. When those to be married bring children into the new family, the couple might be asked about their intention as parents. For example, the minister might ask, "Will you welcome *these children* into your home and regard *them* as children of God, *gifts* from God entrusted to you to bring to God's word and the holy supper, to teach the faith, and to nurture with prayer?" When to do so is appropriate, children might be asked about their desire to be part of the new family. Whenever children are involved, extreme care is taken so that questions do not in any way coerce or manipulate, since to do so is contrary to the dignity and equality afforded the children by baptism.

When planning this part of the service, many families find it helpful to think of the declaration of intent as a fitting replacement for the father "giving away the bride."

The minister may then question the assembly. Two alternatives are provided, or the minister may use similar words. The first option is a straightforward question, addressed to the entire assembly. It acknowledges God's grace and asks the assembly to commit to upholding and caring for the couple in their life together. This may be the better option when the family is addressed specifically. The second alternative names the assembly as family, friends, and all gathered with the couple, and identifies specific ways the assembly is to support and care for them in their life together. This may be the preferred option when the family is not addressed directly. When all those gathered assent to work to sustain the couple in their life together, using the words "We will," the presiding minister leads the assembly in the prayer of the day.

Prayer of the Day

If the ministers and the wedding party are gathered at the baptismal font, they move to a place in front of the church for the prayer of the day. As indicated above, the assembly may sing a hymn of praise during the procession. The nature of the service and the configuration of the worship space determine where the wedding party stands. For example, the traditional arrangement is for the ministers to stand in front of the altar, facing the assembly. The bride and groom stand before the ministers flanked by their attendants. Alternatively, the wedding party might go to places designated for them within the assembly, where they remain for the readings and the sermon, and the ministers go to their places. The presiding minister then leads the prayer of the day from the chair. This arrangement is especially appropriate when marriage is part of the principal service of the Sunday assembly.

When all are in place, the presiding minister invites the assembly to pray ("Let us pray"). After a brief silence in which the assembly enters into common prayer, the presiding minister prays the prayer of the day, possibly lifting the hands in a posture of prayer (see Fig. 3.3, p. 66). Two prayers of the day are provided in the rite (LE 678). Both praise God for revealing divine love, joy, and presence through Jesus; ask God to be present in this wedding; and anticipate the eternal marriage feast of Christ and the world. When marriage is celebrated as part of Sunday worship, one of these prayers follows the prayer of the day appointed for the Sunday or festival. After the prayer of the day, the assembly sits for the readings.

Word

The Word portion of the service includes two or three scripture readings, sermon, and a hymn of the day. When marriage is celebrated within the congregation's regular worship service, the readings are those appointed for the Sunday or festival. When marriage is part of a service of Holy Communion, the established pattern is a reading from the Old Testament, a reading from the New Testament letters, and a reading from one of the gospels. The gospel reading is the last reading; it may be preceded by a sung acclamation and be proclaimed by the minister who is preaching. The assembly stands for this reading. A psalm may be selected as a response to a reading from the Old Testament. The assembly might also sing appropriate hymns and songs in response to the readings. Alternatively, vocal or instrumental music might be interspersed among the readings.

Inviting the couple to select the readings affords an important opportunity to discuss a biblical understanding of marriage as grounded in God's unconditional love and faithfulness. As part of marriage preparation, couples might be given a list of appropriate readings, which they are to discuss. (See Appendix C, p. 237.) The couple might then share with the pastor why they chose the readings they have. The couple inviting family members, members of the wedding party, and friends to proclaim the readings makes the service personal and may add meaning to the proclamation. Those invited to proclaim scripture need to be able to read with confidence.

The readings are normally followed by a sermon, which is preached by the presiding minister or another pastor. The wedding sermon declares God's delight in the couple and blessing on their life together. The promise of the gospel is proclaimed in such a way that the couple and the assembly turn to and trust in God's unconditional love and faithfulness as the source and foundation of marriage and all loving relationships. See pages 195–198 for more helps on preaching for a wedding. A period of silence for reflection follows the sermon. Under certain circumstances, it may be appropriate to omit the sermon and trust scripture to proclaim God's presence, love, and faithfulness.

In response to the sermon, the assembly may join in praising God and proclaiming the gospel by singing the hymn of the day. This hymn provides the best opportunity for the entire assembly to actively participate in the service and is therefore included whenever possible. The hymn of the day expresses God's love and faithfulness and is one the assembly can and will sing. If the members of the wedding party sat with the assembly for the readings and sermon, they take their places before the altar during the hymn of the day. At the conclusion of the hymn, the assembly is seated for the marriage rite.

Marriage

The central actions of marriage are the couple exchanging vows and rings, and the assembly acclaiming their marriage and praying for God's blessing upon their life together. To mark the transition from the service of the word to the central action of marriage, the ministers may lead the couple or the wedding party to a place closer to the altar for the exchange of vows and rings. The couple may move to this place during the hymn of the day or at the presiding minister's invitation to declare their vows. The manner in which the central actions of marriage are conducted makes it clear that the bride and groom are committing themselves to each other in marriage with the assembly witnessing, acclaiming, and praying—rather than the minister or the church marrying the couple.

Exchange of Vows

Using the words provided in the rite (or similar words), the presiding minister may invite the couple to declare their vows to one another. The bride and groom's first or Christian names are used in this invitation, as they were in baptism. The couple faces each other and may join hands. Each partner promises faithfulness to the other. Ideally, the bride and groom memorize their vows so that they can declare them on the day of their wedding and recall them every day of their marriage. The presiding minister functions as the chief witness. The presiding minister might observe the declaration of vows standing with hands joined or holding the book. If the bride or groom needs to be reminded of the words of the vows, the presiding minister quietly prompts them rather than speaking the words in a way that suggests that the couple is repeating an oath made to the church.

Two vows are provided in the leaders edition. They are to be regarded as examples. They show that marriage vows include the promise of lifelong commitment and express the complete sharing that marriage implies. Other possible forms of wedding promises include:

I take you, _____name_____, to be my *wife/husband*, and these things I promise you: I will be faithful to you and honest with you; I will respect, trust, help, and care for you; I will share my life with you; I will forgive you as we have been forgiven; and I will try with you better to understand ourselves, the world, and God; through the best and worst of what is to come until death parts us.

I take you, _____name_____, to be my *wife/husband*. I promise before God and these witnesses to be your faithful *husband/wife*, to share with you in plenty and in want, in joy and in sorrow, in sickness and in health, to forgive and strengthen you, and to join with you so that together we may serve God and others as long as we both shall live.

_____Name_____, I take you to be my *wife/husband* from this time onward, to join with you and to share all that is to come, to give and to receive, to speak and to listen, to inspire and to respond, and in all circumstances of our life together to be loyal to you with my whole life and with all of my being until death parts us.[4]

Those who choose to write their own vows do so with careful guidance. In addition to including the complete sharing and lifelong commitment that characterize marriage, couples are careful not to promise things that are impossible to keep, such as feeling a certain way every day of their marriage.

Giving of Rings

As a sign of the vows they have made to each other, the couple may give and receive rings. Normally, two rings are used. When only one ring is given, the service is modified accordingly. The presiding minister may receive the rings and, holding them in her or his hands, say the prayer provided in the leaders edition (680). The presiding minister then gives the rings to the couple, who exchange them using one of the forms provided or similar words. The first option is the more traditional;

the second, which refers explicitly to the vow, speaks of honor, and invokes the trinitarian name used in baptism, makes the ring a symbol of baptismal vocation, as well as a sign of love and faithfulness. The bride and groom place the rings on each other's left hands.

Acclamation

The presiding minister addresses the assembly and declares that the couple have joined themselves to each other as husband and wife. A form of this declaration is provided in the rite. In places where the form of announcement of marriage is prescribed by law, the presiding minister uses that form instead. The assembly responds, "Amen. Thanks be to God," and may offer its acclamation with applause. A sung acclamation, hymn, or other music may follow.

Other symbols of marriage may be included at this time. These may include ritual actions by the couple. For example, the notes describe the African or African American tradition of the couple jumping over a broom. Other ritual actions are done *to* the couple. Again the notes describe the African or African American tradition of the assembly enfolding the couple in a length of kente cloth. In another tradition, the bride and groom might be crowned with flowers or garlands. Whatever additional symbols of marriage are used, they are placed after the acclamation so as not to obscure or overshadow the central actions of exchanging vows and giving rings. If a unity candle is used, it might be lighted at this time.

Marriage Blessing

The bride and groom then kneel for the marriage blessing. The presiding minister may extend a hand over the couple while praying the blessing. The parents may step forward and lay a hand on their children's heads or shoulders. Two prayers of blessing are provided. The first is directed to God. It recalls God's love in Christ, asks for the abundance of the Spirit in the couple's life together, and anticipates their participation in the marriage feast with all the saints. This blessing is particularly appropriate for Christians who regard marriage as a baptismal vocation. The second blessing is addressed to the couple and emphasizes God's gift of marriage. This blessing is more appropriate for couples who may desire a service that is less overtly Christian or does not connect baptism, marriage, and Christian vocation. Where appropriate or desired, a prayer for the gift of children may be added. Following the marriage blessing, the parents (or others) may speak additional words of blessing and encouragement.

Prayers of Intercession

The marriage portion of the service concludes with the couple and the assembly turning to God in prayer. The prayers of intercession celebrate this marriage as a response to and expression of God's love for the world. The assembly's focus expands from this couple to the world and its needs. Two sets of prayers are provided in the leaders edition (681–684). The invitation to prayer in each set makes clear that the assembly prays in response to the great, divine love that is experienced on this day. The first set of prayers enfolds the couple in the assembly's ongoing prayers for the church, human community, the nations and those who govern, justice and peace, and for all in need. The second set moves from the couple and their life together to the assembly and the world, and includes a petition in which those who have died are named. Both sets end each petition with the words, "Gracious and faithful God," and the congregational response, "hear our prayer." These responses are included in the assembly edition. The prayers in the leaders edition may serve as a starting point for crafting or adapting petitions for the specific occasion.

The couple and assembly stand for the prayers of intercession. The prayers are best led by someone other than the presiding minister, to indicate that they are an action of the assembly. This is another significant way of including a friend or family member in the service. Alternatively, the prayers might be offered by someone who leads the intercessions in the Sunday assembly. The intercessions might be led from a lectern or reading desk. The presiding minister typically prays the concluding prayer to the prayers of intercession, and the assembly responds, "Amen."

A service without communion continues with the Lord's Prayer. The presiding minister may introduce the Lord's Prayer, using one of the two options provided. The choice of which form of the Lord's Prayer will be used depends upon the practice of the congregation and the nature of the assembly. The Lord's Prayer is perhaps the part of the service in which the most people can easily and comfortably participate. The choice of versions may honor this consideration. It cannot be assumed, however, that people know either of the two versions of the Lord's Prayer from memory; the text should be provided by referring to the book or by including it in a worship aid.

Meal

As discussed above, in holy communion the church shares so intimately in the love of Christ that the image of the bride and bridegroom has been used to express this love. The decision to include this intimate sharing in Christ's love as part of the marriage rite depends upon the nature of the assembly. When holy communion is included, the service continues with the exchange of peace. After the presiding minister and the assembly greet each other with the peace, the couple may share the kiss of peace (an amorous kiss is not appropriate at this moment) and the members of the assembly may greet one another in Christ's peace. During the peace, the wedding party moves to places provided for them within the assembly, such as the front pews, for the celebration of the supper.

Following the peace, family members or friends of the bride and groom may bring the bread and wine forward as an offering hymn is sung; this is an excellent way to involve children in the service. Family and friends may assist in distributing communion. All who are baptized are welcome at the table; to restrict the bread and wine to the couple or the wedding party is contrary to God's gift of the sacrament. Appropriate music, especially congregational singing, enhances the spirit of joy and community. When all have communed and the congregation is singing, the wedding party might reassemble before the altar for the Sending. The meal concludes with the prayer after communion, which is provided in the rite and led by an assisting minister.

Sending

If it has not been included earlier in the service, the greeting of peace may be shared. The presiding minister and assembly greet each other with the peace of Christ. The couple may then greet each other with a kiss of peace, and the members of the assembly greet one another with a gesture and words of peace.

The presiding minister then proclaims God's blessing on the assembly. Two forms of blessing are provided. Both vividly declare God's blessing on the life journey that lies ahead for the couple in particular but for the entire assembly as well. An assisting minister then dismisses the assembly, which responds, "Thanks be to God." The service may conclude with a hymn or instrumental music as the wedding party and ministers depart. The order of procession is often the opposite of that used in the gathering, except that, when used, the cross and torches always lead the procession.

The manner in which weddings are celebrated is a congregation's most significant proclamation of the church's theology of marriage. Therefore, the proclamation of God's word as the promise of the gospel, and prayers for God's blessing upon the couple in their life together, are prominent. Everything in the service is in keeping with baptismal dignity and equality. Most important, God's love and faithfulness are emphasized, rather than that of the bride and groom. In these ways, the church celebrates the worldly estate of marriage as a gift that God intends to bring joy and life to the couple and, through them, to the world. Responding to this gift, marriage becomes a baptismal vocation and a sign of God's coming reign.

Appendixes

Nairobi Statement on Worship and Culture

Contemporary Challenges and Opportunities

LUTHERAN WORLD FEDERATION

from Christian Worship: Unity in Cultural Diversity

This statement is from the third international consultation of the Lutheran World Federation's Study Team on Worship and Culture, held in Nairobi, Kenya, in January 1996. The members of the Study Team represent five continents of the world and have worked together with enthusiasm for three years thus far. The initial consultation, in October 1993 in Cartigny, Switzerland, focused on the biblical and historical foundations of the relationship between Christian worship and culture, and resulted in the "Cartigny Statement on Worship and Culture: Biblical and Historical Foundations." (This Nairobi Statement builds upon the Cartigny Statement; in no sense does it replace it.) The second consultation, in March 1994 in Hong Kong, explored contemporary issues and questions of the relationships between the world's cultures and Christian liturgy, church music, and church architecture and art. The papers of the first two consultations were published as *Worship and Culture in Dialogue*.[1] The papers and statement from the Nairobi consultation were published as *Christian Worship: Unity in Cultural Diversity*.[2] In 1994–1995, the Study Team conducted regional research, and prepared reports on that research. Phase IV of the Study commenced in Nairobi and will continue with seminars and other means to implement the learnings of the study, as LWF member churches decide is helpful. The Study Team considers this project to be essential to the renewal and mission of the Church around the world.

1. Introduction

1.1. Worship is the heart and pulse of the Christian Church. In worship we celebrate together God's gracious gifts of creation and salvation, and are strengthened to live in response to God's grace. Worship always involves actions, not merely words. To consider worship is to consider music, art, and architecture, as well as liturgy and preaching.

1.2. The reality that Christian worship is always celebrated in a given local cultural setting draws our attention to the dynamics between worship and the world's many local cultures.

1.3 Christian worship relates dynamically to culture in at least four ways. First, it is *transcultural,* the same substance for everyone everywhere, beyond culture. Second, it is *contextual,* varying according to the local situation (both nature and culture). Third, it is *counter-cultural,* challenging what is contrary to the Gospel in a given culture. Fourth, it is *cross-cultural,* making possible sharing between different local cultures. In all four dynamics, there are helpful principles which can be identified.

2. Worship as Transcultural

2.1. The resurrected Christ whom we worship, and through whom by the power of the Holy Spirit we know the grace of the Triune God, transcends and indeed is beyond all cultures. In the mystery of his resurrection is the source of the transcultural nature of Christian worship. Baptism and Eucharist, the sacraments of Christ's death and resurrection, were given by God for all the world. There is one Bible, translated into many tongues, and biblical preaching of Christ's death and resurrection has been sent into all the world. The fundamental shape of the principal Sunday act of Christian worship, the Eucharist or Holy Communion, is shared across cultures: the people gather, the Word of God is proclaimed, the people intercede for the needs of the Church and the world, the eucharistic meal is shared, and the people are sent out into the world for mission. The great narratives of Christ's birth, death, resurrection, and sending of the Spirit, and our Baptism into him, provide the central meanings of the transcultural times of the church's year: especially Lent/Easter/Pentecost, and, to a lesser extent, Advent/Christmas/Epiphany. The ways in which the shapes of the Sunday Eucharist and the church year are expressed vary by culture, but their meanings and fundamental structure are shared around the globe. There is one Lord, one faith, one Baptism, one Eucharist.

2.2. Several specific elements of Christian liturgy are also transcultural, e.g., readings from the Bible (although of course the translations vary), the ecumenical creeds and the Our Father, and Baptism in water in the Triune Name.

2.3. The use of this shared core liturgical structure and these shared liturgical elements in local congregational worship—as well as the shared act of people assembling together, and the shared provision of diverse leadership in that assembly (although the space for the assembly and the manner of the leadership vary)—are expressions of Christian unity across time, space, culture, and confession. The recovery in each congregation of the clear centrality of these transcultural and ecumenical elements renews the sense of this Christian unity and gives all churches a solid basis for authentic contextualization.

3. Worship as Contextual

3.1. Jesus whom we worship was born into a specific culture of the world. In the mystery of his incarnation are the model and the mandate for the contextualization of Christian worship. God can be and is encountered in the local cultures of our world. A given culture's values and patterns, insofar as they are consonant with the values of the Gospel, can be used to express the meaning and purpose of Christian worship. Contextualization is a necessary task for the Church's mission in the world, so that the Gospel can be ever more deeply rooted in diverse local cultures.

3.2. Among the various methods of contextualization, that of dynamic equivalence is particularly useful. It involves re-expressing components of Christian worship with something from a local culture that has an equal meaning, value, and function. Dynamic equivalence goes far beyond mere translation; it involves understanding the fundamental meanings both of elements of worship and of the local culture, and enabling the meanings and actions of worship to be "encoded" and re-expressed in the language of local culture.

3.3. In applying the method of dynamic equivalence, the following procedure may be followed. First, the liturgical *ordo* (basic shape) should be examined with regard to its theology, history, basic elements, and cultural backgrounds. Second, those elements of the *ordo* that can be subjected to dynamic equivalence without prejudice to their meaning should be determined. Third, those components of culture that are able to re-express the Gospel and the liturgical *ordo* in an adequate manner should be studied. Fourth, the spiritual and pastoral benefits our people will derive from the changes should be considered.

3.4. Local churches might also consider the method of creative assimilation. This consists of adding pertinent components of local culture to the liturgical ordo in order to enrich its original core. The baptismal *ordo* of "washing with water and the Word", for example, was gradually elaborated by the assimilation of such cultural practices as the giving of white vestments and lighted candles to the neophytes of ancient mystery religions. Unlike dynamic equivalence, creative assimilation enriches the liturgical *ordo*—not by culturally re-expressing its elements, but by adding to it new elements from local culture.

3.5. In contextualization the fundamental values and meanings of both Christianity and of local cultures must be respected.

3.6. An important criterion for dynamic equivalence and creative assimilation is that sound or accepted liturgical traditions are preserved in order to keep unity with the universal Church's tradition of worship, while progress inspired by pastoral needs is encouraged. On the side of culture, it is understood that not everything can be integrated with Christian worship, but only those elements that are connatural to (that is, of the same nature as) the liturgical *ordo*. Elements borrowed from local culture should always undergo critique and purification, which can be achieved through the use of biblical typology.

4. Worship as Counter-cultural

4.1. Jesus Christ came to transform all people and all cultures, and calls us not to conform to the world, but to be transformed with it (Rom. 12:2). In the mystery of his passage from death to eternal life is the model for transformation, and thus for the counter-cultural nature of Christian worship. Some components of every culture in the world are sinful, dehumanizing, and contradictory to the values of the Gospel. From the perspective of the Gospel, they need critique and transformation. Contextualization of Christian faith and worship necessarily involves challenging of all types of oppression and social injustice wherever they exist in earthly cultures.

4.2. It also involves the transformation of cultural patterns which idolize the self or the local group at the expense of a wider humanity, or which give central place to the acquisition of wealth at the expense of the care of the earth and its poor. The tools of the counter-cultural in Christian worship may also include the deliberate maintenance or recovery of patterns of action which differ intentionally from prevailing cultural models. These patterns may arise from a recovered sense of Christian history, or from the wisdom of other cultures.

5. Worship as Cross-cultural

5.1. Jesus came to be the Savior of all people. He welcomes the treasures of earthly cultures into the city of God. By virtue of Baptism, there is one Church; and one means of living in faithful response to Baptism is to manifest ever more deeply the unity of the Church. The sharing of hymns and art and other elements of worship across cultural barriers helps enrich the whole Church and strengthen the sense of the *communio* of the Church. This sharing can be ecumenical as well as cross-cultural, as a witness to the unity of the Church and the oneness of Baptism. Cross-cultural sharing is possible for every church, but is especially needed in multicultural congregations and member churches.

5.2. Care should be taken that the music, art, architecture, gestures and postures, and other elements of different cultures are understood and respected when they are used by churches elsewhere in the world. The criteria for contextualization (above, sections 3.5 and 3.6) should be observed.

6. Challenge to the Churches

6.1. We call on all member churches of the Lutheran World Federation to undertake more efforts related to the transcultural, contextual, counter-cultural, and cross-cultural nature of Christian worship. We call on all member churches to recover the centrality of Baptism, Scripture with preaching, and the every-Sunday celebration of the Lord's Supper—the principal transcultural elements of Christian worship and the signs of Christian unity—as the strong center of all congregational life and mission, and as the authentic basis for contextualization. We call on all churches to give serious attention to exploring the local or contextual elements of liturgy, language, posture and gesture, hymnody and other music and musical instruments, and art and architecture for Christian worship—so that their worship may be more truly rooted in the local culture. We call those churches now carrying out missionary efforts to encourage such contextual awareness among themselves and also among the partners and recipients of their ministries. We call on all member churches to give serious attention to the transcultural nature of worship and the possibilities for cross-cultural sharing. And we call on all churches to consider the training and ordination of ministers of Word and Sacrament, because each local community has the right to receive weekly the means of grace.

6.2. We call on the Lutheran World Federation to make an intentional and substantial effort to provide scholarships for persons from the developing world to study worship, church music, and church architecture, toward the eventual goal that enhanced theological training in their churches can be led by local teachers.

6.3. Further, we call on the Lutheran World Federation to continue its efforts related to worship and culture into the next millennium. The tasks are not quickly accomplished; the work calls for ongoing depth-level research and pastoral encouragement. The Worship and Culture Study, begun in 1992 and continuing in and past the 1997 LWF Assembly, is a significant and important beginning, but the task calls for unending efforts. Giving priority to this task is essential for evangelization of the world.

Chicago Statement on Worship and Culture

Baptism and Rites of Life Passage
LUTHERAN WORLD FEDERATION

from Baptism, Rites of Passage, and Culture

This statement is from the fourth international consultation of the Lutheran World Federation's Study Team on Worship and Culture, held in Chicago, United States, in May 1998. The members of the Study Team represent five continents of the world and have worked together for five years. The first consultation, in Cartigny, Switzerland, in 1993, focused on the biblical and historical foundations of the relationships between Christian worship and culture, and produced the "Cartigny Statement on Worship and Culture: Biblical and Historical Foundations." The second consultation, in Hong Kong in 1994, explored contemporary issues and questions in the relationships between the world's cultures and Christian liturgy, church music, and church architecture/art. The papers of these first two consultations were published as *Worship and Culture in Dialogue*.[1] The third international consultation, held in Nairobi, Kenya, in 1996, focused on the Eucharist in its relationships to culture, and issued the "Nairobi Statement on Worship and Culture: Contemporary Challenges and Opportunities." The papers and statement from the Nairobi consultation were published as *Christian Worship: Unity in Cultural Diversity*.[2] The 1998 Chicago consultation examined the dynamics by which world cultures relate to Holy Baptism and certain rites of human passage (healing rites, burial rites, marriage rites). This Chicago Statement builds upon the prior Cartigny and Nairobi Statements, applying their insights to the topics considered at the Chicago consultation.

1. Introduction

1.1. The foundational event in the life of any Christian community is the "one Baptism" (Eph. 4:5) which constitutes the Church to be a "royal priesthood," proclaiming the mighty acts of the life-giving God for all the world (1 Pet. 2:9). Baptism is the burial of Christians together with Christ in order that they may be raised with him to newness of life (Rom. 6:4) as signs of God's new creation. It is the "washing of water by the Word" (Eph. 5:26) which proclaims and gives the forgiveness of sins and, at the same time, identifies the Christian community with Jesus Christ who identifies himself with outsiders and sinners and all the needy world. It is the outpouring of the Holy Spirit who draws the baptized into communion with the Triune God and with each other. As such, Baptism always introduces the newly baptized into life in a local community of Christians, but in communion with all the churches of God. And Baptism has a life-long significance, giving Christians the dignity and responsibility of their vocation in Christ. All other changes and transitions in the life of a Christian must be seen to reflect this basic transition and this basic dignity: "Once you were not a people, but now you are God's people" (1 Pet. 2:10). Baptism thus informs and shapes rites related to the life-cycle.

1.2. Rites of passage are those communal symbolic processes and acts connected with important or critical transitions in the lives of individuals and communities. In almost all cultures, giving birth, coming to adulthood, marrying, reconciling, leave-taking, passage into and sometimes through sickness, and dying and grieving, among several other transitions, are marked by diverse communal rites that express the process of separation, liminality (the transitional or "in between" stage), and incorporation. To accompany people in many of these moments of transition, the Christian community celebrates rites of passage. These rites whereby the Church invokes God's care and providence for people in transition/liminality find their efficacy in the power of the Word. Foremost among these rites observed by the Church are those associated with sickness, funerals, and marriage. For Christians, however, these are rites that extend or renew or conclude their original and essential rite of passage through the waters of Baptism. Therefore, it is good that Baptism should be often remembered and affirmed in these diverse life-cycle rites. And, for Christians, these ways of marking life's transition are appropriately celebrated in the community of the baptized.

1.3. All Christian worship, whether the sacraments or rites of passage, relates dynamically to culture in at least four ways. First, worship is *transcultural,* the same substance for everyone everywhere, beyond culture. Second, worship is *contextual,* varying according to the local natural and cultural contexts. Third, worship is *counter-cultural,* challenging what is contrary to the Gospel in each given culture. Fourth, worship is *cross-cultural,* making sharing possible between different local cultures.[3]

1.4. Among the various methods of contextualization, those of dynamic equivalence and creative assimilation are particularly useful.[4] Dynamic equivalence is the re-expression of components of Christian worship with elements from a local culture which have an equal meaning, value, and function. Creative assimilation is the addition of elements from local culture to the liturgical *ordo* to enrich its original core.

1.5. The design of worship space, the selection of music, and other elements of all rites should never be dismissed as matters of indifference or of personal choice. Rather, they stand under the imperative to do everything in accordance with the Gospel of Jesus Christ, in ways that make clear the baptismal values in the rites.

2. Baptism

2.1. The *transcultural* nature of Baptism arises from God's gift of this "visible Word," this tangible proclamation of the Gospel, to all the Church in all the world. Water, the tangible earthly element of the sacrament, is everywhere available where human life exists. But the pattern or *ordo* of Baptism is also a universal ecumenical inheritance.[5] Baptism involves: a) formation in the one faith (traditionally known as the catechumenate)[6], (b) the water-bath, and c) the incorporation of the baptized into the whole Christian community and its mission. This latter incorporation is expressed by the newly baptized being led to the table of the Lord's Supper, the very table where their baptismal identity will also be strengthened and re-affirmed throughout their life. The events around the water-bath itself have also come to be practiced in a widely used pattern which is very nearly transcultural. In a gathering of the Christian assembly, in which the Word is proclaimed, the following events usually occur: God is praised and thanked over the water; together with the Church, the candidates and their sponsors renounce the forces of evil and confess the universal Church's faith in the Triune God; water is used generously in the Triune Name of God; prayer is made for the Holy Spirit's gifts; and several "explanatory symbols"—e.g., anointing, hand-laying, signing with the cross, and often also clothing and illuminating—may accompany this prayer, disclosing and teaching something of the powerful act which God does in Baptism. Any contextualization of Baptism or of the rites of passage will depend upon the churches allowing these transcultural characteristics of Baptism to be continually renewed in their midst. "We should do justice to the meaning of Baptism and make of our practice a true and complete sign of the thing Baptism signifies."[7]

2.2. But this transcultural gift needs to be *contextualized* in each local place. The local community will have its own ways of teaching and passing on the faith to baptismal candidates and their families, forming them in heart and life as well as mind. These ways may best be developed in connection with other local Christians, in witness to the baptismal unity of the whole Church. The assembly of Christians will have its own ways of gathering. The space for Baptism may be locally designed, as long as this design recalls the need for the baptismal event to take place in the presence of the worshiping assembly, with the generous use of water. In many places this may mean that communities will recover the use of fonts or pools which enable Baptism by immersion (as Luther so strongly advocated[8]). The traditional "explanatory symbols" of Baptism may need to be replaced, by the means of dynamic equivalence, or reinforced, by the means of creative assimilation, so that the power of the water-bath may be more clearly perceived in local context. Each local church will need to ask: what local symbols may express the gift of the Spirit, the adoption of a new identity, baptismal dignity and vocation, death and resurrection, and the unity of the community, and do so without obscuring the central importance of the water and the Word? The "explanatory symbols" should never overshadow the water-bath itself.

2.3. Baptismal unity will never be that of an "insider" group. Baptism, which constitutes the Church, also calls Christians to identify in solidarity with all people. Its celebration will therefore have certain *counter-cultural* elements as well. The poor will be baptized with at least as great a dignity as the rich. Women and men, children and adults, and people from all ethnic/class/caste backgrounds will stand here on equal footing, equally in need of God's mercy, equally gifted with the outpoured Spirit. Baptism, which creates members of the local community, also at the same time creates these people as members of the one universal Body of Christ. Baptism calls us to unity, not to division.[9]

2.4. As the churches once again find this gift of God renewed in their midst, they may also be assisted by *cross-cultural* gifts between the churches which share the one Baptism. The hymns and music of one church may helpfully illuminate the meaning of Baptism in another church in a different culture. One local church's use of baptismal space (fonts/pools and the surrounding area) may suggest possibilities to other churches, elsewhere. And, new "explanatory symbols" discovered or developed by local churches in one area may be used by Christians in other places, who may thereby discover a depth of meaning in Baptism they had not previously imagined.

3. Healing Rites

3.1. When we call on Jesus as the Christ for healing, we appeal to what is close to his heart: concern for those who suffer because of physical illness and other afflictions of the human spirit. Through rites of healing, the Church, represented by its pastors and the local community, invokes the comforting presence of Christ and the Spirit, especially in serious illness which can cause anxiety, break the human spirit, weaken faith, or isolate the human person from society and even from the church community. Churches which have no such healing rites may wish to consider developing them, thereby ministering to and expressing solidarity with those who suffer (1 Cor. 12:22-26).

3.2. Anointing, hand-laying, and the prayer of faith, whenever possible in the presence of the community, are the core elements of Christian rites of healing. They are handed down to us by apostolic tradition (Mark 6:13; Mark 16:17-18; Jas. 5:14-15). They are *transcultural* in the sense that they have been preserved, though possibly re-expressed ritually in the course of contextualization. The Eucharist itself is a primary transcultural expression of the Church's concern for the sick. The congregation's care of the sick includes the eucharistic celebration by the pastor (together with representatives of the congregation) in the home or hospital (or other) room of the sick person, or the ministry of sharing the Word and bringing the Holy Communion from the Sunday assembly to those who, because of illness or disability, are unable to be present in that assembly. All the rites of healing and all the extensions of eucharistic ministry are intended to surround people who are isolated or excluded with God's gift of the baptismal community.

3.3. To enrich and make Christian rites of healing understandable to the people (the task of *contextualization*), it is necessary to identify elements of local rites of healing that can suitably, after critical evaluation, be substituted for elements of the traditional Christian rites through dynamic equivalence, or as will more often be the case, illustrate the original core of the rite through creative assimilation. Elements of local rites of healing include pertinent gestures, symbols, and material elements that can be integrated into Christian use.

3.4. In situations where certain types of illness are regarded as the result of sorcery or witchcraft, Christian catechesis and health education should be instituted. In no way should elements of healing related to sorcery or witchcraft be integrated into Christian rites. The *counter-cultural* aspect of Christian healing should also challenge practices based on those superstitions which sometimes lead to injustice and cruelty toward persons suspected of witchcraft, as well as such health practices that are based on wealth or egocentrism, or such modern institutions that demean the dignity of the sick.

3.5. The biblical readings and prayers should stress that the Church's rites of healing embody Christ's concern for the sick, that they express faith in the power of Christ's death and resurrection, and that they are intended primarily to heal (make whole) the entire person as well as to enable the community to pray for the curing of an illness (whether physical or mental). Rites of healing should include varying provisions for situations of acute, chronic, and terminal illnesses.

4. Funeral Rites

4.1. Christian funeral rites conclude the passage from this world to God (John 13:1) which began at Baptism. They celebrate the baptized's *transitus* or Exodus and mark the day of her or his *dies natalis* (birthday) unto eternal life. At the same time, they accompany the bereaved in the time of loss by the comforting words of Scripture and the support of the Christian community and its singing.

4.2. The funeral practices of Christians have traditionally included the following elements, arranged as a pattern: a) washing, anointing, and dressing the body—rites reminiscent of Baptism; b) a communal vigil (wake) and then a service of the Word or the Eucharist rites expressing the baptismal community; and c) a final commendation and a procession to the place of entombment while hymns or paschal psalms are changed rites alluding to the Exodus.

4.3. In some places outside Christian tradition, a number of the aforementioned rites already exist, such as the washing and clothing of the body and the funeral procession. In such cases the work of *contextualization* is to infuse these rites with baptismal and paschal dimensions through reading and singing from the Word of God and through prayers.

4.4. It is clear that texts, gestures, dirges, and symbols that contradict the foundational Christian faith in the resurrection cannot be integrated into the rite: this is a *counter-cultural* task in developing funeral rites. Another counter-cultural task necessary in some contexts is the avoidance of practices (e.g., expensive coffins, elaborate meals) which impose a severe financial burden on the family of the deceased. On the other hand, Christian funeral rites might include provision for funeral processions as the final stage of the paschal journey in which the community accompanies the dead and the bereaved.

4.5. When cremation is practiced, Christian rites should provide biblical readings and prayers that affirm the faith in the resurrection and norms for the appropriate disposition of the ashes.

4.6. The tradition of chanting or singing psalms during funerals should be encouraged, as should the use of the local and worldwide treasury of hymnody. In all cases, the texts and music should appropriately express the Christian faith.

4.7. Christians have always shown care and respect for cemeteries and other places where the faithful who "sleep in Christ" await the day of his coming. Efforts should be made to express the Christian character of the diverse burial places used by our churches. As well, church buildings where the Eucharist is celebrated in the presence of the body should be designed interiorly for such occasions.

5. Marriage Rites

5.1. The process of transition in which a couple moves from being unmarried to being socially recognized as married may be regarded as itself transcultural in its shape and general character. Still, for Christians, the truly *transcultural* gift is: a) the proclamation of the Word of God in connection with such a transition, and b) the prayer for God's blessing on the couple and their household. The Word of God and the nuptial blessing are the universal Christian additions to the human process of marriage.

5.2. But these additions are made within a ritual which will have deep cultural connections, and here is the task of *contextualization*. The ways in which the process of marrying is unfolded, the ways in which the couple is betrothed, in which their assent is expressed, in which the society gathers around them—these all may be richly different from culture to culture. The type of music used in the celebration may borrow from the local musical tradition, provided that both music and text are appropriate to the communal intention to proclaim the word of God and pray for blessing. As well, the marriage rite may take place in the church, or in the home or in another assembly place. However, when a civil marriage has taken place and the couple comes to the Christian community asking for the nuptial blessing, the consent and marriage vows need not be repeated in the church.

5.3. There are *counter-cultural* aspects of weddings. It is important that the rite maintain and express the baptismal dignity of the parties to the marriage. Thus, the couple must both freely assent to the wedding, and neither bride nor groom should be dealt with as if "property." Furthermore, the status of being married must be seen as neither better nor worse than the status of anyone else in the assembly—these all are the baptized. Baptism is their basic dignity and vocation, and a particular marriage will be seen as one wonderful unfolding of that vocation for the sake of the life of the world. It may be that such baptismal dignity will come to expression by the wedding being held within the context of the Eucharist of the assembly. Or it may be that the nuptial blessing will express the vocation of baptized Christians who are married. In any case, the Church may do well to resist the spread of consumerist or dowry-system patterns of marriage which are often inappropriately expensive without expressing authentic Christian values.

5.4. Among the *cross-cultural* gifts which the churches may share with each other may be new ways in which the baptismal vocation of the married is brought to expression—in signs, songs, or gestures—in a local dialogue with the communal cultural traditions of marriage.

6. Call to the Churches

6.1. We who have served on the Study Team offer our work during 1993–1998 to the glory of God and for the renewal of the Church. We call on the Lutheran World Federation and its member churches to receive this work in ways that will renew their life and mission. Such reception involves the translation of the LWF Worship and Culture Statements and books into local languages, and their wide distribution; local, regional, and/or subregional workshops and meetings of various sorts; pastors' retreats; courses in seminaries and theological institutions; regional newsletters on worship and culture for networking and communication; articles in ecclesial and academic periodicals; consultations with parishes; consultations with architects, artists, and musicians; and so forth. Reception also involves sharing with ecumenical partner churches, seminaries, and journals, and other ecumenical efforts.

6.2. We continue to call on all member churches of the Lutheran World Federation to undertake further intentional study and efforts related to the transcultural, contextual, and counter-cultural natures of Christian worship, and its cross-cultural sharing. We call on all member churches to recover the centrality of Baptism for their life and worship, and as the foundation of rites of human passage, and to do so whenever possible in ecumenical partnerships with wide participation. The challenge is to develop and use forms of worship which are both authentic to the Gospel and relevant to local cultural contexts.

Propers and Hymns for Life Passages

HEALING

The Festival of Luke, Evangelist (October 18) is a traditional day for a service of healing. In addition, the appointed gospels make the following Sundays and weeks especially appropriate for a service of healing:

Advent 3A	Lectionary 12C
Epiphany 3A	Lectionary 13B
Epiphany 4B	Lectionary 14B
Epiphany 5B	Lectionary 15C
Epiphany 6B	Lectionary 16B
Epiphany 7B	Lectionary 20A
Lent 4A	Lectionary 21C
Lent 4B	Lectionary 23B
Easter 6C	Lectionary 27C
Lectionary 9 B,C	Lectionary 30B
Lectionary 10A	

When a service of healing takes place at a time other than a primary Sunday service, selections may be made from the following or other appropriate propers.

Scripture Readings

OLD TESTAMENT

Exodus 16:13-15	*Manna in the wilderness*
1 Kings 17:17-24	*Elijah restores the widow's son to life*
2 Kings 5:9-14	*Healing of Naaman*
Isaiah 11:1-3a	*The gifts of the Spirit*
Isaiah 35:1-10	*The promise of God's coming*
Isaiah 42:1-7	*The suffering servant*
Isaiah 53:3-5	*With his stripes we are healed*

Isaiah 61:1-3 · *Good tidings to the afflicted*
Jeremiah 29:10-14 · *God's presence in an unknown future*
Ezekiel 36:26-28 · *A new heart I will give you*

PSALM

Psalm 13 · *My heart is joyful because of your saving help*
Psalm 20:1-6 · *The Lord answer you in the day of trouble*
Psalm 23 · *You anoint my head with oil*
Psalm 27 · *The Lord is the strength of my life*
Psalm 91 · *God shall give the angels charge over you*
Psalm 103 · *God forgives you all your sins*
Psalm 121 · *Our help is in the name of the Lord*
Psalm 130 · *My soul waits for the Lord*
Psalm 138 · *You will make good your purpose for me*
Psalm 139 · *Where can I go from your Spirit?*
Psalm 145 · *The eyes of all wait upon you*

NEW TESTAMENT

Acts 3:1-10 · *Peter and John heal the lame man*
Acts 5:12-16 · *Healings in Jerusalem*
Acts 10:36-43 · *Apostolic preaching*
Acts 16:16-18 · *The slave girl with the spirit of divination*
Romans 8:18-23 · *We await the redemption of our bodies*
Romans 8:31-39 · *Nothing can separate us from the love of God*
2 Corinthians 1:3-5 · *God comforts us in affliction*
Hebrews 12:1-2 · *Jesus, the perfecter of our faith*
James 5:13-16 · *Is any among you sick? Prayer of faith*
1 John 5:13-15 · *Faith conquers the world*

GOSPEL

Matthew 5:2-10 · *The beatitudes*
Matthew 8:1-3, 5-8,13-17 · *Jesus healed many*
Matthew 26:26-30, 36-39 · *The last supper; Jesus' prayer in the garden*
Mark 1:21-28 · *Healing of the man with the unclean spirit*
Mark 1:29-34a · *Healing of Peter's mother-in-law and others*
Mark 5:1-20 · *Healing of man possessed by a demon*
Mark 5:22-24 · *Request for healing over Jairus' daughter*
Mark 6:7, 12-13 · *They anointed many with oil who were sick*
Luke 17:11-19 · *Your faith has made you well*
John 5:1b-9 · *Do you want to be healed?*

John 6:47-51	*I am the bread of life*
John 9:1-11	*Healing of the man born blind*

Gospel Acclamation

Alleluia. Come to me, all you that are carrying ⎮ heavy burdens,
   and I will ⎮ give you rest. *Alleluia.* (Matt. 11:30)

Proper Preface *(see p. 231 for musical setting)*

It is indeed right, our duty and our joy,
that we should at all times and in all places
   give thanks and praise to you,
O Lord, almighty and merciful God, through our Savior Jesus Christ:
our Good Samaritan, who tends the wounds of body and spirit
with the oil of consolation and wine of hope;
   the Sun of righteousness,
who raises us to life on his healing wings.
And so, with all the choirs of angels,
with the church on earth and the hosts of heaven,
we praise your name and join their unending hymn:

Continue with "Holy, holy, holy."

Color *of the season*

Hymns

242	Awake! Awake, and greet the new morn
607	Come, ye disconsolate
323	God loved the world
673	God, whose almighty word
612	Healer of our every ill
483	Here is bread
698	How long, O Lord
332, 611	I heard the voice of Jesus say
860	I'm so glad Jesus lifted me
615	In all our grief
466	In the singing
595	Jesus loves me!
616	Jesus, remember me
808	Lord Jesus, you shall be my song
610	O Christ the healer, we have come

Proper Preface—Healing

It is indeed right, our du - ty and our joy,

that we should at all times and in all places give thanks and praise to you,

al-mighty and merciful God, through our Sav - ior Je - sus Christ:

our Good Samaritan, who tends the wounds of body and spirit

with the oil of consolation and the wine of hope; the Sun of righ-teous-ness,

who raises us to life on his heal - ing wings.

And so, with all the choirs of an - gels,

with the church on earth and the hosts of heav - en,

we praise your name and join their un - end - ing hymn:

FUNERAL

Scripture Readings

At the processions:

Psalm 23	*The Lord is my shepherd*
Psalm 90	*Our dwelling place in all generations*
Psalm 118	*God's steadfast love endures forever*
Psalm 130	*Out of the depths I cry to you*
Isaiah 41:10	*Do not be afraid, for I am with you*
Romans 14:7-9	*Whether we live or die, we are the Lord's*
Revelation 1:17-18	*Do not be afraid, I am the first and the last*
Revelation 14:13	*Blessed are the dead who die in the Lord*
Matthew 11:28-29	*Come to me, all you who are weary*
John 11:25-26	*I am the resurrection and the life*
John 14:27	*Peace I leave with you*

OLD TESTAMENT

Job 19:23-27a	*I know that my Redeemer lives*
Ecclesiastes 3:1-15	*For everything there is a season*
Isaiah 25:6-9	*God will swallow up death forever*
Isaiah 40:1-11, 28-31	*Comfort, O comfort my people*
Isaiah 43:1-3a, 18-19, 25	*I am about to do a new thing*
Isaiah 55:1-3, 6-13	*Everyone who thirsts, come to the waters*
Isaiah 61:1-3	*The spirit of the Lord God is upon me*
Jeremiah 31:8-13	*I will turn their mourning into joy*
Lamentations 3:22-26, 31-33	*The steadfast love of the Lord never ceases*

PSALM

Psalm 42:1-7	*As a deer longs for flowing streams*
Psalm 46:1-7	*God is our refuge and strength*
Psalm 121	*I lift up my eyes to the hills*
Psalm 143	*Hear my prayer, O Lord*

NEW TESTAMENT

Romans 5:1-11	*Peace with God through Jesus Christ*
Romans 8:31-35, 37-39	*Who will separate us from the love of Christ*
1 Corinthians 15:12-26	*Christ, the firstfruits, has been raised*

2 Corinthians 4:7-18	*We have this treasure in clay jars*
1 Thessalonians 4:13-14, 18	*Teaching about those who have died*
Hebrews 12:1-2	*Surrounded by so great a cloud of witnesses*
1 Peter 1:3-9	*A living hope through Jesus' resurrection*
Revelation 7:9-17	*God will wipe away every tear*
Revelation 21:2-7	*I saw the holy city, the new Jerusalem*
Revelation 22:1-5	*The Lord God will be their light*

GOSPEL

Matthew 5:1-10	*Blessed are those who mourn*
Matthew 11:25-30	*Come to me, all you who are weary*
Mark 16:1-7	*The resurrection of Christ*
Luke 24:1-9, 36-43	*The resurrection of Christ*
John 1:1-5, 9-14	*The light shines in the darkness*
John 6:37-40	*I will raise them up on the last day*
John 10:11-16	*I am the good shepherd*
John 11:21-27	*I am the resurrection and the life*
John 14:1-6	*In my Father's house are many rooms*
John 14:25-27	*Peace I leave with you*

Especially at the death of a child:

OLD TESTAMENT

Isaiah 40:1, 6-11	*God will gather the lambs*
Isaiah 43:1-3a, 5-7	*I have called you by name, you are mine*
Isaiah 65:17-20, 23-25	*A new heaven and a new earth*
Isaiah 66:10-14	*As a mother comforts her child*

PSALM

Psalm 23	*The Lord is my shepherd*
Psalm 42:1-7	*As a deer longs for flowing streams*
Psalm 121	*I lift up my eyes to the hills*
Psalm 139:7-12	*The gracious omnipresence of the Lord*
Psalm 142:1-6	*With my voice I cry to the Lord*

NEW TESTAMENT

Romans 8:31-35, 37-39	*Who will separate us from the love of Christ?*
1 Thessalonians 4:13-14, 18	*Teaching about those who have died*
1 John 3:1-2	*See what love the Father has given us*

GOSPEL

Matthew 5:1-10	*Blessed are those who mourn*
Matthew 18:1-5, 10-14	*A child is the greatest in the kingdom*
Mark 10:13-16	*Let the little children come to me*
John 10:11-16	*I am the good shepherd*

Gospel Acclamation

Alleluia. Jesus Christ is the firstborn ∣ from the dead;
  to him be glory and dominion forev- ∣ er and ever. *Alleluia.*
  (Rev. 1:5, 6)

OR

Alleluia. O God, you have ∣ been our refuge
  from one generation ∣ to another. *Alleluia.* (Ps. 90:1)

Proper Preface (*see p. 236 for musical setting*)

It is indeed right, our duty and our joy,
that we should at all times and in all places
give thanks and praise to you,
O Lord, almighty and merciful God, through our Savior Jesus Christ,
who rose from the dead
and in whom our hope of resurrection dawns.
The sting of death has been removed
by the glorious promise of his risen life.
And so, with all the choirs of angels,
with the church on earth and the hosts of heaven,
we praise your name and join their unending hymn:

Continue with "Holy, holy, holy."

Color *of the season*

Hymns

629	Abide with me
377	Alleluia! Jesus is risen!
422	For all the saints
770	Give me Jesus
721	Goodness is stronger than evil
483	Here is bread
637	Holy God, holy and glorious

Proper Preface – Funeral

It is indeed right, our du - ty and our joy,

that we should at all times and in all places give thanks and praise to you,

al-mighty and merciful God, through our Sav - ior Je - sus Christ,

who rose from the dead, and in whom our hope of res - ur - rec - tion dawns.

The sting of death has been re - moved by the glorious

prom - ise of his ris - en life.

And so, with all the choirs of an - gels,

with the church on earth and the hosts of heav - en,

we praise your name and join their un - end - ing hymn:

MARRIAGE

Scripture Readings

OLD TESTAMENT

Genesis 1:26-28	*Woman and man created in God's image*
Genesis 2:18-24	*Companionship rather than loneliness*
Proverbs 3:3-6	*Loyalty and faithfulness written on the heart*
Song of Solomon 2:10-13	*The voice of the beloved*
Song of Solomon 8:6-7	*Many waters cannot quench love*
Isaiah 63:7-9	*God's steadfast love lifts up the people*
Jeremiah 31:31-34	*The new covenant of the people of God*

PSALM

Psalm 67	*May God be merciful to us and bless us*
Psalm 100	*We are God's people*
Psalm 117	*The steadfast love of the Lord*
Psalm 121	*The Lord keeps watch over you*
Psalm 127	*Unless the Lord builds the house*
Psalm 128	*Happy are they who follow in God's ways*
Psalm 150	*Let everything that breathes praise the Lord*

NEW TESTAMENT

Romans 8:31-35, 37-39	*If God is for us, who is against us*
Romans 12:1-2, 9-18	*A living sacrifice and genuine love*
1 Corinthians 12:31—13:13	*The greatest gift is love*
Ephesians 3:14-19	*The greatness of Christ's love*
Ephesians 5:1-2, 21-33	*Walk in love, as Christ loved us*
Philippians 4:4-9	*Rejoice in the Lord always*
Colossians 3:12-17	*Clothed in gifts of God*
1 John 3:18-24	*Let us love in truth and action*
1 John 4:7-16	*Let us love one another for love is of God*

GOSPEL

Matthew 5:1-10	*The beatitudes*
Matthew 5:14-16	*You are the light, let your light shine*
Matthew 7:21, 24-29	*A wise person builds upon the rock*
Matthew 19:3-6	*What God has united must not be divided*
Matthew 22:35-40	*Love, the greatest commandment*
Mark 10:6-9	*They are no longer two but one*

John 2:1-11   *The wedding at Cana*
John 15:9-17   *Love one another as I have loved you*

Gospel Acclamation

Alleluia. Happy are they who | fear the Lord,
  and who follow | in God's ways. *Alleluia.* (Ps. 128:1)

Proper Preface *(see p. 239 for musical setting)*

It is indeed right, our duty and our joy,
that we should at all times and in all places
give thanks and praise to you,
O Lord, almighty and merciful God, through our Savior Jesus Christ.
You made us in your image;
male and female you created us.
You give us the gift of marriage
and call us to reflect your faithfulness
as we serve one another in the bond of covenant love.
And so, with all the choirs of angels,
with the church on earth and the hosts of heaven,
we praise your name and join their unending hymn:

Continue with "Holy, holy, holy."

Color *of the season*

Hymns

644	Although I speak with angel's tounge
648	Beloved, God's chosen
816	Come, my way, my truth, my life
585	Hear us now, our God and Father
312	Jesus, come! for we invite you
836	Joyful, joyful we adore thee
839, 840	Now thank we all our God
308	O Morning Star, how fair and bright!
488, 489	Soul, adorn yourself with gladness
586	This is a day, Lord, gladly awaited

Proper Preface – Marriage

It is indeed right, our du - ty and our joy,

that we should at all times and in all places give thanks and praise to you,

al-mighty and merciful God, through our Sav - ior Je - sus Christ.

You made us in your image; male and female you cre - a - ted us.

You give us the gift of mar - iage and call us to reflect your faithfulness

as we serve one another in the bond of cov - e - nant love.

And so, with all the choirs of an - gels,

with the church on earth and the hosts of heav - en,

we praise your name and join their un - end - ing hymn:

Endnotes

Chapter Two

1   Although the practice of celebrating baptism apart from a regular worship service of the congregation runs counter to the normative experience of Lutherans for several generations, anecdotal evidence of baptism occurring outside of the usual worship of the congregation is available in personal histories, pastoral diaries, and historical studies. While "private" baptism was a phenomenon that occurred particularly in mission situations without a resident pastor, it has occurred at other times as well. [See Henry Melchior Muhlenberg, *The Notebook of a Colonial Clergyman*. Condensed from the Journals of Henry Melchior Muhlenberg. Translated and edited by Theodore G. Tappert and John W. Doberstein. Second Fortress Press paperback edition. (Minneapolis: Fortress Press, 1998). See also S. Anderzén, *Teaching and Church Tradition in the Kemi and Torne Laplands, Northern Scandinavia*. (Umeå, Sweden: Scriptum 42, 1996).]

2   Luther's own baptism occurred on November 11, 1483, only a day following his birth. The date of his baptism was significant in that his name came from the saint commemorated on that day, Martin of Tours.

3   *The Book of Concord: The Confessions of the Evangelical Lutheran Church*, Robert Kolb and Timothy J. Wengert (eds.), Charles Arand, tr. (Minneapolis: Fortress Press, 2000), 465n218.

Chapter Three

1   *Baptism, Eucharist, and Ministry*, 18b.

2   Craig A. Satterlee, *Ambrose of Milan's Method of Mystagogical Preaching* (Collegeville, Minn.: Liturgical Press, 2002), 179.

Chapter Four

1   Robert D. Putnam, *Bowling Alone: The Collapse and Revival of American Community* (New York: Simon & Schuster, 2000).

2   Loren B. Mead, *The Once and Future Church: Reinventing the Congregation for a New Mission Frontier* (Washington, DC: Alban Institute, 1991), 51.

Chapter Five

1 Arthur C. Repp, *Confirmation in the Lutheran Church*, (Saint Louis: Concordia, 1964), 22.

2 Amy Nelson Burnett, "Martin Bucer and the Anabaptist Context of Evangelical Confirmation," *The Mennonite Quarterly Review* 68 (January 1994): 111–112.

3 Frank W. Klos, *Confirmation and First Communion: A Study Book*, (Minneapolis: Augsburg Publishing House, 1968), 64–65.

4 Paul Turner, *The Meaning and Practice of Confirmation: Perspectives from a Sixteenth-Century Controversy*, (New York: Peter Lang, 1987), 67–68.

5 *Confirmation: A Study Document*, trans. Walter G. Tillmanns, (Minneapolis: Augsburg Publishing House, 1963), 30–31.

6 Herbert G. Schaefer, "Confirmation—Its Meanings and Development in Church History," *Theology and Life* 10 (December 1987): 116.

7 *Confirmation: A Study Document*, 30.

8 *Minutes*, Liturgical Texts Committee, Inter-Lutheran Commission on Worship, (Archives of Cooperative Lutheranism, ELCA Archives, Chicago), 1969–1974.

9 See the *Constitutions, Bylaws, and Continuing Resolutions of the Evangelical Lutheran Church in America* (particularly the following provisions: 10.52.; 12.41.13; 13.32.; 13.42.; 13.52.; S8.21. C8.02.b.; C8.02.c.; C10.02.; C10.04.; C11.01.b.; C12.01.).

10 *Model Constitution for Congregations of the Evangelical Lutheran Church in America.* C8.03.

Chapter Six

1 Frank Senn, "The Confession of Sins in the Reformation Churches," in *The Fate of Confession*, ed. Mary and Power Collins David (Edinburgh: T & T Clark, 1987), 107–8.

2 Dietrich Bonhoeffer, *Spiritual Care*, trans. Jay C. Rochelle (Philadelphia: Fortress Press, 1985), 60–61.

3 Leroy Aden, "Pastoral Counseling as Christian Perspective," in *The Dialogue Between Theology and Psychology*, ed. Peter Homans, vol. 3, (Chicago: University of Chicago Press, 1968), 163.

4 Lyman T. Lundeen, "Forgiveness and Human Relationship," in *Counseling and the Human Predicament*, ed. Leroy Aden and David G. Benner (Grand Rapids, Mich.: Baker, 1989), 192–93.

5 Bonhoeffer, *Spiritual Care*, 63.

6 Thomas C. Oden, *Ministry Through Word and Sacrament*, vol. 2, Classical Pastoral Care Series, ed. Thomas C. Oden (New York: Crossroad, 1989), 58.

Chapter Seven

1   *Apostolic Tradition*, 5. As printed in Geoffrey J. Cuming, *Hippolytus: A Text for Students* (Bramcote, Nottinghamshire: Grove, 1976), 11.

Chapter Eight

1   S. Anita Stauffer, ed., *Baptism, Rites of Passage, and Culture* (Geneva: Lutheran World Federation, 1999), 21.

2   Melinda A. Quivik, *A Christian Funeral: Witness to the Resurrection* (Minneapolis: Fortress Press, 2005), 38.

3   Quivik, *A Christian Funeral*, 51.

Chapter Nine

1   Frank C. Senn, *The People's Work: A Social History of the Liturgy* (Minneapolis: Augsburg Fortress, 2006), 217-221.

2   Stephanie Coontz, *Marriage, A History. From Obedience to Intimacy or How Love Conquered Marriage* (New York: Viking Penguin, 2005), 177.

3   *Lutheran Book of Worship* Ministers Edition, 36.

Appendix A

1   Geneva: Lutheran World Federation, 1994. Also published in French, German, and Spanish.

2   Geneva: Lutheran World Federation, 1996. Also published in German.

Appendix B

1   Geneva: Lutheran World Federation, 1994. Also published in French, German, and Spanish.

2   Geneva: Lutheran World Federation, 1996. Also published in German.

3   For further explanation and examples of this fourfold dynamic, see the Nairobi Statement, 2.–5.

4   For methodology and criteria, see the Nairobi Statement, 3.2.–3.6.

5   Parallel to the LWF Worship and Culture Study has been work by the WCC Commission on Faith and Order. A part of that work has focused on Baptism; regarding the ordo for Baptism, see the statement on "Becoming a Christian: The Ecumenical Implications of Our Common Baptism," 1997.

6   Pre-baptismal catechumenal formation is not merely education; rather, it involves the whole person being formed by the Holy Spirit in the Word, prayer, worship, Christian community, and service in the world.

7   Martin Luther, "The Holy and Blessed Sacrament of Baptism," 1.

8   Martin Luther, "Large Catechism," 4; "The Holy and Blessed Sacrament of Baptism," 1; "The Blessed Sacrament of the Holy and True Body of Christ," 3; and "The Babylonian Captivity of the Church," Luther's Works, vol. 36, 67-8.

9   See the papers of the Strasbourg Institute/LWF consultation on this subject, in *Baptism and the Unity of the Church,* ed. Michael Root and Risto Saarinen (Geneva: WCC Publications; Grand Rapids, Mich. and Cambridge: Eerdmans, 1998).

Bibliography

Anderzén, S. *Teaching and Church Tradition in the Kemi and Torne Laplands, Northern Scandinavia.* Umeå: Scriptum 42, 1996.

Austin, Gerard, O.P. *Anointing with the Spirit.* New York: Pueblo Publishing Company, 1985.

Baptism, Eucharist, and Ministry, Faith and Order Paper 111. Geneva: World Council of Churches, 1982.

Bradshaw, Paul F., Maxwell E. Johnson, and L. Edward Philips, trans. and ed. *The Apostolic Tradition: A Commentary.* Hermeneia Series. Minneapolis: Fortress Press, 2002.

Brugh, Lorraine, and Gordon Lathrop. *The Sunday Assembly.* Using *Evangelical Lutheran Worship*, vol. 1. Augsburg Fortress, 2007.

Evangelical Lutheran Worship. Pew Edition and Leaders Edition. Minneapolis: Augsburg Fortress, 2006.

Evans, Abigail Rian. *Healing Liturgies for the Seasons of Life.* Louisville, Ky.: Westminster John Knox Press, 2004.

Holy Baptism and Related Rites, Renewing Worship 3. Minneapolis: Augsburg Fortress, 2002.

Indexes to Evangelical Lutheran Worship. Minneapolis: Augsburg Fortress, 2007.

Johnson, Maxwell E. *The Rites of Christian Initiation: Their Evolution and Interpretation.* Revised and expanded edition. Collegeville, Minn.: The Liturgical Press, 2007.

Kavanagh, Aidan. *The Shape of Baptism: The Rite of Christian Initiation,* Studies in the Reformed Rites of the Catholic Church, Vol. 1. New York: Pueblo Publishing Company, 1978.

Klos, Frank W. *Confirmation and First Communion: A Study Book.* Minneapolis: Augsburg Publishing House, 1968.

Kolb, Robert, and Timothy J. Wengert, ed. *The Book of Concord: The Confessions of the Evangelical Lutheran Church.* Minneapolis: Fortress Press, 2000.

Koontz, Stephanie. *Marriage, A History. From Obedience to Intimacy or How Love Conquered Marriage.* New York: Viking Penguin, 2005.

Kuehn, Regina. *A Place for Baptism.* Chicago: Liturgy Training Publications, 1992.

Larson-Miller, Lizette. *The Sacrament of Anointing of the Sick.* Collegeville, Minn.: The Liturgical Press, 2005.

Lutheran Book of Worship, Pew Edition and Ministers Edition. Minneapolis: Augsburg Publishing House; Philadelphia: Board of Publication, Lutheran Church in America; St. Louis: Concordia Publishing House; 1978.

Muhlenberg, Henry Melchior. *The Notebook of a Colonial Clergyman*. Condensed from the Journals of Henry Melchior Muhlenberg. Translated and edited by Theodore G. Tappert and John W. Doberstein. Minneapolis: Fortress Press, 1998.

Occasional Services: A Companion to Lutheran Book of Worship. Minneapolis: Augsburg Publishing House; Philadelphia: Board of Publication, Lutheran Church in America, 1982.

Pfatteicher, Philip H. and Carlos R. Messerli. *Manual on the Liturgy*. Minneapolis: Augsburg Publishing House, 1979.

Principles for Worship. Renewing Worship 2. Minneapolis: Augsburg Fortress, 2002.

Quivik, Melinda A. *A Christian Funeral: Witness to the Resurrection*. Minneapolis: Augsburg Fortress, 2005.

Ramshaw, Gail, and Mons Teig. *Keeping Time: The Church's Years*. Using *Evangelical Lutheran Worship*, vol. 3. Minneapolis: Augsburg Fortress, 2008.

Repp, Arthur C. *Confirmation in the Lutheran Church*. Saint Louis: Concordia Publishing House, 1964.

Rite of Christian Initiation of Adults. Collegeville, Minn.: The Liturgical Press, 1988.

Satterlee, Craig A. *Ambrose of Milan's Method of Mystagogical Preaching*. Collegeville, Minn.: The Liturgical Press, 2002.

———. *Presiding in the Assembly*. Minneapolis: Augsburg Fortress, 2003.

Schattauer, Thomas H. "Healing Rites and Transformation of Life: Observations and Insights from within the Evangelical Lutheran Church in America." *Liturgy* 22:3, July–September 2007.

Senn, Frank C. *Christian Liturgy: Catholic and Evangelical*. Minneapolis: Fortress Press, 1997.

———. *The People's Work: A Social History of the Liturgy*. Minneapolis: Fortress Press, 2006.

Spinks, Bryan D. *Reformation and Modern Rituals and Theologies of Baptism: From Luther to Contemporary Practices*. Burlington: Ashgate Publishing Company, 2006.

Stauffer, S. Anita, ed. *Baptism, Rites of Passage, and Culture*. Geneva: Lutheran World Federation, 1999.

———. *Christian Worship: Unity in Cultural Diversity*. Geneva: Lutheran World Federation, 1996.

The Use of the Means of Grace. A Statement on the Practice of Word and Sacrament. Minneapolis: Augsburg Fortress, 1997. Also included as an appendix in Brugh and Lathrop, *The Sunday Assembly*, above.

Turner, Paul. *Confirmation: The Baby in Solomon's Court*. Mahwah, N.J.: Paulist Press, 1993.

———. *The Meaning and Practice of Confirmation: Perspectives from a Sixteenth-Century Controversy*. New York: Peter Lang Publishing, 1987.

Walters, Paul, and James Armentrout. *Christ in Your Marriage*. Minneapolis: Augsburg Fortress, 2007.

Welcome to Christ: Lutheran Rites for the Catechumenate. Minneapolis: Augsburg Fortress, 1997.

Welcome to Christ: A Lutheran Introduction to the Catechumenate. Minneapolis: Augsburg Fortress, 1997.

Welcome to Christ: A Lutheran Catechetical Guide. Minneapolis: Augsburg Fortress, 1997.

Welcome to Christ: A Sponsor's Guide. Minneapolis: Augsburg Fortress, 2002.

Welcome to Christ: Preparing Adults for Baptism and Discipleship. Videotape. Minneapolis: Augsburg Fortress, 1998.

Whitaker, E. C. *Documents of the Baptismal Liturgy*, Revised and expanded edition by Maxwell E. Johnson. Collegeville, Minn.: Pueblo, 2003.

Yarnold, Edward, S.J. *The Awe-Inspiring Rites of Initiation: The Origins of the R.C.I.A.* Collegeville, Minn.: The Liturgical Press, 1994.

Index